ROUTLEDGE LIBRARY EDITIONS:
TRADE UNIONS

Volume 16

TRADE UNIONS IN THE DEVELOPED ECONOMIES

TRADE UNIONS IN THE DEVELOPED ECONOMIES

Edited by
E. OWEN SMITH

Routledge
Taylor & Francis Group
LONDON AND NEW YORK

First published in 1981 in the UK by Croom Helm Ltd.

This edition first published in 2023
by Routledge
4 Park Square, Milton Park, Abingdon, Oxon OX14 4RN

and by Routledge
605 Third Avenue, New York, NY 10158

Routledge is an imprint of the Taylor & Francis Group, an informa business

British Library Cataloguing in Publication Data
A catalogue record for this book is available from the British Library

ISBN: 978-1-032-37553-3 (Set)
ISBN: 978-1-032-39441-1 (Volume 16) (hbk)
ISBN: 978-1-032-39444-2 (Volume 16) (pbk)
ISBN: 978-1-003-34975-4 (Volume 16) (ebk)

DOI: 10.4324/9781003349754

Publisher's Note
The publisher has gone to great lengths to ensure the quality of this reprint but points out that some imperfections in the original copies may be apparent.

Disclaimer
The publisher has made every effort to trace copyright holders and would welcome correspondence from those they have been unable to trace.

Trade Unions in the Developed Economies

EDITED BY
E. OWEN SMITH

Library of Congress Cataloging in Publication Data

Trade unions in the developed economies.
    Includes indexes.
    1. Trade-unions—Case studies. I. Owen Smith, E.
HD6483.T673   331.88'09172'2   81-51469   AACR2

ISBN 0-312-81222-1

CONTENTS

ACKNOWLEDGEMENTS

The editor wishes to make two important acknowledgements. First, he again wishes to place on record his appreciation of the able secretarial help provided by Mrs Gloria Brentnall. He also hopes that the book will prove a small consolation to his family for the various physical and mental absences — especially during their Christmas holidays, 1980 — that this book entailed. The proof stage was reached during the Easter holidays, 1981 and his wife assisted him in compiling the Name Index.

INTRODUCTION

Eric Owen Smith

The aim of this book is to offer a collection of studies on the growth, structure and policies of trade unions in seven developed economies. The contributors, with the exception of Dr Hearn, are economists interested in the general affairs of the country concerned. They were asked to analyse the growth, structure and policy of trade unions in that particular country. As far as possible the early growth of trade unions has been summarised so that a post-Second World War analysis could be undertaken. In all cases, however, many important features of collective bargaining were evident before this date. Basically, the *growth* section contains an examination of the extent to which conflict between the parties has either increased or decreased. This often, though not always, necessitates an appraisal of the roles of the government, the courts and third-party involvement. All developments are viewed against a backcloth of general economic developments and the statistical data generally deal with trends rather than particular developments at any one point in time. The *structure* section contains an analysis of how changes in the structure of the labour force have been reflected by changes in the structure of trade unions. Inter-union relations are examined in this and other contexts. Finally, the *policy* section contains an analysis of the main bargaining issues and the methods employed to achieve these goals.

Australia (Chapter 1) affords an excellent example of a country where the wage determination process is subject to a high degree of third party involvement. In order for this system to operate, a detailed set of rules governing collective bargaining as a whole have been introduced. In consequence, Australian unions are in general highly centralised and trade union growth has been stimulated. Trade union policy has recently consisted of challenging certain aspects of arbitration and technological change. Significantly, the arbitration system was introduced following a period of intense industrial unrest and, as in the case of the United Kingdom, there has been a resurgence of conflict of late. There are two further features common to both Australia and the United Kingdom. First, the high level of trade unionisation ('density') which has recently displayed an expansionary trend. Secondly, there is a complex trade union structure. Australia resembles France, Japan and Sweden in that all four countries have several central union organisations, although there have been significant changes in Australia and Japan in recent years.

France's trade unions (Chapter 2) are characterised by their financial weakness, and by their political and religious divisions. The sympathies of the central trade union confederations range from Communist to Catholic. Numerous regional and factory unions are affiliated to the various confederations. On the other hand, the employer associations are much stronger. At the factory level, too, there is very little effective collective bargaining – this time due to the relatively more powerful position of the individual employer. Trade union density is quite low, although non-unionists often support their organised colleagues. As in West Germany, the propensity to strike has been reduced by rising material prosperity, but in 1968 the whole country was convulsed with strike action. Normally, however, the typical French strike is of short duration due to the financial weakness of the unions. Finally, in contrast to the growing trend among their Australian counterparts, French trade unions do not typically employ professionally qualified staff.

Obvious social differences apart, the striking feature about trade union growth and policy in *Japan* (Chapter 3) is the number of similarities to Germany. Indeed, the most significant exceptions are structural in character: they lie in the amount of plant bargaining and the number of enterprise unions in Japan, where France or the USA are in some respects the more appropriate analogues. But in both Japan and Germany trade unionism has been outlawed on two occasions, the most recent case being prior to and during the Second World War. In both countries trade union leaders were imprisoned. In both countries (following the war) the occupational forces initially stimulated the formation (Japan) or reconstruction (Germany) of strong trade unions. The emergence of the Cold War put an end to the unqualified encouragement of trade unionisation by the occupation authorities. The 1950-52 co-determination controversy in Germany is directly analogous to the resistance to management's attempts to reimpose paternalistic control at the Omi Silk Company in 1954. Employees in both countries, along with France, enjoyed rapidly rising living standards during the post-Second World War era. A concomitant of this has been the relative industrial harmony over the period taken as a whole. Annual bargaining tends to be ritualistic in nature. High fringe benefits are another common feature, as was the existence of a dual labour market – that is 'temporary' indigenous (Japan) or foreign

(Germany) workers who did not enjoy secure employment in the event of a recession. Japan's central trade union organisations are generally opposed to the capitalist system. One third of Japan's trade union members remain outside these organisations because they prefer not to engage in political debate. In the United Kingdom the dichotomy between TUC and Labour Party affiliation is more marked: white-collar unionists are virtually all affiliated to the TUC, but relatively few are affiliated to the Labour Party.

It is apparent from Chapter 4 that *Sweden's* white-collar employees have succeeded where their counterparts in the UK failed, namely in establishing central organisations which are independent of the manual worker's central organisation. As in other countries the central organisations' policy tends to be mainly dictated by the larger affiliates. Collective bargaining is highly centralised and co-ordinated, although there were some unofficial disputes in the late 1960s. (There was also a serious lockout/official strike in 1980.) As in West Germany, one finds a large element of industrial unionism, at least among the 25 unions organising manual workers. White-collar workers, on the other hand, tend to be organised on a loose cartel basis. Trade union density is extremely high, even though there is an absence of closed shop provisions. However, the growing white-collar trade union movement is an area of uncertainty and difficulty. Public sector unionism, in common with so many of the other countries covered in this book, is expanding rapidly. The private sector employers' association has become increasingly concerned about the role of the public sector as pay leader – a feature also discernible in the UK. In Sweden, the private employers insisted in 1980 that they should remain the bell-wether in shaping what happens during the annual pay round. As in the UK, there was a great deal of industrial relations legislation in the 1970s. As in West Germany, there were developments in the field of industrial democracy.

In the case of the *United Kingdom* (Chapter 5), the recent conflict contrasts with the consensus and co-operation which extended from the late 1920s to the 1950s. The 1940s and 1950s marked a period of high employment and generally improving living standards. Trade union density remained constant. The consensus was gradually ruptured by both shop floor and employer militancy – with some of the government's legislation exacerbating the situation in the 1970s. All kinds of legislation – including provisions against unfair dismissal – became increasingly important in the field of collective bargaining. Rising tax liability undermined real wage growth. (The Swedish government informs negotiators of its fiscal strategy before each wage round, but this has not prevented real wages from falling.) Trade union density increased dramatically. However, trade unions are financially weak. Significantly, white-collar unionism was mainly responsible for the expansion in union membership, as in Australia. Nevertheless, the duration of strikes has not reached the levels recorded before and after the First World War. There has been a notable, growing trend in the 1970s for the parties to draw up more formal procedure agreements which often stipulate, among other things, third party involvement in dispute resolution.

Employers in the *United States of America* (Chapter 6) were particularly opposed to the rise of trade unionism. They were also much less likely to be organised themselves and collective bargaining, when it eventually emerged on a wider scale, was nearly always decentralised. As in Japan, West Germany and the United Kingdom, the law also constrained the rise of unions in the USA. Rather like the United Kingdom's case, 'enabling' legislation was necessary before trade unionism could get off the ground. Also like the United Kingdom this legislation was to be a controversial issue. Even after the merger of the craft and industrial orientated central federations in 1955, there was still a good deal of inter-union conflict. Further rifts were caused by the expulsion of several trade unions from the central federation for corruption. Unlike Australia, Sweden, the UK and West Germany, trade union density has fallen of late. The reasons for this decline are explored in some depth. The local union in the USA is generally more powerful and better organised than its counterparts elsewhere, although some centralisation is taking place. Finally, it should be noted that the USA is the home of business unionism. Add to this the complete lack of any labour or socialist party in American politics, and the contrast with every other study in this book becomes most marked.

In *West Germany* (Chapter 7) there is a detailed legal code which permeates every aspect of collective bargaining. In many areas this law is judge made — and the judiciary takes a dim view of the economic disruption caused by strike action. Moreover, the employers are powerfully organised. They may legally lock out employees whose union has called a strike at other establishments in their money wage bargaining region. Before a union may legally call a strike, it must observe a demanding procedure, although it must be emphasised that German trade unions are financially strong and no constraint in this respect operates. Rising economic prosperity and real wages since 1948 have further reduced the amount of conflict, as has the absence of workplace bargaining. Although union density is fairly high, inter-union competition has undermined their ability to organise the growing white-collar labour force. In any case, German trade unions owe their origins to the political and religious organisations who founded and fostered their growth. Hence, the movement remains to the fore in securing more general political aims, including an extension of industrial democracy.

The basic political lesson emerging in all cases seems to be clear. In all highly industrialised countries the kind of relationship which should exist between the trade unions and the state presents one of the leading problems of our time (Flanders, p.96). Trade union legislation in Britain has, for example, been enacted and repealed by Labour and Conservative governments in turn. In promising the TUC the repeal of the Conservative Employment Act, 1980, if and when Labour were returned to office, the then Labour Party leader (James Callaghan) made three conditions. First, 'there must be a complete understanding between us both before we assume office. We need a new partnership to work together.' Secondly, 'we must agree on the need for planned and orderly change necessary in the industrial system. Not all the changes will be pleasant . . .' Thirdly, 'we must define a fresh relationship between the state and the trade unions once and for all' (*The Times*, 3 Sept. 1980, p.1). The Conservative Secretary of State for Employment (James Prior), in introducing his 1981 *Green Paper* on trade union immunities (a topic discussed in Chapter 5), made a similar point. He said: 'the continuing absence of a well defined, stable, and acceptable relationship between government on the one hand and trade unions and employers' associations on the other had contributed to damaging dissension' (*The Times*, 16 Jan. 1981, p.1).

In consequence trade unions and politics are inextricably intertwined. The British Labour Party was founded by the early trade unions, whereas the political and religious movements formed trade unions in most continental countries (cf. Kahn-Freund, p.47). Continental unions, however, had to use their strength to achieve political goals common to the working class a whole, whereas British unions concentrated on the labour market and job control (loc. cit.). In the USA there was a political development which resembled that of Britain (ibid., pp.48 and 60n). In Australia, France, Germany and Japan serious inter-union conflict has been caused by political differences. Nowadays, many large white-collar trade unions in Britain are not affiliated to the Labour Party, but the essential political importance of accommodating trade unions remains a topical and critical issue, irrespective of party political predilections.

This political importance of trade unions derives from the economic implications of collective bargaining. About 80 per cent of all employees in Sweden were unionists (Chapter 4). By 1978, 54 per cent of the labour force in Britain were members of trade unions (Chapter 5). This so-called density ratio was 43 per cent in the FRG (also in 1978 – see Chapter 7), while in the USA about 30 per cent of the non-agricultural labour force are organised (Chapter 6; Rees, 1979, p.115). In Australia, density was as high as 57 per cent in 1973; in France it may have been lower than 20 per cent in 1968; in Japan it was 33 per cent in 1978 (chapters 1, 2 and 3, respectively). Moreover, many employees who are not members of trade unions effectively have their wages fixed in accordance with the outcome of collective bargaining by way of convention, third-party decision or defensive employer tactics (Trevithick and Mulvey, p.86). In other words, the effects of collective bargaining extend beyond the limits of its coverage (Rees, 1979, p.115). Wage inflation is therefore largely the outcome of the process of collective bargaining – as is demonstrated by the studies contained in this book.

The increase in labour's share in the national income might also be attributable to the rise of trade unions, although this is a controversial and highly inconclusive area. For example, a union may succeed in negotiating a short-run increase in money wages but this may induce an employer (or employers) to substitute capital equipment in the long run (Rees, 1977, pp.88-90). In order to arrive at this so-called 'share', one calculates the total income from employment in relation to the national income. For example, the development of labour's share in the Federal Republic of Germany (FRG) displays an increasing trend: it increased from 58 per cent in 1950 to 71 per cent in 1979 (Bundesminister für Arbeit, *Statisches Taschenbuch 1980*, Table 1.5). Among the many factors which affect the share of wages, one in particular is of overriding importance in the case of the FRG. Between 1950 and 1979 the numbers of self-employed decreased. During the same time period, the proportion of employed persons in the total labour force rose from 68 per cent to over 86 per cent (ibid., Table 2.5). This process was mainly the result of a migration from agriculture and the artisan trades which led particularly to an increase in the service sector of employment. One can eliminate the influence of this factor by calculating how labour's share would have developed, if the structure of the labour force had remained constant — say by using the 1960 structure as a base.

Labour's share is dramatically changed when calculated in this manner. In the 1950s there was a continual increase in the income from entrepreneurship and wealth (Meissner and Unterseher, pp.40-42). This was associated with the post-war recovery of the West German economy, the increase in investment and the considerable formation of private productive resources promoted by tax measures. Since 1960, however, the imputed share of labour has begun to increase again: labour market strains have been increasingly felt for most of this period. Hence a fall in labour's share from 65 per cent in 1950 to 60 per cent in 1960 was translated into a recovery to 64 per cent by 1979 (Bundesminister für Arbeit, *Statisches Taschenbuch 1980*, Table 1.5). This latter rising trend was interrupted during the 1969 'profits explosion' and there has been a similar fall from 66 per cent in 1974, when unemployment increased. Trade union 'pushfulness' may be postulated as one variable underlying developments in labour's share since its recovery (Pen, pp.162-6 and 199-206).

One recent estimate indicates that in *relative* terms trade unions in the USA may have increased their members' differential over non-unionised workers by 20 per cent (Rees, 1977, p.74). On other cross-sectional bases the effect in both Britain and the USA may be even larger according to *which* union/non-union differential (inter-industry, occupational, sex, etc.) is being considered and whether inflationary pressure is more pronounced than usual (ibid., pp.70-75, and Metcalf in Blackaby, p.50). On a time-series basis, trade unions generally appear to have a once and for all impact in terms of raising their members' differentials over non-unionised labour (the so-called 'impact effect'). Thereafter, they seem to retain this lead while market forces also pull in the same direction. Over the whole span of a trade cycle, money wage levels are perhaps no higher than they would have been without trade unions. As a result of the presence of trade unions, however, rises probably came sooner and cuts, if any, later (the so-called 'ratchet effect'). Average pay would therefore have been higher (Phelps Brown, p.184). The effect of unions on resource misallocation, that is to say because wages have been higher, but employment and productivity lower, than in a competitive equilibrium position, seems to have been minimal: the loss of output was probably in the order of 0.14 per cent of national income. The costs of unemployment and restrictive work practices are much higher (Rees, 1979, pp.149-51). In other words, the impact of unions on relative wages is only one of the many variables which contribute to the typically uncompetitive nature of labour markets (Rees, 1977, p.88). Evidence from Sweden (Chapter 4) even suggests that heavily organised labour markets may be under greater pressure to innovate. All that has been said in this paragraph could, to varying degrees, be extended to cover the other economies studied in this book. The notable exception (at present) is Japan where an entirely different system of wage differentials operates.

Governments, employers and the courts in different countries have reacted in various ways to the rise of trade unionism, although in general, historical terms the movement met with determined opposition. Nowadays, the right to strike may be embodied in a constitution, statute or custom, but in practice the right will always be qualified. For example, in the FRG strikes may only be called by union leaders after a collective agreement has expired and a 75 per cent majority have voted in favour of strike action; social security benefits are not paid to strikers' families and picketing is strictly limited. The British Conservative government is attempting to move in a similar direction.

Lengthening experience of high levels of employment (until 1974) and the growing complexity and integration of productive processes have both endowed even the smallest work group with the potential power to disrupt production. The costs of disputes have risen as the capital/labour ratio has increased: employers are anxious to ensure optimum use of increasingly expensive plant and equipment. This does not mean to say that workers cannot also incur financial losses as a result of strikes. The financial ability of unions, especially in France and Britain, to anything like compensate for loss of earnings out of strike funds is limited. Most union assets are not easily realised. In the FRG these assets consist of huge businesses entirely owned by the unions. Furthermore, social benefits for the families of strikers, where they exist, do not necessarily imply that strikes will increase if such benefits are a constant proportion of net earnings: the pattern of stoppages could remain the same, once the parties in industrial disputes readjust to these payments. An analysis of all these crucial economic factors essentially requires, first, an estimate of the extent to which the growing latent power of trade unions is utilised and, secondly, the relative economic welfare significance of strikes in terms of lost output. Some observers would argue that such diverse factors as machinery breakdowns and sickness cause greater output losses than strikes. Moreover, some countries view strike action with complete abhorrence while other countries appear quite nonchalant. For example, France was brought to a standstill for weeks in 1968 and redundant steel workers blocked motorways and railways in 1979 but the French are not obsessed by strikes, whereas the German political system would quake at such action.

Indeed, the German oft-frustrated need to maintain an ostensible political consensus can be seen in the system of co-determination. The works council system obviates the conflict inherent in British plant bargaining. On the other hand plant bargaining in Japan arose from a preference for consensus rather than conflict. Plant bargaining is weak in France and Australia, but not in the USA. Industry-wide pay bargaining remains supreme on the continent of Europe, while in Britain there is a longer tradition workplace bargaining (Brown in Blackaby, pp.130-31). In Britain, the problem of accommodating rank and file pressure is made more acute by the existence of lay officials and plant bargaining in many industries. These lay officials (shop stewards) have more power than their counterparts in the USA. Such pressure does not exist in the FRG because the trade union organisation at plant or company level plays second fiddle to the works council. The latter is necessarily a more company-orientated organisation. Hence trade unions in the FRG and Sweden tend to be centralised organisations which negotiate national or regional agreements, while local implementation and supplementation is left in the FRG to the works council. Centralisation in Britain has also taken place away from the formal bargaining structure in so far as the central trade union and employer organisations have become the consultative organs to which government frequently turns. There has therefore been a process of polarisation both upwards and downwards, but the formal bargaining structure has not adjusted to this change (Kahn-Freund, p.84).

Lockouts are often thought of as the equivalent weapon to strikes on the side of the employer, and these are still used, or threatened, in the FRG. Their use in Germany has sparked off considerable controversy, where the legal validity of lockouts has been challenged and they are not always seen as analogous to strike action in bargaining power terms. The employer's power, according to this latter hypothesis, lies in his ability to withdraw or reduce employment opportunities by means of his investment decisions. His pricing decisions affect real wages. All this undermines trade union bargaining power. To allow lockouts, the argument concludes, exacerbates an already unequal balance of power. Employers in France also wield relatively more power, while in the USA there is evidence of even more overt anti-union practices.

However, strike action and other collective sanctions such as overtime bans are only one way in which trade unions achieve and maintain bargaining power. In the USA and Britain the closed shop (i.e. compulsory union membership) is used as a method of controlling labour supply. The closed shop is also legal in Australia. But this practice is illegal in Italy, France and Germany (ibid., pp.54 and 61n). The right to union membership and to participate in union decisions are therefore important legal issues in English-speaking countries, but not among Italian, French and German lawyers (ibid., p.53). Continental unions find other ways to discriminate in favour of union members (ibid., p.55). In any case, legislative protection against unfair dismissal came much earlier in the FRG than Britain. Such protection also now exists in France, Italy and other European countries though not in the USA (ibid., p.72). In Japan it is regarded as a social norm. However, protection against unfair dismissal creates potential legal difficulties for employers in countries where the closed shop exists because they must proceed carefully if they dismiss a non-union member.

So far the trade unions have been analysed as if they were homogeneous entities. However, the gains made by trade unions do not go to these organisations as such but to their rank and file members (Rees, 1979, p.117). Agreements must often be ratified by the membership and officials sometimes face elections. An official coming up for re-election will therefore be anxious to conclude agreements which are perceived by the membership as generous. On the other hand, an official will normally wish to retain his negotiating reputation with employers in terms of realism and even reliability. His dilemma is therefore one of perceiving and satisfying his membership's aspirations, but reaching agreement and compromising with employers.

A universal problem for trade union officials involves selecting negotiating goals. Optimum levels of wages, employment, fringe-benefits and trade union membership are all obvious, but competing, variables which will feature in a negotiating strategy (Rees, 1977, pp.49-51). A dynamic factor will be comparisons with other work groups. Constraints will be the demand for the product and the substitutability of non-union labour or capital (ibid., pp.66-9 and Rees, 1979, p.66).

Taking these factors into account, both the trade union and the employer will enter negotiations having prepared a claim and offer respectively (Hunter, p.229). In accordance with the celebrated model of collective bargaining postulated by Hicks, both sides will indulge in threats, bluff, charges and counter-charges in order to elicit more precise information on the likely position of the opposing party (Hicks, pp.140-47; Shackle, *passim*). Negotiations are nearly always the only way of achieving a settlement. Note that Hicks suggests that disputes are the result of faulty negotiation and inadequate knowledge. More recent writers regard strikes as an inevitable feature of the institutionalised market economy (Fisher, p.79). Nevertheless, the extraction of information is a necessary feature of the negotiating process, if only because expectations about the behaviour of the other party and estimations of the time likely to be required to reach a settlement will be modified. In the event of a threatened or actual breakdown in negotiations, an industrial dispute is still not inevitable for the negotiators may agree to involve a third party — that is a conciliator, mediator or arbitrator. This takes different forms in the various countries covered by this book, but it will improve the flow of information and allow new solution positions to be explored (Hicks, pp.147-52; Hunter, p.231).

Hence, neither party knows what the other side's sticking point will be, nor is the length of strike each side is able and willing to tolerate known. This in turn will be a function of the probable cost to each side, or the speed with which foregone income can be recovered. Relative bargaining power, as already indicated, will vary according to product and factor market conditions. The costs of agreeing and disagreeing therefore enter into the general bargaining stance and power of each party (Burkitt, pp.66-9).

Rising real income will generally have a soporific effect on the bargainers, as was the case in post-Second World War France, Japan and Germany. On the other hand, during the 1970s Britain, Sweden and the USA recorded smaller gains (or even losses) in real pay (Saunders in Blackaby, pp.192-3). Significantly, the rate of change in prices is an important determinant of union growth in these countries (Bain and Elsheikh, p.106).

In short, trade unions are very important. It is essential that policy prescriptions involving these institutions be based on accurate information. The contributors all hope that this volume will be of assistance in this respect.

Bibliography

Bain, G.S. and Elsheikh, F., *Union Growth and the Business Cycle* (Basil Blackwell, Oxford, 1976)

Blackaby, F. (ed.), *The Future of Pay Bargaining* (Heinemann, London, 1980)

Burkitt, B., *Trade Unions and Wages* (Bradford University Press, 1975)

Fisher, M., *Measurement of Labour Disputes and Their Economic Effects* (OECD, 1973)

Flanders, A. in W. Galenson (ed.), *Comparative Labor Movements* (Prentice-Hall Inc., 1952)

Hicks, J.R., *The Theory of Wages* (Macmillan, 2nd ed. 1963)

Hunter, L., 'Economic Issues in Conciliation and Arbitration', *British Journal of Industrial Relations, XV* (2) (1977), pp.226-45

Kahn-Freund, O., *Labour Relations* (Oxford University Press, 1979)

Meissner, W. and Unterseher, L. (eds.), *Verteilungskampf und Stabilitaetspolitik* (Kohlammer, Stuttgart, 1972)

Metcalf, D., 'Unions, Incomes Policy and Relative Wages in Britain', *British Journal of Industrial Relations, XV* (2) (1977), pp.157-75

Pen, J., *Income Distribution* (Penguin, 1974)

Phelps Brown, E.H., *The Economics of Labor* (Yale University Press, 1962)

Rees, A., *The Economics of Trade Unions* (Chicago University Press, 2nd ed. 1977)

—— *The Economics of Work and Pay* (Harper and Row, 2nd ed. 1979)

Shackle, G.L.S. in J.T. Dunlop (ed.), *The Theory of Wage Determination* (Macmillan, 1966)

Trevithick, J.A. and Mulvey, C., *The Economics of Inflation* (Martin Robertson, 1975)

1 AUSTRALIA

Les Cupper and June M. Hearn

Introduction

Australian unions in their formative years and indeed until the turn of the last century closely followed the pattern of union development in Britain. The savagery of the union-employer, union-government collective bargaining conflicts of the 1890s provided a backdrop for the introduction and acceptance of a system of industrial conciliation and arbitration which in the twentieth century has become all pervading. It is widely believed that no other feature of Australian industrial relations has influenced the growth, structure and policies of trade unions as much as this omnipresent tribunal structure.

Absent, to a large extent, are the strong union shop committees, elsewhere the main bargaining agents for workers. In Australia, the highly centralised (at the state and national levels) union organisations, officially registered and protected, undertake almost exclusively the unions' major activities. Whilst a good deal of direct negotiation occurs between the central union officers and employers, this is always in the shadow, and often under the official auspices, of the various conciliation and arbitration tribunals. Some unions, for example, Australia's largest, the Amalgamated Metal Workers and Shipwrights Union (AMWSU) have systematically attempted to build and maintain a network of local and shop-committee organisations, but the strength of most unions remains at the centre because of the organisational viability afforded through registration within the tribunal structure. Australian union officials have needed to develop the special skills required by the system — preparation of logs of claims, submissions, advocacy, examination and cross-examination of witnesses, etc. — skills of a quasi-legal nature. Many unions are loath to rely on their own 'bush lawyer' talents and employ legally qualified advisers. The whole process has worked towards putting the spotlight on central union bodies and leading union personnel. This is not to say that Australian rank and file unionists are totally or even substantially dormant. The many instances of rejection of union leaderships' recommendations by mass meetings clearly reflect this, as do the occasions of expressed dissatisfaction with the arbitration system's decisions through protests, 'wild-cat' strikes, etc. But these are rarely serious challenges to the basic cut and thrust of the industrial 'law and order' mechanism.

Overall, then, whilst this chapter discusses important factors such as the state of the economy, changing technology, demographic influences, political considerations, etc., in shaping Australian unionism, prominence is given to the unions' dependence upon, and support for, a centralised system of conciliation and arbitration, occasional lapses notwithstanding. In toto, the chapter should provide a recognisable, though necessarily sketchy, profile and analysis of Australian trade unions.

Trade Union Growth

Origins

Trade societies established in the Australian colonies in the 1830s and 1840s were the precursor to Australian unionism which in substantial form dates from the 1850s and earns for Australian organised labour the title of 'veteran' by international standards (Gollan). Between 1850 and 1880, unions, following the British pattern yet predating Britain in adopting on a large scale the 'new unionism' (extending beyond a single trade base), were established in a wide range of crafts and industries; a number of inter-union co-ordinating bodies were formed; some world 'firsts' including the 8-hour day (1856) were chalked up; and the roots of one distinctive labour political party were planted. The stage was being set for the emergence of a powerful, national labour movement to coincide with the birth of Australia as a nation state. This birth of a nation, with the advent of federation in 1901, was preceded by chronic 'labour pains' in the 1890s which threatened the very life of most of the existing trade unions, caused the death of many and spawned still others.

In sharp contrast to the decades of economic boom before the 1890s, especially in the 1850s/1870s which covered the period of the gold rushes, the last decade of the nineteenth century was one of acute depression. Trade unions, attempting to retain rather than extend their strength, discovered that the odds against them were too great. The issues in the main centred on the unions' insistence on approved terms and conditions of employment and the right to organise as against the employers' refusal to recognise union organisation and their determination to offer 'the right to work' to any person, unionist or not, on their own terms and conditions. With trade slack and unemployment rampant, it was relatively easy for the employers to hold sway in this trial of strength. The battles were concentrated in the maritime, mining and shearing industries, the numbers of strikers reaching 50,000 at one time with thousands more workers displaced because of the strikes and lockouts. The events are referred to, euphemistically, in labour circles as the 'Great Strikes'. In fact, from a union viewpoint they epitomised desperation, defeat and disillusionment.

1900-1928

Union recovery from the 1890s depended heavily on the advent of the federal conciliation and arbitration system in 1904 with the purpose of preventing and settling industrial disputes of an interstate character. The system, above all, guaranteed formal recognition for federally registered unions, gave legal force to industrial awards and agreements determined within its jurisdiction and, very early in the course of its history, became Australia's centralised minimum wage fixing agency. Undoubtedly the opportunity for legal registration and consequent near monopoly of coverage over relevant groups of workers was a powerful stimulus to union growth, a factor long recognised by labour historians and recently acknowledged by econometricians (Bain and Elsheikh; Sharpe). Indeed, the system depended upon unions for its operation. Although there are no accurate statistics concerning union membership before 1912, it is estimated that the number of unionists rose from approximately 100,000 in 1900 to 500,000 in 1914, largely because of the protection of the industrial tribunal structure (Gollan).

The overriding motivation for unions to choose to work within the machinery of conciliation and arbitration was pragmatic — employers would be forced to accept unions as legitimate parties in determining terms and conditions of employment and unions would have a reasonable guarantee of organisational survival. However, the system was not universally welcomed by Australian unionists. The period was one of world-wide social and political unrest. Doctrines of class war via the American-based Industrial Workers of the World (Wobblies) and from European Marxist movements (especially after the 1917 Russian revolution) imbued many Australian unionists with a determination to expose the arbitral machinery as a capitalist ploy to suppress and manipulate the workers; there remained, in short, an active minority with a preference for direct confrontation with employers and, eventually, the state. The tensions, controls and economic constraints imposed by the advent of the First World War added to the strength of those groups who labelled the arbitration system as a mouthpiece for the ruling class. The 'general strike' of

1917 reflected this approach. The lack of unity among the various anti-arbitration factions, the failure to arouse sufficient grass-roots support for the concept of direct industrial action as *the* strategy for unionists, the strength of the employing class and the machinery of the state, plus the practical advantages of the system to unions as previously discussed, all continued to ensure the viability of the legal industrial framework. Nevertheless the system has always had a small hard core of critics on ideological grounds.

The early part of the twentieth century marked the birth of the ALP (1901) as a distinct, national political party of labour. The remarkably early electoral success of the ALP made possible legislation to extend the franchise, regulate conditions in factories, exclude non-European migrants (perceived as threatening working conditions), introduce social welfare measures such as old age pensions, exercise some control over monopolistic trade practices and generally facilitate pro-labour reforms. Formed largely by active unionists and with direct union-party organisational links (approximately two-thirds of Australian unionists are currently directly affiliated through their individual unions to the Labor Party), the ALP, alongside arbitration, served to institutionalise industrial conflict to a large extent and to encourage unions to develop within a highly centralised, legalistic and overtly political framework. Within this framework the various parties in the industrial relations arena have learnt to accommodate each other. Especially pertinent to this accommodation process has been the growth of central co-ordinating bodies, most notably the Australian Council of Trade Unions (ACTU), which was established in 1927 at a time when unions had undergone several years of growth reaching an average density of 55 per cent of the workforce. The period was also one of bitter demarcation disputes resulting from increased mechanisation, the spread of process work and the growth of the manufacturing sector of the economy. In the 1920s it was still possible to discern the skilled tradesman but often as not his union would also encompass or compete to encompass many other categories of workers not clearly identifiable under the old trade or craft definitions. Inter-union rivalry over organisational jurisdiction provided a strong impetus for the formation of the ACTU. Possibly the most important 'conditions' achievement of Australian unions by the end of the 1920s was the 44-hour working week.

1929-1945

As in the 1890s, forewarned but not forearmed, Australian unions were ill-equipped to protect their members from the onslaught of the 1929/33 depression. Miners, waterside workers and building workers took on employers and governments in vain attempts to resist wage cuts of 20 per cent and more. Massive unemployment reduced the unions' capacity to organise and to engage in direct action. In 1930, strikes accounted for a loss of 1,500,000 work days, whereas in 1933 only 111,000 days were lost. Union membership similarly declined by 115,000 between 1930 and 1933; the proportion of the workforce unionised had dropped from 52.7 per cent to 44.4 per cent in the same period. The slight economic recovery leading up to the Second World War assisted unions to make some gains but generally their position remained weak. The most notable advances were made by unions led by more militant (including communist) leaders, for example, the Miners Federation. Their success was symptomatic of a wave of militancy that was just beginning to break on the union scene when war began.

The Second World War differed from its predecessor in that, at least by 1941, there was a total unison between the trade unions and the (Labor) government in pursuit of an all-out war effort. The fact that Australia was supplying materials as well as manpower meant that full employment for the first time in many years was a feature of the economy. Union agreements with government policies such as wage-pegging, and extended working hours, were entered into on the understanding that they were merely postponements of concessions to be granted after the war. Industrial disputes were not entirely absent but industrial peace was mostly the order of the day.

Post Second World War

The immediate post-war years witnessed an expansion and greater centralisation of secondary industry, a corresponding growth in unionism and an end to the moratorium on many union claims, signalled by a spate of industrial unrest, for example, the historic 1949 coal miners' strike. This was also a period of bitter inter-union and intra-union conflicts, particularly between communist and anti-communist 'Industrial Groups' (Rawson, 1971). Torrid struggles took place in the Clerks, Ironworkers, Railways, Engineering, Building and Waterside Workers Unions and impacted the labour movement generally. The culmination of this conflict was the split in the ALP and the formation of the Democratic Labor Party (DLP) in the mid 1950s.

This was a period of intense politicisation of unions, some of which carry the legacy of wounds to this day. Arguably, the political in-fighting did little to improve the image of unionism in the wider community.

Australian union membership peaked at 61 per cent of the workforce in 1954 before entering a steady decline. The decline in aggregate union membership reflected both the changes in the structure of the labour force and the inability of Australian unions to adjust quickly to changed circumstances. Unionisation in the growth sectors of the economy, particularly the private sector service areas, could not keep pace with the rate of expansion in the workforce nor offset the impact on union membership of the reduced employment opportunities in the traditional strongholds of unionism (coal mining, shipping, stevedoring and railways), the metal trades and engineering industries aside. As a consequence, the period 1954-71 saw, on the one hand, an increase of 36 per cent in actual unionists, and, on the other, a 10 per cent reduction in overall union density (Rawson, 1978). The dominance of non-labour governments (usually less disposed to grant union preference clauses and check-off arrangements) and a Court decision which overturned the validity of compulsory unionism in Queensland (union density falling from 71 per cent in 1966 to 54 per cent in 1973), were further factors contributing to the decline in union density (ibid.).

The slump was not arrested until 1971 and by 1973 the proportion of unionists among wage and salary earners had climbed to 57 per cent. This revival was even more meritorious in the light of the economic downturn experienced in the manufacturing sector during the early 1970s. Two factors contributing to the revival were compulsory unionism agreements and a marked growth in public sector employment. During the late 1960s and the early 1970s (in the wake of a High Court judgement upholding an important Arbitration Commission decision granting preference to unionists), several non-manual unions negotiated compulsory unionism (and check-off) agreements with large private sector employers. Although the agreements were generally restricted to new or future employees, their impact led to dramatic membership increases in unions covering retailing, clerical, banking and insurance workers. The Shop Distributive and Allied Employees' Association, for example, trebled its membership between 1969 and 1971 and in the process rose from the eighteenth to the third largest union. Public sector employment, already highly organised, expanded during the early 1970s. As a consequence, most unions covering federal and state public servants, including teachers, recorded membership increases well in excess of the national growth rate for the period 1971/6. In part, the growth in public sector unionism was fanned by the pronouncements and actions of the federal Labor government (1972/5); for example, an announcement by the Minister for Industrial Relations that an additional week's annual leave would only accrue to union members (a proposal that was later withdrawn) led to a rapid swelling in the ranks of the relevant federal public sector unions. In contrast to the growth in non-manual unions, membership of most large manufacturing unions (including the metal trades) either declined or increased by less than the average growth rate for the period 1971/6. Building industry unions, generally, however, more than held their own. Table 1.1 provides a more complete picture of the service industry/non-manual led revival.

Concomitant with the growth in non-manual unionism was the dramatic increase in unionisation among women workers. The number of female unionists rose by 63 per cent between 1969 and 1975 compared with a 26 per cent rise among male unionists (Rawson, 1978). This increase in turn reflects the greater concentration of female employees in the non-manual and service areas. It has recently been estimated that just over half the female unionists are located in the professional, technical and clerical occupations, compared with 23 per cent of male unionists (Australian Bureau of Statistics (ABS) Survey: 6.65, 1977). However, despite this recent growth and the fact that five of Australia's eight largest unions have more female than male members, overall, seven in ten unionists are male. Moreover, female union officials (full-time industrial staff) remain under-represented in union hierarchies. In 1979, a study of some 450 full-time positions in 36 non-manual unions found that only 14 per cent were filled by females (Cupper, 1980) – a similar situation to that for non-British migrant representation in union leadership (Hearn).

The policies of the ALP government (1972/5) in supporting union claims for equal pay, the introduction of maternity leave, increased annual leave entitlements and, from April 1975, the implementation of a form of social contract whereby a degree of industrial restraint was traded off for an expectation of automatic wage increases in line with cost of living movements (see Policy section), all contributed to a climate conducive to an overall image of union success and strength; so much so that fears of excessive union power were being voiced as a substantial element in the non-Labor parties' (eventually

Table 1.1: Membership of Unions with 10,000 or more Members, 1979 (showing per cent change since 1976 and since 1969)

	Membership (000)	Per cent change since 1976	since 1969
Amal. Metal Workers & Shipwrights	158.5	−3	+6
Shop, Distributive & Allied Employees	145.0	+7	+263
Aust. Workers	135.3	−3	−15
Aust. Teachers*	125.4	+25	+43
Fed. Clerks	99.8	−4	+51
Fed. Liquor & Allied Industries Employees	97.5	−19	+144
Transport Workers	95.1	+2	+29
Fed. Miscellaneous Workers	92.6	+1	+27
Aust. Bank Employees	67.7	+4	+78
Electrical Trades	66.2	−9	+6
Fed. Storemen & Packers	66.2	+8	+154
Fed. Ironworkers	65.7	−1	0
A'asian Meat Industry Employees	53.3	+17	+20
Printing & Kindred Industries	51.7	−7	−3
Fed. Municipal & Shire Employees	50.3	+16	+5
Aust. Railways	50.2	+14	+5
Administrative & Clerical Officers	48.3	−1	+79
Building Workers (BWIU)	47.4	−7	+8
Aust. Postal & Telecommunications	46.2	0	+16
A'asian Society of Engineers	41.9	−31	−43
Public Service Assn of NSW	41.8	+6	+60
NSW Nurses	40.2	na	+168
Royal Aust. Nursing	39.4	+10	+365
Vehicle Builders	39.3	0	+12
Aust. Public Service Assn (4th Division)	35.3	−5	+194
Clothing & Allied Trades	33.4	−11	−5
Health and Research	33.4	0	+57
Aust. Textile Workers	28.8	−13	−31
Municipal Officers	28.0	+6	+40
C'wealth Bank Officers	28.0	+6	+40
Fed. Engine Drivers	26.9	−8	+8
Aust. Telecommunications Employees	25.7	0	+8
Public Service Assn of SA	24.1	+13	+136
Aust. Building Construction Employees & Builders Labourers	24.0	−18	+89
Aust. Insurance Employees	22.2	+12	+62
Amal. Society of Carpenters & Joiners	20.6	+18	+59
Assn of Architects, Engineers, Surveyors & Draughtsmen	20.1	−14	+39
Vic. Public Service Assn	20.0	na	+77
Operative Painters	19.6	−10	−19
Aust. Transport Officers	18.4	+2	+60
Queensland State Service	18.4	0	+70
SA Institute of Teachers	17.8	+20	+31
Civil Service Assn of WA	15.3	+9	+46
Assn of Professional Engineers	15.1	−5	+36
Musicians	14.9	−9	+32
Aust. Timber Workers	14.7	−11	−14
Fed. Rubber Workers	14.3	+1	−2
A'asian Coal & Shale (Miners)	13.6	+20	+23
Aust. Tramway & Motor Omnibus Employees	12.5	+2	−2
Aust. Fed. Union of Locomotive Enginemen	12.0	+5	+2
Food Preservers	11.0	+77	+69
Waterside Workers	10.0	−17	−46

Note: *The membership of this union has been compared with a total membership, in 1969, of the unions which now comprise it (see Structure section).

Source: Rawson and Wrightson, 1981.

successful) bid for office in December 1975.

Since 1976, union density has stabilised (approximately 57 per cent of wage and salary earners) and a plateau appears to have been reached. Indeed, unions may even be hard pressed to maintain their current proportion of membership considering the levelling off in public sector employment, the cessation by the Federal Liberal-National Party coalition government of certain public sector unions 'check-off' arrangements in retaliation against direct action, a far from expansionary manufacturing sector, post-Second World War record levels of unemployment, and the not unrelated introduction of labour-saving computer-based technology in the service industries. An untapped frontier of unionisation may well be in the management sphere, especially in the light of overseas experience (Ford and Lansbury).

It should be noted that the 1970s represented not only a growth period for unionism but, especially with the 'wages explosion' of 1973/4, the drift away from arbitration and a preference for settlements outside the system, rising militancy among white collar/ professional unionists (Lansbury, 1977), plus a continuing high rate of inflation, was also a time of considerable industrial unrest. Between March 1973 and March 1974, there was a 342 per cent increase in the number of working days lost as compared with the previous year (Allan *et al.*).

The pattern of industrial disputes, with an emphasis on the last decade, is presented in Tables 1.2 and 1.3 and Figure 1.1.

Table 1.2: Proportion of Industrial Disputes by Industry, Australia, 1913-1978

			Industry		
	Coal mining[a]	Manu-facturing	Con-struction	Stevedor-ing[b]	Other
1913-20	51	20	3	15	11
1921-30	73	11	3	8	5
1931-40	74	11	2	3	10
1941-50	76	13	1	7	3
1951-60	55	15	5	19	6
1961-65	20	40	12	20	8
1966-70	11	48	16	13	12
1971-75	8	38	12	12	30
1976-78	11	41	11	9	28

Notes:
a Includes other mining 1913-25.
b Includes other transport 1913-50
Sources: ABS *Labour Reports*, 1915-70; *Industrial Disputes*, 1978.

Figure 1.1: Industrial Disputes and Working Days Lost, Australia,

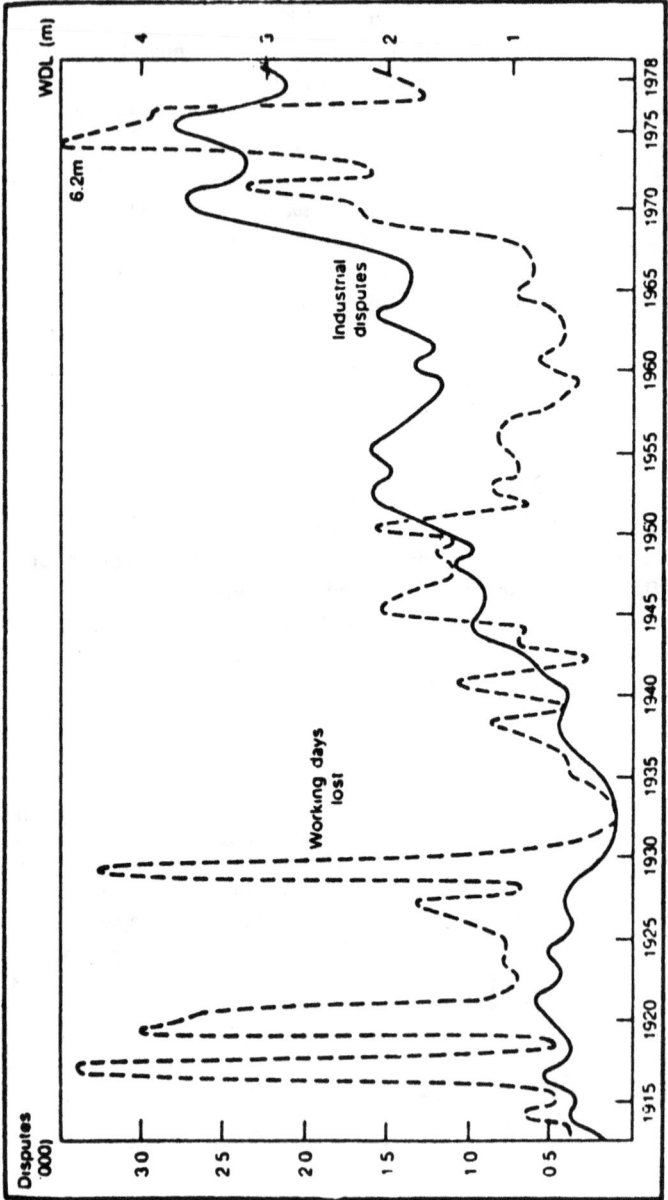

Sources: ABS, *Labour Reports*, 1915-53; and *Labour Statistics*, 1978; Plowman *et al.*

Table 1.3: Annual Statistics of Industrial Disputations, 1970-1979

	1970	1971	1972	1973	1974	1975	1976	1977	1978	1979
Number of disputes	2738	2404	2298	2538	2809	2432	2047	2090	2277	2032
							(2055)*			(2040)**
Number of workers involved ('000)	1367.4	1326.5	1113.8	803.0	2004.8	1298.0	615.5	596.2	1075.6	962.7
							(2189.9)*			(1862.9)**
Number of working days lost ('000)	2393.7	3068.6	2010.3	2634.7	6292.5	3509.9	1741.7	1654.8	2130.8	3063.6
							(3799.2)*			(3964.4)**

Notes:
* Figures in brackets are those including effects of Medibank stoppages (opposition to the dismantling of a national health insurance scheme).
** Figures in brackets are those including effects of Western Australian Union officials' dispute (opposition to restrictions on right of assembly).

Sources: Australian Bureau of Statistics, *Labour Report*, No.58, 1973; *Industrial Disputes* (Catalogue No.6321.0); *Industrial Disputes* (Catalogue No.6322.0).

Government-Union Relations: Recent Initiatives

A perennial problem confronting Australian governments, dealing with
unions which operate within a legal framework yet repeatedly flout the
industrial laws, is how to impose effective penalties for breaches of the
rules without bestowing upon the transgressing unions a martyrdom
they could not hope to achieve single-handed. The Conciliation and
Arbitration Act embodies powers for prosecuting parties in breach of
industrial laws (including awards and agreements) but in the past decade
these have rarely been invoked. The most celebrated exercise of such
powers occurred in 1969 when a tramways union official was gaoled
for contempt of court for refusing to surrender his union's records to
the Industrial Court after the union had decided not to pay fines for
engaging in strikes in defiance of Court orders. The resulting nationwide industrial chaos and unified stance of unions in opposition to the
use of industrial penal powers succeeded in securing the early release
of the union official in quite bizarre circumstances. (It came to an end
when an anonymous donor paid the union's fines and the union official
was released from gaol without, however, ever 'purging' his contempt
of court.) This experience made employers distinctly reluctant to
initiate prosecutions against recalcitrant unions. It was in this context
and with a general 'get tough with unions' mandate that the Liberal-
National Party government established the Industrial Relations Bureau
(IRB) in 1977 under an amendment to the Conciliation and Arbitration
Act. It was intended that the Bureau would protect the worker not
wishing to be a unionist, would police the operation of the industrial
laws and regulations and, most importantly, initiate prosecutions against
any breaches, the latter designed to compensate for the undoubted
unwillingness of employers to utilise their own powers to initiate
prosecutions under the former (pre-IRB) Act. To date, the IRB has had
a succession of 'celebrated' failures in its actions against unions but in
1980 it did survive a High Court challenge by Australia's largest union,
the AMWSU, contesting the validity of its powers. The fate of this
relatively new and, among unions as well as many employers,
unpopular industrial relations enforcement agency is uncertain.

   In addition to the IRB, the government has introduced a plethora of
legislation aimed at curtailing union activities designed to disrupt or
dislocate production of goods and/or provision of services. In
particular, there are measures to prevent the operation of secondary
boycotts during strikes, laws against public servants causing industrial
disruption denial of unemployment benefits to workers laid off
because of strike action by fellow-unionists, as well as proposals for

the introduction of 'secret ballots for strikes' legislation (Mitchell). In
general, it would be true to say that since the departure of the last
Labor government in 1975, the conservatives have been committed to
union control through legislation, although it must be conceded that
so far there has been a heavy reliance on threat, and proceedings have
been implemented cautiously. The unions, too, have largely resorted
to bark rather than bite in their responses to government initiatives
which, if fully pursued, could seriously restrict their growth and
operations.

Trade Union Structure

One of the Australian trade union movement's most distinguishing
characteristics is its multiplicity of employee organisations. No fewer
than 315 trade unions service a total membership of 2.85 million
unionists. This fragmentation is not surprising given the movement's
craft origins the subsequent grafting on of semi-skilled and unskilled
employees, flirtation with industry unionism, the organisational
protection accorded unions by various conciliation and arbitration
systems and union and tribunal preference for using 'occupation' in
determining union eligibility. Nor is it surprising that the classical
union typology – craft, industrial and general unions – fits
uncomfortably with the realities of Australian union structure *viz.*
horizontal organisation 'based on one or more specified occupations,
which may or may not be qualified by reference to a specific industry
or to formally acquired skills' (Martin).
   The distribution of unionists among unions is far from uniform.
Seven unions (with memberships in excess of 80,000) account for
28 per cent of total membership and 98 unions with fewer than 500
members constitute a little more than half a per cent of total
membership. Indeed, 189 unions (those with memberships of
less than 2,000) account for only 3.8 per cent of total membership.
ABS data reveal that 174 unions operate in one state only but that
these single-state unions account for only 19 per cent of total
membership. Of the remaining interstate or federated unions, 89 are
truly national in that they operate in each of the six states. Of further
note is the relative uniformity in union density as between states
(54 to 63 per cent).
   Union density tends to be less uniform between industries. In 1976,
for example, in excess of 70 per cent density was recorded in the

communications, electricity, gas and water, transport and storage, and public administration and defence (notably public sector employment) compared with 20 per cent density in agriculture, timber and fishing. Less than three in ten persons employed in the wholesale and retail trades are unionised (ABS, *Labour Statistics*, 1977).

The multi-union character of Australian industry — 'it would not be unusual . . . for more than 20 unions to have members in a large enterprise' (Myers Report, vol.1, p.139) — is not confined to the private sector. No fewer than 88 unions have coverage in Federal government employment (which in turn reflects the diversity of occupational categories), 37 of whom recruit exclusively among the federal public sector employees. The remainder also have members in the private sector or state public service or authorities. The size of 'pure' public sector unions ranges from the large general unions, such as the Administrative and Clerical Officers Association and the Australian Postal and Telecommunications Union (with memberships in excess of 40,000), to the small occupationally-based unions such as the Commonwealth Medical Officers' Association boasting a couple of hundred members. The penetration of 'mixed' unions into Federal government employment varies. For example, the Federated Miscellaneous Workers Union has only 2 per cent of its members in the public sector, whereas the Association of Architects, Engineers Surveyors and Draughtsmen of Australia has approximately 40 per cent, but their focus is generally confined to occupations where the pay and conditions closely match those outside the public sector and where employees are mobile between the sectors.

In part, the fragmentation of Australian union structure is offset by the presence and activities of the Australian Council of Trade Unions, the major co-ordinating peak or inter-union body. In September 1979, the occasion of its last biennial Congress, the ACTU had 138 affiliated unions representing an estimated 2,360,000 unionists or approximately 85 per cent of the unionised workforce. Affiliates, ranging in size from the AMWSU with 158,000 members to unions with less than 50 members, are allocated to eight Industry Groups. Table 1.4 records the distribution of unions (and unionists) among the respective 'Industry' Groups, gives an indication of the growth of non-manual unionism in the services area, and the stability cum decline of the traditional strongholds of unionism, for example, manufacturing and the Australian Workers Union, referred to in the previous section.

The ACTU's position as the dominant inter-union council was further strengthened in 1979 following the disbandment of ACSPA,

Table 1.4: 'Industry' Groups of Unions Affiliated to the Australian Council of Trade Unions (September 1969 and 1979)

Group	No. of unions		Membership	
	1969	1979	1969	1979
Metal Industry	9	10	295,579	321,951
Transport	20	27	157,451	205,321
Services	30	42	348,448	502,150
Food and Distributive Services	21	18	155,678	376,006
Australian Workers Union (AWU)*	1	1	148,507	117,620
Manufacturing	15	16	183,748	178,896
Building	16	14	128,201	138,584
Australian Council of Salaried and Professional Associations (ACSPA)**	—	10	—	226,196

Notes:
* The Australian Workers Union (then Australia's largest union) joined the ACTU in 1969 on the condition that it receive the status of a separate Industry Group and membership of the ACTU Executive.
** The ACSPA group was formed in 1979 to accommodate the new non-manual affiliates stemming from the ACTU-ACSPA merger. Prior to the merger a number of unions were affiliated to both ACSPA and the ACTU. These dual affiliates were given the option of joining the new ACSPA Industry Group but, with the exception of two state constituents of the Australian Teachers Federation, decided to remain in their existing groupings.
   Other inter-union councils (1977) included the Australian Federation of Police Associations and Unions (25,945), the Australian Public Service Federation (123,152), the Australian Teachers Federation (114,556) and the Council of Professional Associations (34,641).

Source: Derived from Plowman *et al.* (Appendix 8.1).

the then leading non-manual or 'white-collar' peak body. ACSPA affiliates (associations with members employed as salaried officers in professional, commercial, technical or similar occupations), with some notable exceptions (the Australian Banking Employees Union and two state teacher unions with a combined membership of 90,000), affiliated with the ACTU, swelling the Council's numbers by approximately 162,000 members (Cupper and Hearn). More recently, the Federation of College Academics have voted to join the ACTU. In contrast, a proposal by the Federation of Australian University Staff Associations to affiliate with the ACTU was rejected by its member associations. The ACTU-ACSPA merger was the culmination of ten years of negotiations and may well be 'one more indication of the diminishing organisational and behavioural gap between manual and white collar unions in general' (Martin, p.29). It should be noted, however, that where plebiscites were conducted among the union membership (as distinct from decisions taken by union councils) to decide the question of affiliation, the voting proved to be very close. The terms of the ACTU-ACSPA merger, particularly favourable to ACSPA regarding representation on the ACTU Executive, reflected the ACTU's desire to achieve closer organisational unity and a recognition of the changing balance of the blue collar/white collar composition of the Australian workforce.

The Council of Australian Government Employee Organisations (CAGEO) is the other major inter-union body. CAGEO's 25 affiliates represent 225,000 unionists employed by the Federal government and/or its statutory authorities. Several CAGEO affiliates are also affiliated to the ACTU and it is almost certain that this public sector peak council will formally merge with the ACTU.

A long-standing objective of the ACTU is unionism structured along industry lines. Despite constant reminders by an array of industry, government and union spokesmen of the need for amalgamation/ mergers and the benefits thereof, rationalisation has proved to be a most difficult task. Numerically, there has been a net reduction of 46 unions since 1968 but by far the largest proportion of this reduction resulted from kindred single-state unions forming federations. (The number of single-state unions fell by 49 over the same period.) To the authors' knowledge, only five amalgamations have occurred in the federal jurisdiction in the past decade, the most notable of which involved the Boilermakers and Blacksmiths Society, the Amalgamated Engineering Union and the Sheetmetal Workers which merged to form Australia's largest union, the Amalgamated Metal Workers Union (AMWU) in 1972. This amalgamation was a forerunner to the AMWU merger with the Federated Shipwrights and Constructors Association (forming the AMWSU) in 1976 and to the current negotiations for a further merger with the strategically placed Federated Engine Drivers and Firemens Association.

All too frequently it is implied that mergers are easily achieved. Nothing could be further from the truth, at least in the Australian context. Federal-state, and indeed, interstate branch rivalries (Barker), threatened redundancies among incumbent officials, the loss of union identity or heritage, ideological incompatability (Carr) and organisational jealousies, quite apart from the exacting legal requirements applied to organisations seeking amalgamations under the Federal Conciliation and Arbitration Act, are but some of the factors militating against formal mergers. Further, the absence of severe economic recession and widespread structural change and the virtual perpetuity guaranteed by the arbitration system, have enabled many smaller unions to avoid the necessity to merge into larger more viable organisational units. It is of note that no unions have attempted to amalgamate under the existing legal requirement (introduced in 1972) that at least 50 per cent of the rank and file of each of the unions seeking amalgamation must cast votes before a majority supporting the proposal can be deemed valid. The union amalgamations that have occurred since 1972 have proceeded under an 'exclusion clause' which does not require the 'host' union to submit itself to a ballot if the membership of the amalgamating union is less than 1/20th of its own membership (Khoury). The 50 per cent plus 'turn out' barrier is currently the subject of review by the National Labour Advisory Council and is expected to be reduced to at least 25 per cent.

However, despite the factors hindering amalgamation, the rationalisation of Australian union structure is not a dead issue. Serious merger negotiations (some already culminating in memorandums of agreement or understanding) are proceeding between the Australian Textile Workers Union (26,108 members) and the Australian Boot Trade Employees Federation (7,600 members); the Seamen's Union of Australia (4,625 members) and the Marine Cooks, Bakers and Butchers Association (500 members); the Federated Ironworkers Association (58,719 members) and the Australasian Society of Engineers (21,703 members); and the two major distributive unions – the Federated Storemen and Packers Union of Australia (62,000 members) and the Transport Workers Union of Australia (65,820 members). The issue of 'one union on the waterfront' is also currently being pursued on Australia's wharves and a special amalgamation conference has been conducted by the leading unions in the postal and telecommunications divisions of the public service.

Reasons for the proposed mergers are many and varied but include economic viability. The textile and boot trade unions, for example, lost between 30 and 50 per cent of their respective memberships in the years immediately following the 25 per cent tariff cuts of 1974. Political and industrial compatibility (postal and telecommunications; transport and distribution) and the pressures of technological change (including demarcation disputes) also underlie the proposed (and recent) amalgamations (Barker). Interestingly, many of the mergers mooted involve medium sized rather than small (less than 2,000 members) unions, a consideration that concerns those who have an inordinate fear of union power.

Recent mergers at inter-union council level (actual and probable), represent major developments in the rationalisation of Australian union structures and should serve as an example for individual unions. The 'new look' ACTU could have up to 160 affiliates representing a wide cross section (2.5 million) of the Australian workforce. The mergers will provide an excellent opportunity for the ACTU to re-examine its internal executive/organisational structure. Indeed, following an unsuccessful move during the 1979 Congress to expand the current Executive to provide direct representation to unions with memberships in excess of 75,000, the ACTU acknowledged that, in the light of changes in the labour force, its current representative structure needed modification and agreed to review this as a matter of high priority. Figure 1.2 outlines the existing ACTU power structure.

Before considering some selected Australian union policy issues, brief comment should be made on two matters related to the structure of the Australian trade union movement. Firstly, Australia's fragmented, largely occupation-based, union structure (and the consequent overlapping jurisdiction) and the recent shifts in the composition of the unionised workforce have provided ample opportunity for inter-union rivalry to raise its head. Regrettably, the absence of reliable data reduces the discussion to mere impressions but inter-union conflict seems to be more disruptive and bitter over issues involving the demarking of a particular type of work (particularly where new technology has eroded, or threatens to erode, the supply of work; for example, building and construction and railways) than over the demarking of unions' jurisdictional coverage, although the two are often interrelated. Inter-union disputes of a 'body-snatching' type, whilst equally sensitive issues, appear less prone to strike action as they are often short-circuited by the legal requirements for organisations registered in the federal system to have their rules (including coverage) approved, and to notify and seek approval from the Industrial Registrar if they wish to alter their rules, for example, to broaden their membership eligibility clause. It is not unusual in these matters for up to 20 unions to oppose formally the proposed rule variation. In arriving at a solution, 'working agreements' as to current (and future) coverage are often reached between the disputing unions. Nor is it unusual for registered unions to oppose vehemently the application for the registration of a new union on the grounds that the employees to be represented by the new organisation may already 'conveniently belong' to a registered organisation. This defence

Figure 1.2: ACTU Executive Structure (1979) (total membership 21)

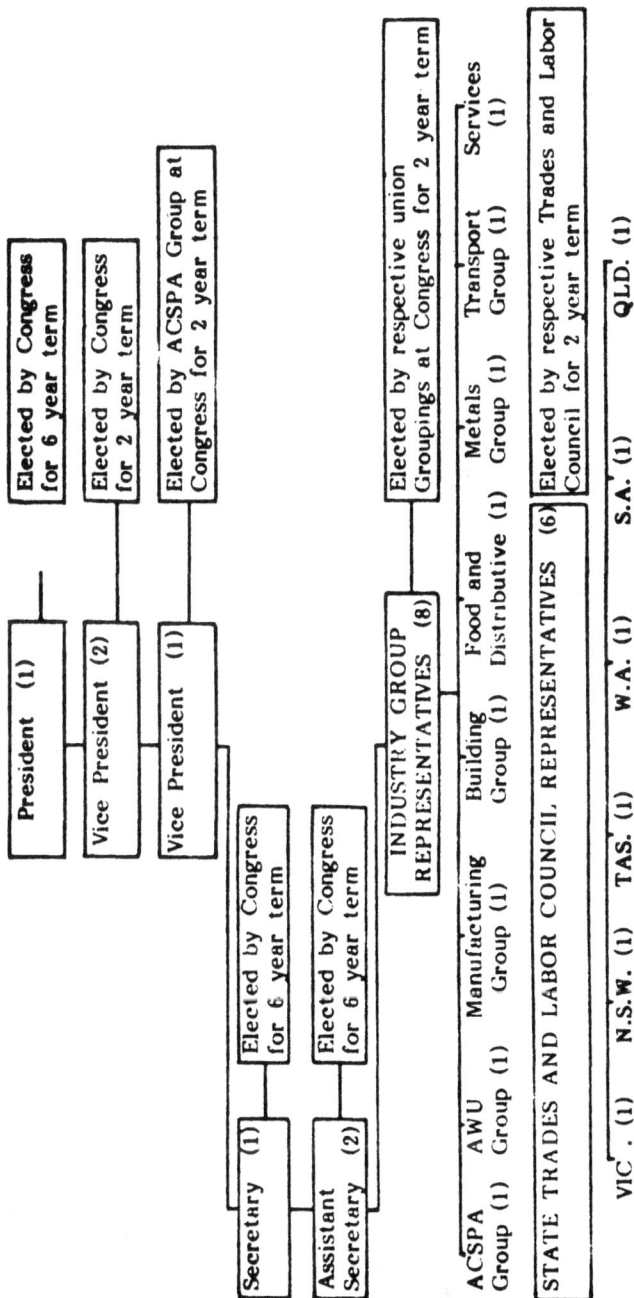

was recently employed by established clerical/administrative unions to frustrate the Australian Computer Professionals Association's attempt to register and gain coverage of workers in the expanding computer industry.

Secondly, the multiplicity of employee organisations coupled with low membership dues has resulted in many unions being poorly staffed and resourced — an oft-cited reason for rationalising union structure. Of particular note, however, is the increasing employment of specialist support (mainly research) staff in the medium sized and larger unions, particularly, but not exclusively, in the non-manual area and the major inter-union councils. The emergence of 'the professionals' or, less kindly, 'the young Turks' (often tertiary educated) within the leadership of Australian unions and their peak councils has led to a marked improvement in the quality of union position papers, submissions and policy recommendations. This development, coupled with public-funded trade union education programmes (Cupper, 1980), represents a substantial challenge to the assumption of many union officials that the 'school of hard-knocks' is the only teacher.

Trade Union Policy

An underlying theme of this chapter has been the close association between Australian union growth and structure and the legally constituted conciliation and arbitration systems. The relationship between union policy (and strategy pursued in support of policy) and the industrial tribunals is equally pronounced, even to the point that Australian unions have been accused of lacking industrial self-reliance (Howard). A less critical view, and one supported by the authors, is that Australian unions are essentially pragmatic, using the socially acceptable tribunal framework when appropriate and pursuing claims outside of the system on other occasions (the two approaches not being mutually exclusive). Australia's industrial dispute record (see Growth section) also suggests that the unions' recourse to direct action has not been unduly inhibited by the presence of 'the rule of law'. In short, a 'best of both worlds' approach has been employed which serves to fan academic and practitioner debate on the respective merits of collective bargaining and compulsory arbitration (Niland). This two-dimensional character of Australian union strategy is perhaps best illustrated by reference to the traditional union concerns of wage determination and job security.

Wage Determination

Dating from the famous Harvester (Basic Wage) Judgement of 1907,
Australian unions have relied extensively on tribunal-determined
minimum award standards. These have operated at the national, industry
and enterprise levels as the basis upon which to build further wage
tiers (for example, over-award payments) by means of direct negotiation
coupled with coercive power. For most of this century the annual/
biennial/quarterly and now the six-monthly National Wage Case presided
over by a full bench of the Federal Conciliation and Arbitration
Commission has been the central means for establishing *national*
minimum standards, for maintaining purchasing power and for
distributing the benefits of national productivity gains among wage and
salary earners generally. While the influence of the National Wage
decision is far reaching (given that state industrial tribunals invariably
adjust their respective awards and agreements in line with the decisions
of the Federal Commission), its importance in overall wage determination
has fluctuated markedly. In 1967/8, for example, the percentage
contribution of National Wage Case increases to the total increase in
the weighted average minimum weekly wage rates for males was 39.5
per cent, rising to 52.6 per cent in 1970/1 and falling to 19.1 per cent
in 1973/4 (Howard, p.93). In the year ending December 1978 (as a
by-product of the wage indexation guidelines discussed more fully
below), a staggering 97 per cent of the movement in the average
minimum weekly wage for males (and 99 per cent for females) was
attributable to National Wage Cases. The residual movement in wages
is either determined within the system by arbitrated decisions,
registered agreements or consent awards, or by collective agreements
emanating from, yet remaining outside of, the tribunal framework
(Yerbury and Isaac).

It is generally recognised that during the 1950s and early 1960s
the majority of wage settlements were arbitrated decisions. Negotiated
agreements, particularly of any substance, were newsworthy events
(De Vyver). The mid to late 1960s witnessed both a marked increase
in direct negotiations and an expansion in the contents (scope) of
agreements. The shift to collective bargaining was due to many factors
but of primary importance was the policy of the Arbitration
Commission in restricting, or attempting to restrict, the rate of wage
increase. As one commentator remarked, 'the Commission would not
grant the increases that unions thought the market would provide thus
they were forced into the bargaining area to obtain the adjustment
that the Commission denied them' (Howard, p.92). An environment

permissive of price increases and characterised by sustained full
employment aided unions in their pursuit of negotiated agreements.
Consent awards and certified agreements dominated the federal
jurisdiction during the early 1970s. Indeed, for the period from
1970 to 1973 approximately three-quarters of the total settlements
within the Commission were of the 'non-arbitrated' variety. A survey
of 60 major unions, conducted during the early 1970s, disclosed that
three-quarters of the respondents claimed to be using direct
negotiations or bargaining procedures in dispute resolution, of which
some 30 per cent were negotiated solely within the conciliation and
arbitration framework, 20 per cent were operating completely outside
the system, while 50 per cent were using a mixed approach (Niland).
This general movement to self-reliance was in part due to increased
legislative support for the Commission's conciliatory, as distinct from
arbitral, functions and the more accommodative stance adopted by
Commission personnel (Cupper, 1976; Isaac).

Australia's new era in pragmatism and direct negotiation received
an abrupt setback in April 1975 when, amid pressure for wage restraint
from a Labor government normally espousing the virtues of collective
bargaining, and after tripartite conferences convened by the
Commission had failed to reach agreement on principles for wage
fixing, the Commission introduced what have become known as the
'wage indexation guidelines'.

The guidelines were a clear attempt by the Commission to regain
a tight rein on wage determination at a time when average weekly
earnings had increased by 28.6 per cent in the previous year,
unemployment had reached 5 per cent of the workforce and inflation
was approaching an annual rate of 20 per cent. Not unrelated, man-
days lost through industrial disputation had increased dramatically
(see Table 1.3) during the 1974 wages scramble. Clearly the movement
to collective bargaining cannot be held responsible for all of these
adverse developments but, given the impact of negotiated settlements
on established wage relativities and the inevitable quest for their
restoration, it was an important contributing factor.

In brief, the guidelines granted wage increases on the following four
grounds: quarterly indexation (based on the six capital city Consumer
Price Index (CPI) movements) unless the Commission could be
persuaded to the contrary (that is, indexation was not to be automatic);
periodic national productivity hearings; wage adjustments for new work
and changes in work; and, as a phasing-in arrangement, claims on
account of 'catch up of community movements'. Subsequent

modifications to the guidelines (May 1976, September 1978 and April 1980) have seen the quarterly CPI/indexation hearings replaced by six-monthly hearings, the resolution of 'anomolies' and 'inequities' made the subjects for special conferences, and a tightening up of conditions under which work value adjustments may be granted. (It has been estimated that by June 1980 some 50 per cent of employees covered by federal awards had received work value increases in the previous two years.) The linch-pin of the indexation package has remained unaltered, namely, 'substantial compliance' as measured by union willingness to temper direct action and to limit movements in the rates of pay outside of national wage (indexation) hearings.

The ACTU welcomed the general tenor of the guidelines, particularly the restoration of an adjustment system in a time of high inflation. (Between 1921 and 1953 a system of *automatic* quarterly adjustments in line with changes in the CPI had operated in the federal jurisdiction.) However, the Council was quick to warn that it 'did not accept that the decision should be interpreted as involving a wage freeze or removing collective bargaining in regard to wages in accordance with the four grounds for wage increases contemplated by the decisions' (ACTU Executive Resolution, 1973). With the advantage of hindsight, this rider proved to be an expression of pious hope as an estimated 90 per cent of Commission matters are now finalised by arbitration (Lansbury). At its most recent Congress (1979), ACTU affiliates reaffirmed their strong commitment to the right to bargain collectively without substantial compliance, denounced the Commission's departure from full percentage wage indexation in the majority of cases (See Table 1.5) and committed the Council to mounting a national wage claim based on productivity increases since 1973/4: a proposal that will test a previously unused tenet of the wage fixation principles.

The ACTU's call for the restoration of purchasing power and the pursuit of improved conditions (particularly shorter hours) has been adhered to by its more strategically placed affiliates, to the extent that in the June 1980 National Wage Case the Commission made the unprecedented decision to discount the CPI movement by 0.5 per cent for non-substantial compliance, noting that, with the exception of 1974, the January/February 1980 lost-time levels were very much higher than in any year since 1961. However, the Commission did not accept government and private sector employer argument that increases in wage movements in the past six months from other than national wage decisions (primarily across-the-board work value increases)

Table 1.5: Wage Adjustments Under Wage Indexation: March Quarter
1975 to March Quarter 1980

Quarter		Wage variation	CPI increase %
1975	March	Full 3.6%	3.6
	June	Full 3.5%	3.5
	September[1]	None	0.8
	December	(0.8% + 5.6%)	5.6
1976	March[2]	Full 3.0% to $125 p.w.	3.0
		Flat $3.80 thereafter	
	June	Full 2.5% to $98 p.w.	2.5
		Flat $2.50, $98-$166 p.w.	
		Partial 1.5% thereafter	
	September	Full 2.2%	2.2
	December	Flat $2.90 for Medibank	6.0
		Partial 2.8% to $100 p.w.	
		Flat $2.80 thereafter	
1977	March	Partial 1.9% to $200 p.w.	2.3
		Flat $2.80 thereafter	
	June	Partial 2.0%	2.4
	September	Partial 1.5%	2.2
	December	Partial 1.5% to $170 p.w.	2.3
		Flat $2.60 thereafter	
1978	March	Full 1.3%	1.3
	June/September	Full 4.0%	4.0
1979	December/March[3]	Partial 3.2%	4.0
	June/September	Partial 4.5%	5.0
1980	December/March[4]	Partial 4.2%	5.3

Notes:
1   As the CPI movement was less than 1 per cent the .8 per cent increase for the
    September quarter was carried over into the December quarter.
2   The March 1976 decision introduced the first of several 'plateau' decisions,
    that is, where a proportionate increase was awarded up to a certain level of
    wages and increases above that level were invariably flat monetary amounts.
3   The Commission has periodically discounted the CPI portion represented by
    government petrol pricing policy. For example, December/March 1978/9
    (.8 per cent), June/September 1979 (.5 per cent), December/March 1979/80
    (.6 per cent).
4   As is discussed in the text of this chapter, the Commission discounted the CPI
    by .5 per cent for the lack of 'substantial compliance' by the union movement
    in the first quarter of 1980.

Sources: Plowman *et al.* (ibid.); Print E3410, Australian Conciliation and
Arbitration Commission, July 1980.

warranted discounting the CPI movement further.

This somewhat lengthy excursion into wage determination serves to highlight the close association between Australian unions and the industrial tribunals in deciding the distribution of the economic cake. It also illustrates the drawbacks of unions becoming enmeshed in a highly centralised and regulated wage fixing apparatus. Recent developments suggest that the Australian union movement has placed itself in a no-win situation. If it meets the requirements of substantial compliance there is no guarantee that real purchasing power will be maintained. If it fails to comply with the guidelines the Commission has indicated its willingness to penalise industrial action by awarding less than full indexation. The ACTU's continued support for indexation in these circumstances prompts two further comments. Firstly, the need to distinguish formal statements of policy on wage objectives from actual experience: '. . .we decided to continue the proceedings . . . because we were satisfied that the ACTU had done what it could to call off the (35 hour week) Campaign (being waged by the Metal unions)' (ibid., p.38), and to balance national/sectional union priorities. Secondly, the concern that to reject totally the indexation package may mean the acceptance of a less orderly and egalitarian wage structure, particularly in the context of widespread unemployment, weighs heavily on the minds of Australian union officials.

Job Security

The maintenance of full employment has always been of concern to Australian unions. Like their overseas counterparts, they have proffered advice to governments (and industrial tribunals) as to appropriate macro-economic policies to achieve reasonable expectations of job security for their members. In recent years, against a background of actual and feared job displacement in depressed economic circumstances, unions have been forced to take cognisance of the unregulated introduction of new technology into Australian industry and the resulting consequences for the form and level of employment. At its 1979 Congress, the ACTU determined its most comprehensive policy yet on this issue.

On a philosophical level, technological change is perceived in terms of optimum rather than maximum development, the former taking into account all the sociological and environmental factors as well as economic values. In particular, the ACTU policy stresses that all who wish to work should have that right and that the benefits of technological change should accrue equitably throughout the community.

In practical terms, to effect the regulation of technological change, the ACTU argues for tripartite (unions/employers/government) consultative structures in the form of committees at national, corporate and industry levels. The desire for legislative backing, as argued in a new and imaginative dimension to its policy, has resulted in the ACTU proposing the enactment of a Technological Change (Impact of Proposals) Act which would require employers to specify details of, and reasons for, proposed changes; provide information and technical data adequate to permit a careful assessment of the desired changes; and describe and analyse the effects and costs of any redundancies upon the community, government services and welfare benefits. Employers would be obliged to consult with the government and the unions following the release of the impact statement. In short, unions would have the right to appraise well-researched proposals.

Individual unions are encouraged to seek obligations via industrial awards and tribunals or agreements from employers to consult and negotiate on issues related to the introduction of new technology. Further, and in recognition that there will be some casualties of technological change, the ACTU has specified as a guide to its affiliates 13 compensation standards, including: a minimum of six months' notice for those to be retrenched; severance pay for retrenched workers based on a minimum of four weeks' pay in respect of each year of employment (an extra week's pay for each year of employment for each person over 35 years of age an an additional 4 weeks' pay for each two years of employment or part thereof in excess of 10 years of employment if over 45 years of age); portability of accrued rights including long service leave and superannuation; the implementation of union-approved retraining programmes and compensation by employers to employees for capital loss in homes where such employees have to transfer to other locations to obtain work.

The ACTU's policy on technological change is a rather belated response to the challenges posed by management-initiated investment in labour-saving technology. In general, individual unions have also been largely reactive in the face of such challenges (Pauncz). Apart from its submission to the Committee of Inquiry into Technological Change in Australia which reported in 1980 (the Myers Report), the ACTU has relied on individual union affiliates to conduct educative programmes among their members and the community generally concerning the dangers of unplanned, uncontrolled changes. Some unions, for example those in the telecommunications and printing industries, have participated in stoppages and strikes and, eventually, negotiated agreements with employers over the introduction of new technology. In the case of the telecommunications industry, repeated instances of industrial dislocation led to the negotiation of draft procedures for the introduction of new technology which are considered by many to be a blueprint for further agreements in other industries. The procedures represent the end-product of over 70 meetings between Telecom Australia unions and management and a mutual desire to avoid a repetition of a bitter dispute in 1978 over the introduction of new equipment. In essence, the three-year agreement attempts to establish explicit rules for considering, assessing and deciding on new technology. Specifically, it provides for consultation (beginning at the 'contemplative' stage and ending with the 'trials and implementations' stage), jointly administered feasibility studies (including reference to the impact of the changes on staff and the community), the sharing of information, joint consideration of the timing of the proposed change, and an obligation on Telecom to pursue policies which will lead to the creation of additional employment within Telecom and associated Australian industries. The success, or otherwise, of the agreement is likely to have a marked effect on the wider acceptance of the broad principles underlying current thinking on the vexed issue of technological change.

The findings of a recent government-sponsored inquiry into technological change, the Myers Report, met with rather trenchant criticism from unions on the grounds that it skirted the major issue of job displacement. At least two important features of the Report, however, represent direct challenges to organised labour. Firstly, the advantages of fewer unions in coping with technological change, that is, the impetus for union amalgamations not yet thoroughly grasped, external constraints notwithstanding (see Structure section). Secondly, the low incidence of unions actually seeking provisions in awards to regulate the introduction of new technology where such provisions are possible (the Industrial Arbitration Act of New South Wales and the South Australian Industrial Conciliation and Arbitration Act). Ironically, the Myers Report recommended that *general* guidelines for the introduction of new technology be established by the Australian Conciliation and Arbitration Commission, which so far has shown a preference for dealing with *particular* cases. Where the Commission has figured, it has been to mitigate detrimental effects on employees rather than encroach on managerial prerogatives to dismiss or retrench workers. Consultative arrangements remain very much the province of direct employer/union negotiation outside of the major tribunal system (as does industrial democracy generally) lending further weight to the 'bob each way' nature of Australian unions' overall industrial strategy – a strategy that has obtained since 1904.

Conclusion

Australian unions have long been the focus of international interest mainly because of their achievements and the national peculiarities of the system in which they operate. Although the die was cast for Australian unionism with the advent of conciliation and arbitration at the turn of the century, this chapter has sought to detail several important post-Second World War developments including: the growth of white-collar and professional unionism, the relatively short-lived forays into 'purer' forms of collective bargaining, the acceptance of a quasi-social contract in the guise of wage indexation, heightened and more widespread union militancy and a parallel expansion of legislative measures designed to curtail union activity, and the limited but growing involvement of unions in the regulation of technological change. In large part, these developments reflected prevailing economic pressures which, to date, however, have not been sufficiently critical to engender wholesale change in the character of Australian unions.

Bibliography

Allan, R.H., Nieuwenhuysen, J.P. and Norman, N.R. in Maunder, P. (ed.), *Government Intervention in the Developed Economy* (Croom Helm, London, 1979), pp.41-71

Australian Bureau of Statistics, *Labour Statistics*, 1977

Australian Bureau of Statistics, No.6.65, 1977

Australian Council of Trade Unions, *Minutes of 1979 Congress*

Bain, G. and Elsheikh, F., *Union Growth and the Business Cycle* (Basil Blackwell, Oxford, 1976)

Barker, D.H., 'The Federated Shipwrights and Ship Contractors Association and the Amalgamated Metal Workers Union: A Case Study in Amalgamation', University of Melbourne Research Paper, October 1977

Carr, B., 'Australian Trade Unionism 1977', *Journal of Industrial*

Relations (March 1978), pp.80-86

Cupper, Les, 'Legalism in the Australian Conciliation and Arbitration Commission: The Gradual Transition', *Journal of Industrial Relations* (December 1976), pp.337-64

—— 'Public Funded Trade Union Education: The Australian Experience', *Industrial Relations Journal* (March/April 1980), pp.57-68

—— Employment in Australian Non-Manual Unions (A Preliminary Report, 1980)

Cupper, Les and Hearn, June M., 'Cross-currents in Australian Trade Unionism', *New Zealand Journal of Industrial Relations* (May 1980), pp.13-27.

De Vyver, F.I., 'The Melbourne Building Industry Agreement', *Journal of Industrial Relations* (April 1959), pp.7-19

Ford, G.W. and Lansbury, R.D., 'The Role of Management in Industrial Relations', in Ford, G.W., Hearn, June M. and Lansbury R.D. (eds), *Australian Labour Relations Readings*, 3rd ed. (Sun Books, Melbourne, 1980), pp.279-99

Gollan, R.A., 'The Historical Perspective' in Matthews, P.D.W. and Ford, G.W., *Australian Trade Unions* (Sun Books, Melbourne, 1968)

Hearn, June M., 'Migrant Participation in Trade Union Leadership', *Journal of Industrial Relations* (June 1976), pp.112-23

Howard, W.A., 'Australian Trade Unions in the Context of Union Theory', in Ford, G.W., Hearn June M. and Lansbury, R.D. (eds.), *Australian Labour Relations Readings*, 3rd ed. (Sun Books, Melbourne, 1980), pp.78-99

Isaac, J.E., 'Wage Determination and Economic Policy', *Australian Economic Review* ((3) 1977), pp.16-24

—— 'Lawyers and Industrial Relations', in Hambley A.D. and Golding J.C. (eds.), *Australian Lawyers and Social Change* (Law Book Co., Melbourne, 1976)

Khoury, D., 'The Federal Law Relating to Union Amalgamation in Australia: Help or Hinderance?', *Journal of Industrial Relations* (March 1978), pp.55-64

Lansbury, R.D., 'The Growth of Unionisation of White Collar Workers in Australia: Some Recent Trends', *Journal of Industrial Relations* (March 1977), pp.33-49

—— 'The Return to Arbitration: Recent Trends in Dispute Settlement and Wages Policy in Australia', *International Labour Review* (September-October 1978), pp.611-24

Martin, R.M., *Trade Unions in Australia*, 2nd ed. (Penguin, Ringwood, 1980)

Mitchell, R., 'Industrial Relations Under a Conservative Government: The Coalition's Labour Law Programme', *Journal of Industrial Relations* (December 1979), pp.435-65

Nieuwenhuysen, J.P. and Sloan, J., 'Wages Policy', in Gruen, F.H. (ed.), *Surveys of Australian Economics* (George Allen and Unwin, Sydney, 1978), pp.91-132

Niland, J.R., *Collective Bargaining and Compulsory Arbitration in Australia* (University of New South Wales Press, Sydney, 1978)

Pauncz, K., 'A Survey of Redundancy Procedures', *Work and People*, 5 (1) (1979), pp.7-12

Plowman, D., Deery, S. and Fisher, C., *Australian Industrial Relations* (McGraw-Hill, Sydney, 1980)

Rawson, D.W., 'The ALP Industrial Groups', in Isaac, J.E. and Ford, G.W. (eds.), *Australian Labour Relations Readings* (Sun Books, Melbourne, 1971), pp.205-22

—— *Unions and Unionists in Australia* (George Allen & Unwin, Sydney, 1978)

Rawson, D.W. and Wrightson, Suzanne, *A Handbook of Australian Trade Unions and Employees' Associations* (Australian National University, Camberra, 1981)

Report of the Committee of Inquiry into Technological Change in Australia (Australian Government Publishing Service, Canberra, 1980)

Sharpe, I.G., 'The Growth of Australian Trade Unions: 1907-1969', *Journal of Industrial Relations* (June 1971), pp.138-54

Yerbury, D. and Isaac, J.E., 'Recent Trends in Collective Bargaining in Australia', *International Labour Review*, 103 (1971), pp.421-52

2 FRANCE

J.R. Hough*

Introduction

Trade unions in France present a number of quite distinct and even remarkable characteristics and they differ in a number of respects from those considered elsewhere in this book. French trade unionism is weak, ineffective, chaotic, and even tragic and it certainly appears true that the trade union movement has failed to establish for itself a position comparable to that of its counterparts in other countries. In the view of one commentator, 'In most of French private industry, genuine collective (bargaining) relations have scarcely been tried' and even if there is room for debate as to whether this judgement is exaggerated, it does echo broadly similar conclusions by other writers. Collective bargaining is, in short, a new practice in France! (Adam *et al.*, p.12; Kendall, p.72; Lorwin, p.190).

It is impossible to understand the present situation in French trade unionism without some knowledge of the special historical, cultural and economic influences which have contributed in no small measure to its development. Nowhere is this more true than when the national trade union confederations are considered, of which there are three major and at least two minor ones: no single national representative body or voice of the trade union movement, on the lines of the TUC in the UK, exists in France. This partly explains, and is partly explained by, the weakness referred to above.

Trade Union Growth

Before the Second World War

France never experienced an industrial revolution along the lines of the British model and many of the developments associated with large-scale

*For helpful comments on a previous draft of this chapter I am grateful to Professor A. Bienaymé of the University of Paris-Dauphine, Monsieur F. Orivel of the University of Dijon, Dr M. Schain of the University of New York, Monsieur J. Menin, Secrétaire Général of the Confédération Générale des Cadres, Monsieur B. de Canecaude, Mr G. Salemohamed and the Editor. No response was received to enquiries which I addressed to the three largest trade union confederations in France. The author accepts final responsibility for any remaining errors.

industrial production for mass markets did not take place until well
into the twentieth century. The French revolution of 1789 and the
revolutions of 1838, 1848 and 1871 all brought elements of economic
change, although they were basically social and cultural movements.
The pattern of change and economic development was slow
throughout the nineteenth century, with the employing and landowning
class largely retaining their wealth and power.

Strands of a socialist movement can be traced back as far as the
revolution of 1789 and certainly by the later years of the nineteenth
century there was a relatively strong, if not united, brand of socialism
in France, intent on both polemical argument and political action.
After many years of intermingled growth, setbacks, policy U-turns,
and internecine strife, socialists of various persuasions achieved power
in the Popular Front government, formed after their major victory
in the general elections of May 1936. Trade unionism developed
initially as the industrial wing of the socialist movement and can be
traced as far back as 1863. The first Confédération Générale du
Travail (CGT) was set up at the Limoges Congress of 1895 but it was
from 1906, with the Charter of Amiens, often cited as the basic
text of French unionism, and the drawing-up of a new constitution
for the CGT, that the birth of a modern union movement may be
dated (Lefranc, 1978, and Reynaud, give detailed accounts of the
historical development).

By 1914 the CGT could claim no more than 400,000 members out
of an estimated 6 million industrial workers in France and the
ensuing years saw remarkable ups and downs in membership: perhaps
2m by 1920, down to 1m by early 1936, up to approaching 5m
during the Popular Front era, down to around 2m by 1939, up to
around 5½ m by 1947, then falling to some 2m in 1957 (Kendall,
p.37).

A quite separate strand in the history of trade unionism evolved
out of the hostility of the leaders of the Catholic Church in France,
and of many of the more right wing Catholics, to much of what the
CGT stood for and especially its involvement with the socialist
movement. This led to the growth of the second major confederation
of unions, for avowedly Christian and denominational members, under
the title Confédération Française des Travailleurs Chrétiens (CFTC);
not until 1964 was the word Chrétiens dropped and the title changed
to Confédération Française Démocratique du Travail (CFDT) and even
then a sizeable minority formed themselves into a new organisation,
the CFTC (Maintenu). When the earlier splitting-off from the CGT of a

significant anti-communist element into a new movement known as
CGT-FO (for Force Ouvrière) is taken into account, the genesis of the
present-day structure of several competing confederations, with only
occasional and spasmodic attempts at mutual co-operation, can be
readily discerned.

After 1945

The French Communist Party (PCF) grew in terms of both membership
and electoral share in the immediate post-war period; it joined General
de Gaulle's government from October 1945, and was soon able to gain
total control of the CGT, with a prominent communist, Benoît Frachon,
installed as General Secretary. Only when one takes full account of
the fact that the French communists faithfully followed whatever was
the current Moscow policy, which in turn was liable to sudden changes
of direction and U-turns, can one begin to understand the tergiversations
and conflicting policy stances of the CGT in the ensuing years (even
though the equation CGT = PCF is much too simple since the
relationship between these two bodies was both complex and subject to
fluctuations). Thus when the overall policy stance dictated by Moscow
was one of the utmost co-operation with the government of the day
in order that the communists within the government could exert
maximal influence in a pro-Russia direction, we find the CGT denouncing
strikes, minimising or resisting wage increases, or privately encouraging
managements to fine striking workers (Kendall, p.56: he cites how during
1945-7 the CGT sought to refuse wage increases offered by Renault
management to its workers). After the dismissal of the five communist
ministers from the government in May 1947, however, the communists
switched back to militant pro-strike policies and thus ended the fragile
post-war unity of the CGT.

The anti-communist members joined the new and rival CGT-Force
Ouvrière (CGT-FO or simply FO) in April 1948, but with a lack of
funds or physical resources (despite, or possibly even because of,
financial support from the American AFL) it was many years before
they could become a noteworthy force within French trade unionism.
CGT retained the allegiance of a majority of unionised industrial
workers and FO's adherents were mainly among white-collar and
government employees. The large teachers' union, Fédération de
l'Education Nationale (FEN), withdrew from both organisations.
As Kendall comments (p.59):

French labour, demoralised, weak and divided, riven by political

schisms, out-manoeuvred by management, was chronically unable
to exert its full weight on either the industrial or political scene.

The policy switches and divisions within the CGT movement as a whole
were viewed with no small pleasure by the main rival confederation,
the CFTC, which recorded steady gains in membership. It too, however,
was rent by a prolonged dispute which had worried the movement
before the war and which dominated every Congress from 1946 to
1964: should the confederation remain avowedly confessional or was
it primarily a movement for workers, many of whose members also
happened to be Christians? Eventually the latter view predominated,
the name was changed to CFDT, and the movement shifted gradually
leftwards, all of which was quietly encouraged by a new generation
of leaders within the French Catholic Church, who tended to think
in less separatist terms.

An examination of political, social and economic events in France
in recent times would probably conclude that the two dates of the
greatest import were 1958, when General de Gaulle was returned to
power, and 1968, when France was gripped by a unique social uprising.
In 1958 the CGT made no secret of their hostility to de Gaulle, the
CGT Secretary, Pierre Le Brun (himself not a communist), rejected
an invitation to join de Gaulle's cabinet as Minister of Labour, and in
the vote on the new constitution tried, not very successfully, to
mobilise workers to vote No. The CFTC, on the other hand, adopted a
policy of wait-and-see and did not issue any voting instructions to its
members. In May 1968 the social unrest which had started amongst
university students soon spread to workers and a large-scale
demonstration in Paris on 13 May brought together the CGT, CFDT,
FO, FEN (together with the National Union of Students); this has
been seen as one of the very rare demonstrations of solidarity by
French trade unionists but in fact from the outset the CGT were
opposed to some of the students' demands and supported the government
over the maintenance of law and order. The general strike, which within
a few days had been joined by some ten million workers, was the first
ever at which workers in private sector industries, the nationalised
industries and the civil service stopped work together (Lefranc, 1978,
p.114). Economic life almost ground to a halt. The veneer of unity
did not last long, however; as soon as the negotiations with the
government began on 25 May, the CGT were pressing for large wage
increases whilst the CFDT's main demand was for union recognition
in the workplace.

In the aftermath of the traumatic events of 1968, both major confederations adopted expressly socialist policy statements, the CGT at its Congress of 1969, and the CFDT the following year. (Their policy approaches had in fact been converging over the preceding few years.) The CGT also urged the need for a single representative trade union organisation whilst the CFDT expressed its belief in workers' participation and in democratic economic planning (as opposed to France's 'technocratic' planning). On the occasion of the socialist-communist 'Common Programme' of political aims, enunciated in 1972, the CGT immediately declared its support and actively campaigned on behalf of the programme whilst the CFDT again reserved its position.

In the later 1970s the gradual deterioration of the national economy and the steady rise in the published unemployment statistics did nothing to aid inter-confederation co-operation. Even *within* each confederation disunity was sometimes apparent; in 1974, for example, Edmond Maire of the CFDT campaigned vigorously against Giscard d'Estaing during the presidential elections but he later had to admit rather ruefully that probably a quarter of his own members had not supported him. The CGT has made strenuous efforts to widen its membership base, particularly towards white-collar workers, but with only slow success. The less radical Force Ouvrière has been more acquiescent than either of the other two major confederations with incomes restraint and the 'contractual' approach of the government; the smaller CFTC and CGC (Confédération Générale des Cadres) have usually followed its lead, as, on occasion, has the FEN (the large teachers' union). It is possible to argue that membership figures alone are an insufficient guide to the overall importance of the various confederations. The CGC, for example, includes mainly white-collar professional workers and executives in positions of some authority, who may well have more influence than is indicated by their relatively low numerical figures. (This view was emphasised in a long article in *Le Figaro* of 7 November 1980.)

Far, therefore, from the trade union movement gradually moving towards unity of policy and action, which was the expressed hope of the CGT as far back as 1919, pluralism is, in the view at least of one of the most perceptive observers, getting worse (Lefranc, 1978, p.120; his view is in contrast to the optimism shown by Kendall).

The National Economy

Transformation of the Economy. From the turn of the century until

1945 France achieved little in the way of industrialisation, economic growth and rise in general living standards. During the two world wars, France suffered severe population losses. Industrial and transport facilities, as well as the socio-economic infrastructure, were destroyed or damaged throughout the country. During the inter-war period, the economy largely stagnated and there was rather little modernisation of, or reinvestment in, industrial plant. Total industrial production in 1938 did not exceed that of 1913 and this level was not attained again until after 1945 (Hough, 1976, gives further details of the economic background). In the ensuing 30 years, however, the French economy underwent a remarkable transformation with high rates of economic growth being recorded almost every year; throughout the 1960s the rate of growth of GNP, at around 5.5 per cent, was higher than in any other member country of the EEC, including West Germany. It is a curious fact that whereas the resurgence of the West German economy has been widely publicised and discussed in many other countries, including the UK, much less attention has been paid to the post-war recovery of France.

A major aspect of the economic change that France has experienced has been the relative decline of the agriculture sector, whether measured as a percentage of total employment or as a percentage of GNP, and the relative increases in the industrial and, especially, the tertiary sectors. In this period agriculture suffered a more rapid decline than ever experienced in any other country (Clout). The index of industrial production, on the other hand, which stood at 40 in 1945 (based on 1938 = 100), had reached 438 by 1970 and 661 by 1974. From 1945 to around 1960 the emphasis was on post-war reconstruction but thereafter the growth continued, now orientated towards an acceleration of industrial concentration, the opening of frontiers within the Common Market, and the integration of French industry in world markets (French Embassy, London, 1977). Of prime importance here has been the acceleration of mass production, as exemplified by the extremely successful motor industry, alongside the development of high-technology, science-based industries, such as electronics and aerospace. Amongst the leading industrial nations of the world, France now ranks fifth, after USA, USSR, Japan and West Germany, and has far outstripped the UK. The average income per head in France is now about 1.5 times that in the UK, whereas in the latter 1940s the reverse was true. (Note: a detailed account of French industrial structure will be given in Hough, 1982.)

Economic Planning. Perhaps the aspect of France's economic resurgence that has aroused greater interest than any other has been the fact that it has been accompanied by a system of national economic planning, to an extent not seen in any other Western industrialised country; not unnaturally there have been numerous attempts to identify whether, and if so how much of, France's economic success could be attributed to this system of planning. (For good accounts of French planning, see Gruchy or Holmes and Estrin; for details of other ways in which the French government has intervened in the economy see Hough, 1979.) From Plan 1, adopted in 1946, to Plan 8, the details of which are now being finalised, successive French governments have, in effect, endeavoured to set out in writing and in great detail the economic prospects and possibilities facing the country over the next five years or so. Rather more than 'indicative', on account of the various financial incentives offered, but a long way short of being 'directive', economic planning in France is not easily categorised. In any event it has changed constantly over the 35 years or so that it has been in existence. That it has played at least some part in aiding France's recovery, perhaps principally by raising the expectations of businessmen and industrialists, seem scarcely open to doubt.

Only in the latter 1970s has this unbroken record of success been seen to falter; the effects of the oil crisis combined with high rates of inflation, unemployment rising steadily to reach 1.4m by 1980, and renewed attention to the severe regional imbalance of the French economy, all combined to make the year-by-year increases in living standards appear far more transient than previously. At the very least France is sharing with her competitors the effects of the general world recession.

Social Reforms. There has been a long series of measures of social reforms relating either directly or indirectly to the interests of trade unions. The major landmarks are summarised in Figure 2.1, which also includes some major developments prior to the end of the Second World War.

Trade Union Structure

For any discussion of the structure of French trade unionism to be meaningful, it must take into account both the radical divisions which exist between the various confederations, the union membership

Figure 2.1: Some Landmarks in Social Policy and Collective Bargaining

1864 — Ban on strikes lifted by law and recognition of right of combination
1884 — Waldeck-Rousseau Act authorising trade unions
1891 — First collective agreement (in coal mines in north of France)
1898 — Act relating to industrial accidents
1910 — Old age pension Act
1919 — Reinforcement of collective agreements legislation
 — Act on eight-hour day
1928 — First social insurance Act
1932 — First family allowance Act
1936 — Acts establishing the right to annual leave with pay, the 40-hour week, and instituting collective bargaining and staff delegates
1945 — Ordinance on Social Security
 — — Ordinance making joint works committees compulsory in firms with more than 50 employees
1946 — The Preamble to the Constitution guarantees the right to strike
1947 — Institution of the statutory complementary superannuation scheme for cadres
1950 — Creation of the minimum growth wage (SMIC)
1955 — Renault agreement linking wages for the first time with productivity increases and raising annual paid leave to three weeks
1956 — Generalisation of the three-weeks leave entitlement
1958 — Extension of complementary superannuation to all wage-earning and salaried categories
1959 — Ordinance on profit-sharing
1962 — Annual leave raised to four weeks at Renault
1966 — Outline Act on vocational training
1967 — Creation of the National Employment Agency providing a better labour-exchange organisation
 — Ordinance on compulsory profit-sharing
1968 — Grenelle Agreements on wages
1969 — First agreement on security of employment, providing for joint employment commissions, the information and consultation of the joint works committee when mass redundancies are proposed, and guarantees in the event of dismissal or transfers
 — Generalisation of four weeks annual leave with pay
 — The first 'progress contract' signed at Electricité de France/Gaz de France
1970 — Declaration of employers and trade unions on the conversion of terms of employment to a monthly basis
 — National agreement on vocational training
1971 — Act on continuous vocational training
1972 — Agreement instituting anticipated superannuation for persons who become unemployed over the age of 60
1973 — Creation of the Wages Guarantee Fund to pay workers the sums due to them if their employer goes bankrupt
1974 — Redundancy compensation agreement providing for payment of 90% of last gross pay for up to one year

Source: French Embassy, London, *Facts and Figures*, Ref. No. A/108/5/75.

strength or weakness, in addition to actual organisational structures to be found within each confederation and its constituent unions. The inter-confederation divisions are, as have already been shown, unlikely to disappear within the foreseeable future and they necessarily weaken the unions' organisational structures at every level. Similarly, strong union organisation is rendered unattainable by the very low membership, and lack of funds, of French trade unions. It is difficult to avoid giving the impression of a vicious circle, with each cause of weakness reinforcing, and in turn being reinforced by, each of the others.

Membership

Membership of trade unions is at a very low level and this must be a root cause of union weaknesses. A major problem for any observer, however, is that no accurate or reliable statistics of union membership exist and, given all the related circumstances that have to be taken into account, it is not at all clear how any valid statistics could be assembled. It is generally agreed that no more than 20 per cent of French wage earners are members of trade unions, but even here there is a problem of defining terms: what exactly is a 'member of a trade union'? It has long been the custom for trade unionists to be issued with membership cards on which stamps should be affixed to correspond to the payment of monthly subscriptions. It has also long been customary, however, for not all the monthly subscriptions to be paid and stamps affixed. Even the cards of the most stable and loyal unionists would not have more than ten, out of twelve, monthly stamps, and the CGT estimated an average of eight stamps per card in 1959 (Chatillon). Some unionists never have more than a small number of stamps on their cards. During the latter months of each year the local union representatives are particularly reluctant to press for payment of monthly subscriptions for fear that their members will decline to re-join the union for the following year.

The membership cards are issued by the national confederations to their constituent unions and by the latter to their members, but at each of these stages many spare cards are available in case of need. Similarly a number of members over the course of the year receive more than one card, e.g. if they move house, or change their job, or transfer to a different union. In any event a membership card with no, or only a few, subscriptions paid, can scarcely indicate membership in any meaningful sense. Clearly, therefore, a count of membership cards is of little use. At the other extreme a count of members with twelve monthly stamps on their cards would give a minimal figure which would be equally misleading. Dr Chatillon suggests the adoption of a norm of at least six stamps, but it seems obvious that what is needed, from the point of view of the development of a soundly-based and adequately-financed unionism, is a completely different system for the collection of subscriptions.

Each of the confederations issues annual membership statistics but these are clearly exaggerated claims. Estimates of the various levels of trade union activity (to be analysed below) were given in *L'Entreprise* of 8 November 1974 (see Figure 2.2 for full titles of the various confederations):

CGT:	2.4m. members, grouped in 37 professional federations, 95 departmental unions, 14,000 'syndicats de base' (company, factory or plant unions)
CGT-FO:	850,000 members, grouped in 36 professional federations, 95 departmental unions, 11,000 'syndicats d'entreprise' (company, factory or plant unions)
CFDT:	770,000 members, grouped in 40 professional federations and national unions, 99 departmental unions, 3,500 'syndicats de base'

These may be compared with Kendall's estimates (p.61) of realistic membership figures which were:

CGT:	1.3m
CGT-FO:	500,000
CFDT:	700,000

Kendall quotes estimates of a total trade union membership of 2.7-3.0m, out of a total active *labour* force of some 20.5m (as shown in the 1968 census) (of whom only some 15m would have been wage earners), i.e. a rate of unionisation of around 13.1-14.6 per cent whereas Chatillon suggests a realistic rate of unionisation would be 20 per cent and Stewart suggests 20-25 per cent. The discrepancies are clearly very wide but they show that the density of unionisation in France is relatively low.

The official definition of a member in the CGT constitution, for what it is worth, is one who pays at least ten stamps per year and Kendall points out that on that basis the CGT's actual membership was almost exactly one half of the figure officially claimed by the confederation. It is not even clear from the above figures which is the

the second largest confederation. Kendall indicates the CFDT and he subsequently speculates whether the CFDT, with a tradition of more soundly-based, dues-paying, unions may eventually emerge as the leading organisation of the French working class. It is difficult to find any evidence to support this and since Kendall's figures are partly based on statistics supplied by the CFDT a word of caution may be necessary.

Quite separate and more indirect attempts at assessing reliable membership statistics have also been made via the elections within industrial plants to the boards which formerly administered social security funds and, more latterly, to the *comités d'entreprise* (works councils) which should exist, to defend the workers' interests in all firms with more than 50 wage earners. (Works councils are further examined in the Policy section below.) Adam quotes official Ministry of Labour statistics to show that in 1970 out of a total of 1,419,727 votes cast some 46 per cent went to CGT candidates, 19.6 per cent to CFDT candidates and 7.3 per cent to CGT-FO candidates, with all union supported candidates taking 88 per cent of the votes. It is not clear what meaning can be attached to these figures since it is clear that the vast majority of workers either did not bother, or did not have the opportunity, to vote; they would seem to support the contention that the CFDT has considerably more support than the CGT-FO but even this is not certain, since the latter's membership tends to be concentrated in the public sector services, where *comités d'entreprise* do not exist.

If all *comités d'entreprise* and similarly elected representative bodies are taken into account, the total votes obtained by all union-supported candidates greatly exceed the number of trade unionists (ignoring problems of double-counting) and this has been taken to indicate implied confidence in the unions by those workers who are not union members. It is certainly true, as will be shown below, that union calls for a strike are often supported by many non-members.

Why are French workers so reluctant to join trade unions? This question is discussed at some length by Chatillon but, perhaps not surprisingly, there does not seem to be any one, simple answer. He asks whether French people are by nature so essentially individualistic that they are philosophically inclined against such banding together, but notes that in some occupations, e.g. typographers and basic-grade schoolteachers, the rate of unionisation in fact exceeds 80 per cent. Similarly he asks whether the reputed antipathy of Frenchmen to the payment of compulsory contributions makes them unwilling to commit themselves to the payment of regular subscriptions, but finds this unlikely since the contributions required are so small. More valid and fundamental causes appear to be the deep-rooted divisions within the trade union movement, which can only cause confusion among potential members, the steady improvements in wages and living standards which all workers have enjoyed since 1945 without, for the most of them, having to join unions (so that these benefits appear as 'free goods'), and the very real fear that joining a union may endanger either their prospects for advancement and their future career or their job itself, so opposed are many French employers still to trade union membership. Given such root causes it is difficult to foresee how the unions will be able to develop into more soundly-based and more representative institutions.

For a period of about six years following the social unrest of 1968 the trade unions recorded significant increases in membership, particularly among workers in private sector firms, but a considerable falling off of membership seems to have followed in the late 1970s. In 1975 the claimed membership figures and areas of strength of all the significant confederations were as set out in Figure 2.2.

Funds and Resources

As Stewart has argued, the importance and influence of French trade unions, both politically and in the workplace, are out of all proportion to their low membership figures. It is true that trade union representatives sit on many national governmental and semi-governmental committees, as well as on the boards of nationalised industries. Moreover, there has often been at least one trade union representative in the government at ministerial level. It does, on the other hand, appear undeniable that the work of the unions is severely hampered by their acute lack of funds, which is an inevitable consequence of their weak membership position. The full-time union executives are clearly rather poorly paid — so much so that in 1971 the employees of the CGT actually went on strike for higher wages — and the unions are unable to employ the services of the highly-qualified specialists, for example in statistics or economics, that complex negotiations now require. They are thus at a severe disadvantage *vis-à-vis* the Patronat, the employers' organisation, who will be well supplied with all the supporting evidence they require. Lefranc, a French trade union leader, has written in graphic terms of the impression this created on their union counterparts from other countries:

Figure 2.2: The Five Representative Confederations*

Confédération Générale du Travail (CGT). The communist-dominated confederation; founded in 1895.
Claimed membership: 2,400,000
Most influential in: steel, metallurgy, building, chemicals, mining, printing, ports and dockyards, electricity and gas, railways

Confédération Générale du Travail — Force Ouvrière or *Force Ouvrière* (CGT-FO or FO). Founded in 1948 from a split in the CGT.
Claimed membership: 850,000
Most influential in: Civil Service, Paris transport, agricultural and food trade, banking, insurance, electrical engineering, building and civil engineering, clothing, leather and hides

Confédération Française Démocratique du Travail (CFDT). Founded in 1919 as the CFTC, transformed in 1964 when formal links with the Catholic Church were severed.
Claimed membership: 770,000
Most influential in: metallurgy, rubber, oil industry, textiles, electrical engineering, banking, insurance

Confédération Générale des Cadres (CGC). Founded in 1944.
Claimed membership: 250,000
Most influential in: sales (travellers and representatives), textiles, metallurgy, chemicals, banking, insurance, paper-cardboard, furniture

Confédération Française de Travailleurs Chrétiens (CFTC). Founded in 1919; broke away and reformed as the CFTC in 1964 when the minority rejected the newly established CFDT.
Claimed membership: 200,000
Most influential in: mining, banking, insurance, air traffic control, oil industry, glass ceramics

---

* All membership figures given here are estimates; the emergence of these confederations was analysed in the Growth section.

Source: French Embassy, London, *Facts and Figures*, Ref. No. A/108/5/75.

Foreign trade unionists view us with a degree of condescension. They have the impression that French trade unionism has not got beyond the developmental phase: whereas in Germany, the United States, and England, the unions have sufficient resources to engage the services of experts, who, covered with diplomas and loaded with figures, are capable of entering into discussions on a basis of equality on various commissions with representatives of the employers and of the public authorities. (Writer's translation from Lefranc, 1970.)

Membership subscriptions are obviously the major source of income for the trade unions but they also receive considerable sums of money from the government, largely geared, nominally at least, towards the education and training of trade union officials. This system has developed largely since 1959, up to which year the unions, and especially the CGT-FO, received annual subsidies from their counterparts in the USA. The sums are now distributed annually by the Ministry of Labour and a major bone of contention for many years, especially on the part of the CGT, has been the basis on which this distribution is effected. The division was strongly biased in favour of the more moderate confederations, the CFDT and the CGT-FO, and not until 1971 was the CGT able to persuade the government that it should receive a greater share of the total sum available. By 1975 the direct payments from the Ministry of Labour for education and training purposes amounted to:

CGT:	Frs. 2,615,000
CGT-FO:	Frs. 2,615,000
CFDT:	Frs. 2,615,000
CFTC:	Frs. 1,100,000
CGC:	Frs. 900,000

Naturally the CGT still feels a grievance over the basis now used; its claim is that if funds were allocated according to size and responsibilities, i.e. per head of membership, it should receive far more than (perhaps twice as much as) the FO and CFDT (Chatillon, p.52).

Finally under this heading mention must be made of strike funds, which are in fact minimal. Even active members have traditionally been unwilling to make the separate payments into strike funds, which in turn has severely limited the possibilities for any long-drawn-out stoppage stoppage and has tended to orientate union policy towards short, sharp strikes, often of only one day's duration. Strike funds are, however, rather stronger in the industrial areas in the north-east, around Lille, and in Alsace and Lorraine, in which localities the nearness of the Belgian and German frontiers, respectively, has always tended to exert definite influences on trade union practice.

An article in *L'Express* (6 December 1980) suggested that the financial problems of the major confederations, and especially the CGT had now become acute and that serious cash-flow difficulties were being experienced at the end of each month.

Organisational Structures

When writing of the organisational structures within French trade
unionists, one observer notes that the 'appearance' is that the
confederations' structure is 'logical, decentralised, under close
membership control, and independent of political parties', whilst the
reality is that:

> communist controls have ended political independence, and
> vitiated both membership control of officials and the autonomy
> of union bodies close to the base (grass roots). The logic of
> national union structure within each confederation is less
> important than the practice of competing unions of the three
> major workers' confederations, several splinter confederations,
> and many unaffiliated unions (Lorwin, p.146).

The former part of this statement appears to relate primarily to the
CGT, whereas the latter brings us back yet again to the rifts in the
movement as a whole.

Nominally the structural pattern provides for a considerable degree
of decentralisation and local democratic control. The national
confederations have little power or autonomy beyond what their
member unions choose to give them and the latter are subject to all
major decisions being taken or confirmed by frequent local assemblies
or conventions. Diagrammatically the organisational structures of the
three largest confederations may be summarised as in Figures 2.3,
2.4 and 2.5.

Figure 2.3: CGT

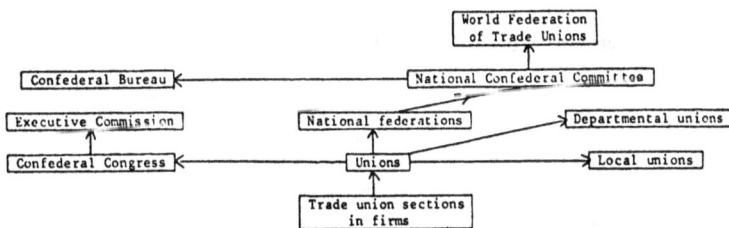

In the case of the CGT, since 1969 the Executive Commission (and no longer the
Confederated Committee) is elected by the Confederated Congress; to ensure
internal unity, the members of the Confederal Bureau must all be on the Executive
Commission.

Source: French Embassy, London, *Facts and Figures*, Ref. No. A/108/5/75.

Figure 2.4: CGT-FO

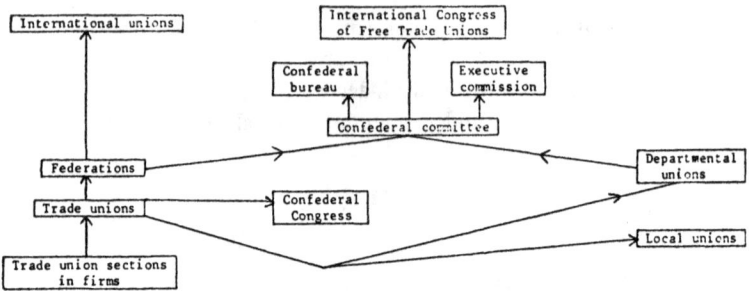

The CGT-FO's structure has remained closest to that of the original organisation of the trade union movement. This organisation reflects the pre-eminent place of the federations and departmental unions. Congress does not appoint any of the leaders and power lies with the confederated organisations which enjoy a wide measure of autonomy.

Source: French Embassy, London, *Facts and Figures*, Ref. No. A/108/5/75.

Figure 2.5: CFDT

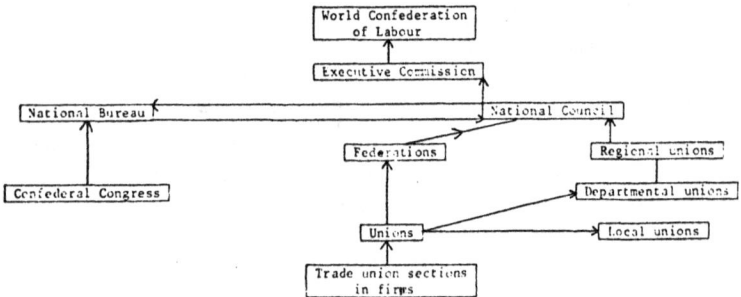

The CFDT has the most original structure. At the CFDT, Congress play a very big part: it elects the National Bureau's 31 members (10 on behalf of the federations, 10 on behalf of the regional unions, 10 on behalf of the National Bureau itself, which has a right of representation, and 1 cadre). The National Council (known at the FO and CGT as the Confederal Committee) is a kind of parliament that meets twice a year. It draws up the list of candidates from which Congress will elect the National Bureau. The Executive Commission has only 10 members, elected by the National Bureau from amongst its ranks.

Source: French Embassy, London, *Facts and Figures*, Ref. No. A/108/5/75.

As might be imagined, the local unions present an almost infinite variety of types and sizes; they may be based on the industrial plant or on the locality whether area, city, or departmental, although the overall tendency is towards being industry-based rather than craft-based.

The largest have several thousand members but the smallest less than ten. The CGT prefers one local (branch) per plant but the CFDT locals (branches) are more occupation-based and may include one for white-collar workers, one for engineers and technicians, and one for production workers, all within a single plant. In theory at least all decisions are taken, on a strictly egalitarian basis, by the periodical general meetings of workers but inevitably considerable executive power rests with the executive committee or general secretary; in the smaller locals (branches) the latter will be a worker on the shop floor but in the largest ones, he will be a full-time, salaried, official. Sometimes his salary may even be paid by the firm, especially in the case of public sector organisations.

Where the local union is not confined to one plant (and even sometimes when it is) it may embrace a number of branches, or sub-divisions. Representatives of local unions meet, in connection with matters of common interest, with colleagues from the same city or from the same Département. (The Département is the basic administrative, political and judicial unit in France.) At the city level trade union often receive assistance, financial or otherwise, such as by the provision of a building, from the local municipality. Of rather more importance than these, however, is the grouping of locals into national unions (sometimes termed 'federations' with rather a loose framework, sometimes, especially in the case of government administrative employees, termed 'syndicats nationaux'), each of which will normally have an executive board, perhaps comprised of locals' secretaries, and a national committee, elected from amongst the membership.

On paper at least ever since 1906 the CGT's policy has been to favour industrial unions at the expense of craft unions and until 1939 considerable success was achieved in, for example, mergers involving respectively practically all the railway unions, several regional agricultural unions and a number of electrical workers' unions. Some earlier opposition to this process on the shop floor seems to have been overcome but many craft unions still remain. Within each confederation, a single railway workers' union and a single metalworkers' union have been achieved but elsewhere divisions remain. Victor Feather, writing of the possible development of factory unions in the UK, succinctly remarked:

There could be a French situation of thousands of completely autonomous local and factory unions, without responsible central

control or guidance or a central organisation which could advise
employers nationally and negotiate authoritatively with
governments . . .

Within the CFDT the industrial unionism question has tended to be
focused on the position of white-collar workers who are far more
prominent in this confederation than in the CGT.

The Confederations

The confederations themselves are most directly involved in the
formulation of national policy, in direct dealings with various
government bodies, and in international representative meetings. It
is the confederations, too, that are seen by the general public as the
voices (not always in harmony) of the French trade union movement
through contacts with the mass media. The permanent full-time
officials of each confederation are subject to a national committee
which in turn is answerable to periodic, usually biennial, conventions
or congresses. The latter are, in theory at least, the supreme decision-
making bodies but inevitably they can be swayed or manoeuvred
by the executive. The delegates, representatives of local unions, often
see the proceedings as an opportunity to voice their feelings of
dissatisfaction over developments since the previous assembly two
years previously. Barjonet describes the proceedings as 'une Grande
Mess' (a High Mass — a complex church service in which the movements
of all the participants are known beforehand). In smaller, biannual,
meetings of representatives there are, according to the same writer:

one or two speeches of magisterial quality, delivered by the top
leaders, received in a religious silence and followed in the midst
of general indifference by inevitably laudatory contributions of
the federation and department chiefs.

In the case of the CGT, 12 to 14 full-time *secrétaires confédéraux*
meet regularly in the Bureau Confédéral (BC), under one *secrétaire
général*, and in practice this body is sufficiently well organised to be
able to exercise sway over the Commission Administrative (CA) of
some 35 elected representatives. Since the whole apparatus is firmly
under the control of the French Communist Party the question of
which committee controls which is in practice rather academic. The
general trend over the last 30 years has been for the party to seek
more centralised control, at the expense of the local unions.

Regarding the national committees and conventions of the three major confederations, in the earlier years the voting systems in use were weighted in favour of smaller units and this principle has been retained in both the CFDT and the FO. In the CGT, however, since 1946 voting has been based on numbers represented (as in the TUC in the UK) which does, of course, allow the large industrial centres to dominate the proceedings.

The position of Secretary General is not as prominent as might have been expected and within each of the confederations there has been a tradition of hostility towards entrusting too much power to any one such figure. In practice, however, as mentioned above, he is the most important member of the Bureau Confédéral which in turn can effectively dominate policy. Certainly the CGT Secretary Generals in the post-war period, Benoît Frachon and Georges Seguy, have been major national figures, as also, to only a slightly lesser extent, have been Edmond Maire of the CFDT and André Bergeron of the FO.

Disillusion

Finally mention may be made of a detailed survey of the state of trade unionism in France conducted by the respected newspaper *Le Monde* and published in a series of articles on 4, 5, 6 and 7 March 1980. This survey presented a picture of disillusion with the unions, a steady loss of membership, and more unwillingness than ever to pay union dues. Examples were quoted of local union sections which had lost 50 per cent to 60 per cent of their membership within the space of a few years. Whilst the reasons for this state of affairs were not entirely clear they appeared to be a mix of (i) profound disappointment among left-wing activists since the loss of the French parliamentary election in March 1978, (ii) the increasing national unemployment, (iii) the deepening economic crisis and fear of retaliatory action by the employers, (iv) disillusion over what trade unions had achieved or could achieve and (v) increased willingness by employers to involve workers in factory decision-making processes in other ways. One union official interviewed was particularly regretful that the unions lost contact with the unemployed (*chomeurs*):

> Trade unions have not managed to maintain contacts with the body of unemployed. Committees have been set up here and there to bring them together but these remain largely empty structures (writer's translation).

The General Secretary of the CGT, Georges Seguy, some ten years ago accepted that the divisions in the unions' ranks were a major cause of their low membership figures, although he went on to argue that these divisions were diminishing in importance over time, a view for which it is difficult to find strong supportive evidence. A second major cause, in Seguy's opinion, was the 'lies and slanders of the enemy and his allies as to the subordination of the CGT to the French Communist Party'.

Trade Union Policy

Collective Bargaining

It will now be apparent that the weak and divided French trade union movement, lacking both financial resources and expert support services, is unlikely to be a strong bargaining force. Indeed, collective bargaining in the sense of meaningful negotiations between two parties of approximately equal strength scarcely exists. Negotiations take place between employers and union representatives in most large factories but, whatever may be the objective strength of the unions' case, it is undermined by (i) their minority membership and (ii) the legal provision for the compulsory arbitration of disputes.

With regard to the former, ever since the 'Matignon' legislation of 1936 (see Figure 2.1) trade union representatives have been entitled to be accorded bargaining status even if they represent a minority of the workforce. The Ministry of Labour lists as 'representative' 61 trade union organisations which could only muster less than 10 per cent of the total vote in *comité d'entreprise* elections, when the great majority of workers do not even bother to vote. Alone of the three major confederations, the CFDT's view is that representation should only be accorded where the figure reaches 10 per cent, thus providing an incentive to recruitment. The provision for compulsory arbitration, also enacted in 1936, has often seemed to remove the real crux of any negotiations and again to make the unions seem impotent in the eyes of the workers. The fact that the representatives of the CGT, under orders from the Communist Party, have often been seen to put forward points which scarcely seemed to be in the workers' interests, did nothing to dispel the feeling of malaise. (For example, *Le Monde* of 5 March 1980 reported union opposition to an employer's attempt to introduce flexitime for his employees.)

The disunity within the trade union movement, both vertically and horizontally, has also chronically weakened the bargaining process.

In large-scale, national negotiations, the employers' united front would often be face to face with over one hundred trade union representatives, by no means united in viewpoint or policy.

Reynaud correctly describes the structure of the employers' organisations as 'très complexe' and notes that the annual listing of the names of all the various national and local representative bodies now covers 350 pages in the Patronat's year-book. The largest and most important of these employers' organisations, the 'Professional Federations', are industry-based and are established for all the major industrial sectors. The overall Confederation, Le Patronat Français, achieves a quite remarkable degree of strength and unity, to the extent that a single, coherent, employers' policy, on each of the major issues of the day, can be identified (Reynaud, ch.2).

Following the civil unrest of May 1968 the Chaban-Delmas government decided to institute, for the first time, meaningful union-employer negotiations to settle wages in the nationalised industries, and a series of bilateral agreements followed in the years 1969 and 1970. It was the government's hope that private sector firms would be influenced by and follow this lead but in reality little of the sort seems to have taken place. Where collective bargaining does exist in private industry in any meaningful sense, the employers have generally been able to refuse to participate either at the level of the plant or at national level, confining the proceedings to the departmental level where the union would be able to muster much less of a show of strength. Where wage levels are negotiated these are frequently fairly nominal; wages actually paid depend greatly on the degree of institutionalised wage drift which follows. The CFDT has been aiming at sectoral agreements, each to cover a part of an industry, but has had rather little success in enforcing such a policy.

French employers continue to refuse to become involved in realistic collective bargaining whenever possible; and still have an attitude to their employees which can only be described as paternalistic. Michelin, for example, which is said to pursue aggressive anti-union policy, is said to have boasted that its workers:

> belonged ... to the Michelin company from cradle to grave. Born in a Michelin hospital, they were educated in a Michelin school, lodged in Michelin houses. When they died, the company, with pious wisdom, paid for a mass to be said for the good of their souls (Kendall, p.83).

Citroën and the former Simca (now within the Peugeot group) were reported to be so anti-union that they refused facilities for posting union notices, fire workers for distributing union literature in the plant and search workers' lockers for incriminating material (Lesire-Ogrel). Kahn-Freund (p.72) attaches considerable importance to the provision against unfair dismissal which was re-enacted in the *Code du Travail*, 1974, but other writers suggest or imply that French employers have little difficulty in circumventing the law (Chatillon; Lesire-Ogrel).

Where negotiations do take place the lack of unity on the unions' side greatly weakens their position; as the official Sudreau Report noted:

> The commitments undertaken in the name of the workers are inevitably precarious. The representative unions are not always signatories to an agreement. Each is free to participate or not in negotiations, to sign or not to sign the agreement, to associate itself ultimately (with the agreement) or to denounce it.

Plant-level bargaining is not strong in France. As Slack noted:

> No tradition of voluntary negotiations exists and there is little to resemble the formalised procedures which ensure continuing bargaining relationships on the North American or British model. Only in 1968 was legislation enacted to grant union officers a recognised status as workforce representatives at plant level . . . A non-member may see the divisions between the unions as a sign of their ineffectiveness in pursuing concrete gains and may even be genuinely confused about union objectives. Furthermore, dealing with a particular union takes on all the appearances of a political act − a non-member may 'conscientiously object' to attaching himself to what he sees first and foremost as a political ideal.

On similar lines a recent comparative study could refer to France as having 'unilateral management regulation of work-place relations', 'the paternalistic setting of the French Works Committee', and the maintenance of a large area of unilateral control by French employers, although it went on to suggest that over time more meaningful work-place organisation is *gradually developing* (Marsden, p.3 − writer's emphasis).

Strikes

It follows from what has already been said about lack of adequate financial base that prolonged, major stoppages are usually out of the question for French unions. Short surprise or irritation strikes, sometimes called 'pin-prick' stoppages, are much more common. They seem both to command considerable support from non-union members and to impress the employers as to the strength of the workers' feelings. One estimate is that the average support for such a strike call is around 50 per cent, which would, of course, normally be sufficient completely to disrupt the productive process, even if union leaders profess to find it disappointing (Reynaud, ch.6). On the other hand, as a French periodical comment on a joint CGT-CFDT day-long series of demonstrations in 1975 pointed out:

> The turn-out was honourable, but the factories continued to function. At the Matignon (the prime minister's residence) they observed the day with interest . . . It was not a great demonstration of force, but it was the best organised by the CGT and the CFDT for a long time (*Le Point*, No.158, 29 September 1975, quoted in Schain).

French union leaders continue to see these short strikes in psychological and even mystical terms. Many of the stoppages are very short; according to official government statistics, in 1952 out of every ten strikes, eight lasted less than one week, five less than one day, and two less than one hour (Lorwin, p.238). However, though prolonged strikes are largely out of the question, it is a rare year in which the total number of man-days lost through strikes is less than several million. Short, wildcat strikes may be called even whilst negotiations with employers are in progress, partly, it seems, as a general expression of feelings on the part of the workers:

> The strike is an affirmation of class consciousness and class action. It is an act of revolt, a moment of dissociation of the worker from the capitalist system (Lorwin, p.235).

Often it may be one of the smaller unions which issues a strike call and gains the support of both non-organised workers and members of the larger unions.

By 1980 this tendency towards short-term strikes was being increasingly questioned, especially within the CFDT. Nevertheless, on the rarer occasions when strikes of longer duration take place a major problem is lack of finance, as has been indicated above. Usually considerable sums do in fact become available from outside sources including the Communist Party (to the CGT), municipalities, special collections in churches with the support of sympathetic priests and even bishops, and also indirectly from employers, in that employer-financed welfare facilities may continue to function.

Traditionally during strikes in France picketing was never so common or taken so seriously as in the UK or the USA. Its use has, however, become far more widespread over the last ten years or so, doubtless influenced by examples of such practice in other countries (Caire).

Findings on (a) average annual working days lost per 1,000 employees, (b) average annual working days lost per striker, (c) average annual number of stoppages per 100,000 employees and (d) average annual number of working days lost per stoppage for 20 OECD countries (1969-78) illustrate the 'pin-prick' hypothesis and France's relative strike position (the 20 countries include all the seven covered in this book). France's ranking was 8, 1, 12, 3 for (a), (b), (c) and (d) respectively, although (c) is partly due to definitional differences (Creigh *et al.*). Like all fairly short-run time series, however, there is an arbitrary element; this particular series, for example, omits the massive 1968 strikes in France but captures the growing trend of longer official strikes in the UK (see Table 5.1 and Table 1.3 for Australian trends).

Political Action

As is to be expected, all the major confederations have links with one or more political parties. As has already been indicated these links are closest in the case of the CGT and the Communist Party, whose activities are closely enmeshed at every level. In the immediate post-war period the frequent switches of policy by the French Communist Party, at Moscow's behest, did nothing to add to the credence or stability of its union counterpart. On paper at least the aims of both CP and CGT include the outright abolition of the capitalist system but in practice policy has often been much less radical and tempered by the opportunism of the moment.

At all levels non-communists, including some Catholics and even priests, have always been present within the structure of the CGT and their value for propaganda purposes is obvious. French trade unions have always lacked an adequate mouthpiece in the form of an effective newspaper or journal for the movement and the CGT are able to make good use of the Paris communist daily *L'Humanité* to put forward their views.

Except for a brief honeymoon period after 1945 the French
Communist Party has always been excluded from the current government
coalition and has thus been out of power. This fact perhaps helps to
explain why the CGT has failed to develop the effective power base of
a strong and active membership in the post-war period.

The links between Force Ouvrière and the Socialist Party have never
been so close at any level. The FO's member unions include many
members of the Socialist Party, which is perhaps hardly surprising in
view of the appeal the unions of this confederation make to a broadly
left-wing but non-militant point of view. The essential reasonableness
of the Socialist Party's point of view has often been seen as its undoing:

> ... neither on workers' material interests nor the hope of peace can
> it compete effectively with the lack of scruple of communist
> propaganda. Only in its anti-clericalism does it make a comparable
> polemic appeal. Otherwise there is a mild ineffectuality, a routine
> and doctrinaire quality, to all its attempts at opportunistic agitation
> (Lorwin, p.292).

The party is far from being in a position to control the FO and the
links between the two are mainly informal, especially via individuals
who are in executive or prominent positions in both movements. Both
have tended to appeal to white-collar and often middle-class quasi-
intellectuals as much as to workers on the factory floor. Many of the
leaders of the FO are not in the Socialist Party; many are members
of no party whilst others are scattered across almost the whole
political spectrum. Indeed the official FO banner still reads 'Against
any political control'.

It was at one time possible to write, as did Lorwin, of quite close
contacts, co-existing with nominal independence, between the CFDT
and the MRP, the former Catholic-orientated, slightly right of centre,
political party; since 1958, however, not only has the CFDT ceased to
have formal connections with church-orientated politics, it has also,
as shown above, shifted away from a confessional stance and towards
the left. Some informal contacts between the two movements remain
at ground level and some church leaders still urge on the faithful the
desirability of supporting the CFDT, but these links are no longer at
all strong. Even in the 1950s, when they were at their strongest,
there were frequent prolonged disputes between the two sides, for
example over such questions as state subsidies to church schools.

Despite, or perhaps because of, the nature of these party-union links, the unions have overall been able to exert rather little real influence on government policies. As one widely-quoted study notes:

> Labour's role is largely a matter of public relations. The real contact is between industry and the State and these two effectively exclude the 'third partner' from serious discussions (McArthur and Scott).

Given this process, it is hardly surprising that much of the most significant legislation that has dealt with the working-class condition has been passed in spite of the vigorous opposition of the trade unions (Schain).

Workers' Participation and Profit Sharing

Partly, perhaps, as both effect and cause of the weak trade union situation, a complex system of workers' participation has evolved in France; on paper at least the worker is now frequently involved in the decision-making process both with his employer and with the government, although in practice the level of participation still falls short of that found in many other comparable countries (Kennedy).

Every concern with 50 or more employees is required by law to establish a *comité d'entreprise* (works council), although the Sudreau Report found that over half the companies in question had not done so. The *comité* is to be composed of employees elected by their fellow workers. It is required to meet at least once a month in a consultative capacity. The *comité* often operates alongside *délégués du personnel*, empowered to take up individual or collective claims or grievances with the management. The legal provisions relating to these and other representative provisions are extremely complex (Arseguel). As an example of how the intentions of the law could be avoided, one firm known to the writer divided itself into two separate fictitious legal entities, each with 49 employees, in order to secure exemption.

One of General de Gaulle's final political acts was to implement a modified profit sharing scheme, enacted in 1967; this scheme was compulsory for all companies with 100 employees or more, whereas an earlier scheme introduced in 1959 had been voluntary. A share in profits, devised via a complex mathematical formula such as perhaps only French legislators could devise, is attributed to the employees and may then be used in various ways; only after a period of five years may it be paid out to the workers in cash (Kennedy). A related Act in 1973 permitting workers to purchase shares in the company in certain circumstances has had rather little effect.

Parallel to the above may be cited the 'contractual' approach to economic policy adopted by the French government under which, nominally at least, employees were consulted and involved in such questions as price controls, productivity improvements and income restraint. In practice the veneer of a 'contract' between the government and other parties over time wore rather thin (Ardagh; Hough, 1979).

The attitude of the trade unions to each of the above developments has been one of ambivalence if not of outright opposition. The overall tendency has been to be suspicious of any such moves which have not originated within the union movement and which would do nothing to incline workers to become members. Further, the CGT, and more latterly the CFDT, have been opposed to any provisions which would tend to reconcile the worker to the existing capitalist system, as opposed to seeking its radical transformation. The consequence, that French trade unions have often been in the position of opposing developments which would seemingly be of direct benefit to the workers, has already been mentioned above. Only very recently has this stance been seriously questioned. Thus a recent critique could refer to the CFDT as:

> affirming the need for [a] return to workplace and branch-level action in support of demands, not only for material improvements but also for increased worker power, leading towards a change in the model of development . . . For some, this marked a reassertion of the *autogestionnaire* conception of social transformation (Martin and Ross).

Another observer traces such a change of tactics back to the consequences of the social unrest of May 1968 but in reality it may stem more recently from the extreme disappointment felt by the Left in France at their failure at the French parliamentary elections in 1978 (Erbès-Seguin).

Conclusion

It is difficult to be optimistic regarding the future of French trade unionism. The root causes of the movement's internal divisions and weaknesses are deep seated and it is difficult to see any signs of a real desire to overcome these. Opposition to the development of strong unions is manifest and well organised on the part of the Patronat and is probably still present, more covertly, on the part of the French government.

The sustained period of high economic growth, lasting for more than 30 years after 1945, brought about steady rises in standards of living throughout France and, if anything, made it more and more difficult for the ordinary working man, or woman, to see why he, or she, should join a trade union. Whether the effects of the oil crises, economic recession and high levels of unemployment in the late 1970s and on into the early 1980s will have any effect on such attitudes it is, as yet, too early to say. One study suggested that the profound radicalism of French workers remained undiminished over time and was reinforced by the nature of French trade unions, but this argument has been refuted as too simplistic by a more recent work and it scarcely seems to conform to the reality of the situation (Gallie; Hamilton).

To an Anglo-Saxon observer at least, until the trade union leaders decide that their top priority must be to put their own house in order, the outlook for a strong and united union movement in France must remain bleak. (One should, however, at least mention the converse point of view, currently emphasised by the CGC, that the disunity of the various confederations is itself a source of strength in that it allows for the expression of a diversity of views and opinions.)

Some ten years ago the Secretary General of the CGT could write of 'the future great unified trade union centre of the French workers, without political fragmentation' (Seguy), but in the real world there seems little prospect of such a hope coming to fruition in the foreseeable future. For much of the 1970s it was possible to view the CGT and CFDT as gradually moving towards a more common platform and approach, producing inter-confederation agreements and issuing joint strike calls from time to time. Since about 1978, however, the CFDT seems to have suspected that the main result of such co-operation was to bolster the position of the Communist Party and as a consequence it has become increasingly wary of any joint ventures.

Indeed, as the older loyal union members gradually retire and are replaced by young workers who feel no such ties of loyalty, one can only forecast that union membership may decline to even lower levels. If and when such a process were to be set in train it is difficult to see how or when it would stop. The prognosis for the future of French trade unions must be more pessimistic than for those in any of the other countries included in this book.

Bibliography

Adam, G. *et al.*, *La Négociation Collective en France* (Paris, 1972)
Ardagh, J., *The New France* (Pelican, 3rd edition, 1977)
Arseguel, A., 'Institutions représentatives du personnel dans l'entreprise' (*Notes et Etudes Documentaires*, No. 4488-9, Nov. 1978)
Barjonet, A., *La CGT*, quoted in Kendall
Caire, G., *La Grève Ouvrière* (Les Editions Ouvrières, 1978)
Chatillon, S., *Pourquoi la Division Syndicale?* (Economica, Paris, 1978)
Clout, H., *The Geography of Post-War France, a Social and Economic Approach* (Butterworth, 1972)
Creigh, S., Donaldson, N. and Hawthorn, E., 'Stoppage Activity in OECD Countries', Department of Employment *Gazette* (November 1980), pp.1174-81
Erbès-Seguin, S., *Democratie dans les Syndicats* (Mouton, Paris, 1975)
French Embassy, London, *French Industry*, Facts and Figures from France, Ref. No. A/118/4/77
—— *Trade Unions in France*, Facts and Figures from France, Ref. No. A/108/5/75
Gallie, D., 'Trade Union Ideology and Workers' Conception of Class Inequality in France', *West European Politics, 3* (1) (Jan. 1980)
Gruchy, A.G., 'The French Planned Economy', ch.6 in his *Comparative Economic Systems* (Houghton Mifflin, 1977)
Hamilton, R., *Affluence and the French Worker in the Fourth Republic* (Princeton, 1967)
Holmes, P. and Estrin, S., *French Planning Today* (University of Sussex, Economics Seminar Paper No. 76/14)
Hough, J.R., 'French Economic Policy', *National Westminster Bank Review* (May 1976)
—— 'Government Intervention in the Economy of France', in P. Maunder (ed.), *Government Intervention in the Developed Economy* (Croom Helm, 1979)
—— *The French Economy* (Croom Helm, 1982)
Kahn-Freund, O., *Labour Relations* (Oxford University Press, 1979)
Kendall, W., *The Labour Movement in Europe* (Allan Lane, 1975)
Kennedy, T., *European Labour Relations* (Lexington, 1980)
Lefranc, G., 'Histoire et évolution récents du syndicalisme français', *Vie Sociale* (August 1970)
—— *Le Syndicalisme en France* (PUF, Paris, 10th edition, 1978)
Lesire-Ogrel, J., *Le Syndicat dans l'Entreprise* (Paris, 1967)
Lorwin, V.R., *The French Labour Movement* (Harvard University Press, 1966)

McArthur, J. and Scott, B., *Industrial Planning in France* (Harvard University Press, 1969)

Marsden, D., 'Industrial Democracy and Industrial Control in West Germany, France and Great Britain', UK Department of Employment, Social Science Branch, Research and Planning Division, *Research Paper No. 4* (Sept. 1978)

Martin, A. and Ross, G., 'Trade Unions and Politics in Western Europe', *West European Politics, 3* (1) (Jan. 1980)

Reynaud, J.-D., *Les Syndicats en France* (Du Seuil, Paris, 1975)

Schain, M., 'Corporatism and Industrial Relations in France', in P. Cerny and M. Schain, *Politics and Public Policy in France* (Frances Pinter, 1980)

Seguy, G., 'Trade Union Democracy', in *World Trade Union Movement* (Prague, May/June 1971)

Slack, E., 'Plant-level Bargaining in France', *Industrial Relations Journal, 11* (4) (Sept./Oct. 1980), pp.27-38

Stewart, M., *Trade Unions in Europe* (Eyre & Spottiswoode, 1974)

Sudreau Report: 'Rapport du comité d'étude pour la reforme de l'entreprise', 1975 (also quoted in Schain)

3 JAPAN

G.C. Allen

Introduction

In the course of two generations Japan has risen from being a
predominantly peasant country with a well-developed infrastructure
but little more than a fringe of large-scale industry into one of the
most advanced industrial societies in the world. As recently as 30 years
ago nearly half the occupied population was to be found in agriculture,
forestry and fishing. Today the proportion has fallen to little more
than one-tenth, and even that figure exaggerates the importance of
agriculture since the majority of the farm households derive a large
share of their income from non-farming occupations. The change has
occurred so rapidly mainly because of Japan's success in importing
and applying the industrial techniques that had been devised in
Western countries. It is this quality of technical assimilation that has
most strongly impressed American and European observers, who have
also noted that Japan has often bettered her instruction, both in the
application of advanced scientific and technological knowledge to
her industry, and in her adaptation of American methods of
management. Yet they have seldom remarked on another aptitude
that has made an outstanding contribution to her economic
performance, namely her capacity for institutional innovation. This
has been displayed most conspicuously in the system of collective
bargaining that has emerged since the Second World War and of which
there were only traces in earlier times.

Trade Union Growth

Trade Unions Before 1940

Before the Second World War trade unions were of little account, for
the whole environment, economic, social and political, was unfavourable
to this development. A few large factories had been established during
the early part of the Meiji period (1868-1912) but the majority of the
workers recruited for them were girls whose industrial life was short,
or the sons of peasants who considered work in factories simply as a
temporary means of supplementing their family incomes. For many
years by far the greater part of the output of industrial goods came from

small workshops in which the relations between masters and journeymen were paternalistic. The growth of heavy industry (shipbuilding and steel) and of sea and railway transport between the end of the Sino-Japanese War (1895) and the Russo-Japanese War (1905-6) led to an increase in the number of permanent, male industrial workers, and these organised unions under the guidance of a national society, the Labour Union Promotion Society, which also sought to persuade the government to enact factory legislation. The leaders of the movement were nearly all members of the intelligentsia who had studied in foreign countries. Progress was cut short when the authorities took alarm and suppressed the unions under the powers of the Public Peace Police Act of 1900. (ILO, Part III, chs. III and IV; Levine, ch.III.)

Trade unions did not resume their development until the First World War, which brought with it an enlargement of the heavy industries and the growth in the size of the permanent industrial labour force. The liberal temper of the Japanese governments in the years immediately after the war removed some of the former political obstacles to the trade unions, and in 1921 the Japan Labour Federation (*Sodomei*) came into existence with a membership of about 100,000, divided among 300 separate unions. The movement was strengthened when the International Labour Office, established in 1919, got to work, for the Japanese government showed itself to be sensitive to criticisms made by that body.

The number of workers organised in unions continued to grow throughout the 1920s and beyond. In 1931 there were 818 unions with an aggregate membership of 370,000 and in 1936 about 1,000 unions with 420,000 members (Levine, pp.63-4). Of this total (the maximum attained in the pre-war period) the Seamen's Union accounted for over a third and the railway unions for another substantial share. It follows that most of the workers in manufacturing industry were unorganised. The reasons are not difficult to find. In 1936-7, despite the rapid economic growth in the preceding quinquennium, the total number of industrial workers reached only 6½ million (excluding construction, a small-scale industry). Of these under 3 million were so-called 'factory' workers, that is, workers in establishments with 5 employees and over (DCI). Nearly half these 'factory' workers were in workplaces with under 30 employees and probably hardly more than a third in workplaces with 200 or more employees (Reubens). Two-fifths of the 'factory' workers, moreover, were women, mostly young girls engaged in what were still Japan's staple manufactures, namely textiles. They were recruited from peasant families by the agents of the mill-owners and they were housed during their working life in dormitories in the mill compounds. They normally stayed in the mills for only two or three years, before returning to their rural families with savings that constituted their dowries. Many of the urban male workers were, as in earlier times, either self-employed craftsmen, or seasonally or temporarily engaged in industry. Those whose whose roots were in the country – the majority – often returned to the family farms in periods of industrial depression. These conditions were highly unfavourable to the development of effective labour organisations, and the trade union leaders were inclined, in consequence, to direct much of their energy into political propaganda as a means of redressing the injustices of the new industrial society.

The world depression between 1929 and 1932 had catastrophic effects on agriculture and on Japan's two main export industries, raw silk and cotton manufactures. The downward pressure on wages and on the incomes of the self-employed that was exerted by the deflationary conditions of the time became irresistible. Even when industrial recovery after 1932 led to a rapid extension of Japan's manufacturing base, the only workers to benefit were those in the expanding heavy industries, especially the armaments trades. Other branches of industry and the service trades found that they could obtain an ample supply of recruits from the still depressed, and over-populated, countryside without raising wages. Indeed, as a contemporary investigation revealed, in those sectors of the economy, real wages actually fell between 1932 and 1936 (Uyeda, pp.279ff). The much increased production of Japan in that period of the *junsenji-keizai* (or quasi-wartime economy) took the form mainly of armaments, investments in heavy industries at home and in Manchuria, and the additional exports required by the worsening of the country's terms of trade with the outside world. Yet it was not only unfavourable economic factors that hampered the rise of effective labour organisations. The collapse of parliamentary government after 1932 and the transference of power to the military cliques put an end to the policy of official toleration. The trade union movement itself was split asunder by quarrels between those who supported the new nationalist policy and those who remained faithful to socialist or liberal principles. With the outbreak of the Sino-Japanese War of 1937 the right-wing unions surrendered their claims to the right to strike, while the left-wing unions were suppressed. In July 1940 the government dissolved all independent labour organisations.

The achievements of the trade unions, even in the period when they were officially tolerated, had been insignificant. Membership never exceeded 5 per cent of the industrial labour force. The right of collective bargaining had been conceded by employers in only a few instances, and standard rates of wages were almost unknown. Only the seamen and inland transport workers had succeeded in creating unions that had to be reckoned with. Wages and conditions of work were determined largely by the compulsions of a market in which the employers enjoyed overwhelmingly superior bargaining power. The best of them accepted a measure of responsibility for their employees' welfare. In the large, well-established firms there was a reluctance to discharge 'regular' employees in times of bad trade, and generous payments were often made to them on retirement. In return the employers expected unquestioned deference to their authority which sometimes extended to the private lives of their workers, including even the arrangement of their marriages. The wages paid varied widely from firm to firm for the same class of worker, and they were made up, at the will of the employer, of basic wages, payments for age, personal character, education, family responsibilities, length of service and punctuality, in varying proportions.

Government regulation did not supply the deficiencies left by the absence of effective trade unions. The first Factory Act, passed in 1911, and designed to protect women and young persons against excessive hours of work, and employment at night, did not come into operation until 1930 (ILO, Part III, ch.1). Even so, the majority of workplaces remained outside its purview. There were regulations that limited the working hours of miners and governed the working conditions of seamen. A modest Health Insurance Scheme, based on the British model, was introduced during the 1920s, together with some provision for workers' compensation in cases of sickness or injury arising out of their employment. In 1936 a law was passed that made compulsory, over part of industry, the hitherto customary payment of allowances to workers on their retirement. But, on the eve of the Second World War, Japan was still without unemployment insurance, the public regulation of wages, and effective official conciliation and arbitration provisions for settling disputes. Such protective legislation as existed did not apply to, or was unenforceable over, the large industrial sector composed of small and medium-sized firms (Ayusawa, pp.104-5).

Trade Unions and the Occupation Authority

For almost seven years, from August 1945 until March 1952 (when the Peace Treaty came into force) the economic and social policy of Japan was governed by directives from the Occupation Authority (Supreme Commander of Allied Powers or SCAP). Although at the beginning of this period the economy was in ruins, SCAP was at first less actively concerned with promoting recovery than with ambitious measures of social and political reform. Its chief object was that of destroying once and for all Japan's capacity to wage war, and of reshaping her institutions so as to establish her as a democracy on the Western model. In some branches of the national life the policy called for sweeping reforms in existing institutions, but since trade unions had been eliminated at the outbreak of the Pacific War and public provision for social welfare was insubstantial, SCAP was presented in this sphere with a *tabula rasa.* It proceeded quickly to introduce measures which soon transformed the country's industrial relations and the status of the workers.

The policy was embodied in a number of laws which the Japanese government was required to enact. They included the Trade Union Act and Labour Relations Adjustment Act of 1946 and the Labour Standards Act of 1947. The first of these was modelled on the American Wagner Act and conferred on workers the right to organise unions, to bargain collectively with their employers and to strike. The only workers to whom these rights were not accorded at that time were certain classes of public servants. Discriminatory acts by employers against trade unionists, and a refusal by them to bargain with union representatives, were forbidden, under penalties. The Trade Union Act and the Labour Relations Adjustment Acts also provided for mediation and arbitration in industrial disputes and for the public regulation of wages. The latter function was entrusted to a National Labour Relations Board and 46 Prefectural Boards which were tripartite in membership and contained official members as well as representatives of the employers and the workers. The Labour Standards Law was designed to introduce the employment standards set out in the recommendations of the International Labour Office. It dealt with limits on the hours of work, the provision of holidays with pay, factory conditions, overtime pay and procedures for dismissal. In establishments with ten or more workers, the employers were obliged to draw up 'employment regulations' by agreement with the trade unions, and to those regulations, once agreed, they had to conform. A system of inspection was devised, and penalties imposed for breaches of the laws. Other enactments covered unemployment benefits, industrial health insurance and compensation for accidents. In 1947 a Ministry of Labour was established. The result was that, within two years of the end of the war, Japan was equipped with a labour code that embodied the standards of advanced Western countries, standards which were not of her own choosing but had been imposed by the victors in the Pacific War. (M of L (1953) and *Year Book*.)

It might have been expected that reforms that stemmed from such origins would have been fragile. In fact, not only did the legal foundations endure, but on those foundations the Japanese, in the course of the next decade, erected a superstructure of trade union organisation and industrial relations which at length made a massive contribution to the country's economic performance. This superstructure, however, took some years to build and, in the early post-war years, the prospects for industrial harmony looked very bleak.

Conflicts and Their Resolution

The workers responded with zest to their changed legal status, and between the end of the war and December 1948 the number of trade unionists rose from none to 6¾ million, distributed among some 34,000 unions (JI of L, *Labour Statistics*; M of L, *Year Book*). These unions, finding managements demoralised by war and defeat and enjoying, at first, the favour of the Occupation Authority, took advantage of their new bargaining strength. Their leaders, many of whom had spent the years of war in prison, were much influenced by socialist, syndicalist or communist ideas. In some instances, they wrested the managerial functions from the employers, and assumed responsibility for the recruitment, dismissal and discipline of the factory workers. At the centre of trade union activity there were the resuscitated All-Japan General Federation of Labour (*Sodomei*) which was in the hands of the right-wing socialists, and the smaller All-Japan Congress of Industrial Labour Organisations (*Sanbetsu*) which was dominated by the communists. The majority of the unions affiliated themselves to one or other of these bodies.

The militancy displayed by the new movement and the disorders that resulted from it provoked SCAP to intervene (Levine, pp.26-7). It put an abrupt end to a general strike in February 1947 and, when the 'Cold War' began in 1948, its enthusiasm for democratic reforms gave place to a determination to turn Japan into a base for the deployment of American power in the Western Pacific. Its labour policy was modified accordingly. In July 1948 the rights of collective bargaining and of striking were withdrawn from civil servants, and Commissioners were appointed by the Cabinet to fix the terms of employment in the public service. At the same time workers in the public corporations, including those employed in the national railways, though still allowed to bargain collectively, lost the right to strike and had to submit to compulsory conciliation and arbitration over matters in dispute. Later the employees of the local authorities and local public enterprises were covered by similar regulations. These arrangements have continued with few changes. At the present time trade unions in the private sector remain covered by the Trade Union Law, those formed from employees in public corporations by the Public Corporation and National Employees Labour Relations Law, and civil servants by the National (or Local) Public Service Law. In 1978, 72 per cent of the trade unionists were in the first category, 10 per cent in the second, and 18 per cent in the third (JI of L (1979), p.13).

The labour movement suffered a further setback as a result of the deflation that followed the application of the Dodge Stabilisation Plan in 1949. After the outbreak of the Korean War in 1950 the government, alarmed by the presence of political activists among the union leaders, took additional power for dealing with general strikes and saw to it that communists were removed from positions of authority. The number of trade unionists fell, and by 1954 the *proportion* of the industrial labour force in trade unions was lower than in 1948. These were years of bitter conflict. There were prolonged strikes of seamen, electricity workers and miners. In 1952 the number of man-hours lost through stoppages reached a peak — 15 million, three times the average of the previous six years. Perhaps most significant of all was the long strike at the Omi Silk Company in 1954, since this was not provoked, like most of the others, by a dispute about wages, hours or redundancy, but it arose from the workers' resentment at the management's attempts to assert the kind of paternalistic control over their lives that had been commonplace before the war (Okochi *et al.*, ch.9).

After the middle 1950s collective bargaining was gradually transformed by the convergence of several changes both in policy and also in industrial conditions. Prolonged nationwide conflicts inspired by political ideology, or sparked off by resistance to managerial strategies, gave place to shorter, local stoppages or 'go-slows'. Managements by this time had begun to realise that the national policy

of giving priority to industrial growth could not succeed unless the
co-operation of the workers in this purpose could be won. At the same
time, the new, science-based industries, to which Japan had turned
for the solution of her economic problem, called for different types
of workers and for different systems of recruitment, training and
hierarchical relationships within the firm, from those familiar in the
past. Managements were thus impelled, and persuaded, to adapt
their employment policy to the needs of the developing
industries and to the social attitudes of the post-war generation of
workers, especially the attitudes of the young men and women
required for the new plants. The mood of the workers themselves
responded to the management's changed policy, not least in
consequence of the benefits, in rising real incomes, that accompanied
economic growth. It is true that periods of strife recurred from time
to time. The first was during the years (1958-62) in which the coal
industry was being run down; in 1960 three-quarters of the days
lost through disputes occurred in the mining industry. Again, at the
beginning of the long recession in 1974 there was a proliferation of
strikes brought about by resistance to wage freezes. The most serious
troubles, however, were confined to the public sector and transport.
From the late 1950s onwards strikes in private manufacturing
industry increasingly assumed an almost ritualistic character and
usually lasted only a few hours. Japan, which in the early post-war
period had been grouped with countries with an unfavourable record
in industrial relations, moved up the scale of enviable performance.
Some data are contained in Table 3.1. During the later 1970s the
number of days lost per worker through strikes or lockouts was much
lower in Japan than in any other industrial country, except West
Germany (JI of L (1979), pp.31-2).

Table 3.1: Number of Working Days Lost through Stoppages

Year	Days lost (thousands)
1970	3,915
1971	6,029
1972	5,147
1973	4,604
1974	9,663
1975	8,016
1976	3,254
1977	1,518

Source: M of L, *Year Book*, 1977.

Trade Union Structure

The type of trade unions and the system of collective bargaining now
prevalent in Japan arose out of the storms and conflicts of the
immediate post-war years. They emerged, as will be shown, from the
impact on the country's social organisation of the urgent needs of
industrialists intent upon rapid expansion. Today, the typical trade
union is the 'enterprise' union (*kigyo betsu kumiai*); that is to say,
workers are organised mainly according to the firms that employ
them (Levine, pp.101-7; Okochi *et al.*, pp.274-8). This explains both the
complex structure, and the large number, of trade unions – see Table 3.2.

Table 3.2: Trade Unions and Members in 1977

Membership	No. of unions	No. of members
5,000 and over	339	5,612,896
1,000 – 4,999	1,372	2,376,153
500 – 999	1,530	1,056,201
300 – 499	1,930	740,899
100 – 299	7,749	1,302,379
30 – 99	12,243	707,725
under 29	8,824	140,759
Total	33,887	12,437,012

Source: M of L, *Year Book*, 1977.

When a firm operates several plants, separate unions are usually formed
for each of them, and they are linked in an organisation that covers all
the firm's workers, irrespective of the 'industry' in which their members
are engaged. As an example, the union of workers in the various Hitachi
plants together make up an 'enterprise' union known as *Hitachi Soren*.
The individual 'enterprise' unions are normally affiliated to regional
or national associations representative of workers in the same trade or
trades, such as the Federation of Metal and Engineering Workers
(*Zenkokukinzoku*). Sometimes the 'enterprise' unions are affiliated to
several national bodies. The various unions of miners employed by
the Mitsui Mining Company are affiliated both to the Miners' Federation
of Japan and to an enterprise-wide association. Many of the national
federations or associations are, in turn, affiliated to one of the few
central labour organisations, most of which can trace their origins to
the pre-war period. During the last 40 years these have been, from time

to time, split up, re-grouped and renamed. At present the chief central
bodies comprise *Sohyo*, with about 36 per cent of total trade union
membership, *Domei*, with 18 per cent, and *Churitsuroren*, with 11 per
cent (JI of L (1979), p.13). Like their forerunners, these bodies are
active politically. *Sohyo* supports the Japan Socialist Party, the
ultimate purpose of which is the overthrow of private capitalism and
the establishment of a socialist society. *Domei*, the Democratic
Socialist Party, seeks rather to strengthen the power of organised labour
over industrial management and central policy-making. One-third of
the trade union members, however, remain outside the central
organisations, since they prefer not to engage in the political debate.

   The ratio of union members to the total number of employees in
1978 was just under 33 per cent, rather lower than in the late 1960s.
About 28 per cent of them are women. This density ratio differs
widely from industry to industry and, also, according to the size of
enterprises. The most completely organised industries are the public
utilities and government service, with transport and communications
(part of which falls within the public sector) close behind (*ibid.*, p.11).
Trade unionism has made little headway in industries where the
typical productive unit is small — agriculture, construction and
distribution. Manufacturing, taken as a whole, occupies an
intermediate position. In the large firms the workers are well organised,
but trade unions have met with little success in attempts to recruit
members among the small and medium-sized firms which, in the
aggregate, are still responsible for a substantial share of industrial
output and employment. The union membership includes a high
proportion of white-collar workers. After the war, these, when
employed in manufacturing, transport and public service, showed
themselves eager to join unions along with their blue-collar colleagues,
and they have often provided leadership. The fact that in Japanese
firms no distinction is drawn between staff and shop-floor workers in
regard to privileges and amenities goes far towards explaining the
former's participation in the 'enterprise unions'. Tables 3.3 and 3.4
provide statistical evidence for the general statements in this paragraph.

   The relations among the various types of organisations call for
examination in some detail. As already explained, it is the enterprise
unions (which in 1978 numbered about 34,000) that normally
conduct negotiations with the employers. However, there are
important exceptions. The seamen are organised in an industrial union,
and the unions formed in part of the public sector (e.g. the state
railway employees and the teachers) approximate to that form. The

Table 3.3: Trade Union Membership in 1978 (per cent of total employees)

Industry	
All industries	32.6
Manufacturing	37.6
Transport and communications	64.4
Electricity, gas, water	75.3
Construction	16.9
Mining	45.3
Agriculture, forestry	22.0
Finance, insurance, etc.	63.3
Government, central and local	74.2
Other service industries	22.5

Source: M of L, *Basic Survey of Trade Unions* (Tokyo, 1978).

Table 3.4: Trade Union Membership in 1969 by Size of Enterprise in Private Industry (per cent of total employed in class)

No. of employees in enterprise	
500 and over	63.6
100 – 499	31.5
30 – 99	9.0
29 or less	3.4

Source: M of L, *Basic Survey of Trade Unions* (Tokyo, 1972).

federations or regional bodies to which many of the enterprise unions are affiliated do not become directly involved in collective bargaining. Their function is primarily that of co-ordinating the policies of the individual enterprise unions. Recently, however, their role has been somewhat modified. The structural changes in industry that accompanied the long depression of 1974-7 induced collaboration in order to meet the problems of wage standstill, or redundancy and, in consequence, the federations took on a new significance. As to the central bodies, in addition to their political activities, they also exert some influence on the strategy of negotiation. Their importance in this respect has grown with the spread of the practice of *Shunto*, the annual 'Spring Offensive', which is now a notable feature of industrial relations.

After the middle 1950s, it became increasingly customary for the unions to put forward their wage claims, almost simultaneously, in

the Spring (Okochi *et al.*, pp.77-9). This timing was found convenient
by employers and workers alike. The practice arose originally
as a means of strengthening the latter's bargaining power during a
period in which labour was still in ample supply; but the employers
soon realised that it was to their advantage also, since it put a stop
to the escalation of a succession of claims. Normally the choice of the
unions to lead the offensive is made centrally and the wage advances
won in the early negotiations tend to determine the subsequent range
of settlements. But the individual enterprise unions do not, by any
means, slavishly respond to guidance from the centre or from
federations. For instance, in December 1980, the General Federation
of Private Railway Workers' Unions (*Shitetsusoren*), with 205,000
members, decided to submit to its constituent unions a recommendation
for a certain wage demand for the Spring Offensive in 1981. But
commentators on the proposal expressed doubt whether the unions
would accept this guidance.

Although the enterprise union as the dominant feature of the labour
movement is to be regarded as a product of the post-war period, its
form was probably influenced by certain practices or attitudes
prevalent in earlier times. Thus employers in the textile industry, as
already described, were long accustomed to recruit their female
operatives from particular regions in the countryside and to provide
accommodation for them during their short working life. Wages and
conditions of work varied widely from firm to firm. The employer
sought to establish a paternalistic relationship with his workers
and would not tolerate attempts by outsiders (e.g. trade union
officials) to participate in any negotiations. The workers, for their
part, were not conscious of sharing a common interest with the body
of employers in the whole industry, and their conditions of
employment were hostile to the appearance of any such consciousness.
Such attitudes were conducive to the development of enterprise
unions rather than occupational or industrial unions. It is true that
the outlook of the skilled, male craftsman who, in previous times,
made up a considerable part of the labour force in the engineering
and metal industries bore a resemblance to that of their Western
counterparts. But, after the war, the type of labour most urgently
required for the new, science-based industries did not consist of
craftsmen but rather of young men who were ready, or even eager,
to be trained by the employer in new techniques, and who looked
forward to a lifetime career with the firm that recruited them. This
applies especially to employment in the large firms, while in the small

firms the relations between employer and employed remained as
always very intimate. Many of the recruits for both types of firm came
from rural areas; between 1955 and 1969 employment in agriculture
and forestry fell from 14 million to 9 million, while that in
manufacturing industry increased from 8.4 million to 13.3 million
(PMO). Naturally enough, the relations that came to prevail in the
factories were strongly influenced by those to which the new recruits
had been accustomed in their native villages. The notion that there
was a bond among workers as a whole, or workers in a particular
industry, closer than that between themselves and their employers
was alien to them.

SCAP's policy played a part in the evolution of the system. From
the outset it had pressed for the formation of joint councils of
workers and employers for collective bargaining within firms, and
this policy was pursued by the National Labour Relations Board set
up by the Labour Relations Adjustment Act of 1946. The
establishment of these councils set a precedent for negotiations at
the level of the enterprise. In the large firms the decisions reached
after the discussions were applied to all their employees. The
headquarters and offices of the unions were often located within
a plant-compound, and at the outset the firms often provided the
buildings and furnishings for the unions. Yet, as the experience
of the early post-war years demonstrated, the unions were not
simply 'company' unions. Far from being subservient to the
management, they at one time usurped its functions. The apparently
paradoxical relationship between unions and employers can be
understood only if one remembers the circumstances of the time.
Since SCAP had called the trade unions into being, managements
felt obliged to act in conformity with its policy. But obviously the
outcome would have been very different if the policy had been
applied to a society that lacked Japan's special qualities.

Trade Union Policy

Wages and Employment Practices

The negotiations at the time of the Spring Offensive usually turn on the
additions to be made to basic wages, but, although those are likely to
be quickly concluded, discussions between unions and management do
not end there. Indeed, they often continue for much of the year and
are directed towards other constituents in the total wage, such as
overtime allowances and the biannual bonuses. These 'other constituents'

are very important. The basic wage, which usually makes up about four-fifths of monthly earnings, varies with age and seniority. A school-leave or a college graduate, is normally recruited by a firm on finishing his formal education and, once established, he expects to remain with the employer for the rest of his working life. His basic wage will rise from year to year and will probably reach its maximum in the quinquennium before he retires, that is to say, between the ages of 51 and 55. Tables 3.5 and 3.6 illustrate these basic features of the pay system.

Table 3.5: Contractual Earnings According to Age of Males in all Industries in 1977 (per month)

Age	Earnings (in thousand yen)
15–17	75
20–24	109
30–34	169
40–44	201
50–54	205
55–59*	175

*The government recently urged an extension of the retirement age and workers are sometimes re-engaged on a 'temporary' basis after retirement — see below.

Source: M of L, *Basic Survey of Wages*, 1977.

Table 3.6: Education and Wages in 1977 (in thousand yen)

Grade of Education	Length of Service		
	1 year	15–17 years	30 years
Lower Secondary School	122	173	212
Upper Secondary School	120	204	282
Junior College	131	251	360
University	137	287	386

Source: M of L, *Year Book*, 1977, pp. 150-1; the wage figures are for monthly contractual earnings.

Besides his basic pay, however, he will receive supplements related usually to his personal circumstances. They include payments in respect of his educational standards, regularity of attendance, punctuality, housing needs, and other matters. At *O-Bon* (midsummer festival) and

at New Year he will also be given bonuses related to the prosperity of
he firm. A prosperous firm may pay bonuses equivalent to four months'
wages, or even more. Finally, the large firms often provide lavish
'welfare' payments in kind. (JI of L (1979-80 a, b and c); Okochi *et al.*,
ch.13.)

It is evident that there is nothing resembling a 'rate for the job'
common to all workers who perform it. As wages are negotiated firm
by firm, they differ for the same type of worker, or for the same job,
both between and within firms. Merit payments and production bonuses
have become increasingly common, but they have not gone far
towards supplanting the conventional system. The recruit, once taken
on, has a guarantee (at any rate, in large firms) of 'lifetime' employment.
Even if he is not promoted to higher grades, he can expect his income
to rise steadily as years go by and, in return for his loyalty, he is
assured of his firm's solicitude for his welfare. These conditions of
employment and the nature of the trade unions leave few occasions
for demarcation or jurisdictional disputes. When technical advances or
market changes render obsolete certain types of skill or experience, the
workers so affected have no reason for resisting technical innovations,
retraining and allocation to new jobs, since their wages remain unaffected.
Some examples of this process will be given later. The structural
adaptability that has distinguished the Japanese economy and has been
a source of its strength owes much to the easy transference of workers
in response to changes in markets. The whole system of employer-
worker relations as it has developed since the war has been well-attuned
to the promotion of rapid growth in a period of high technology and
frequent innovation. It is evident that the various constituents of
the system — enterprise unions (*kigyo betsu kumiai*), seniority wages
(*nenko chingin*) and lifetime employment (*shushin koyo*) — are
integrally associated, and that one of them could hardly survive without
the others.

At one time foreign students of Japan's post-war trade unions and
industrial relations were inclined to regard them as the result of the
adaptation of traditional practices to the new industrialism. The
proposition that they were to be regarded as innovations rather than as
survivals from the past was put forward some 20 years ago by Professor
Taira in a number of illuminating articles (1962 a, b and c). It has
subsequently won support from many other economists and economic
historians. Thus, Professors Karsh and Levine have stated: '. . . what
have often been taken as pre-modern traditions actually were social
innovations or new responses to the industrialising process itself'

(Okochi *et al.*, p.13). Professor Sumiya makes the same point: 'The lifetime employment and length of service wage systems . . . are to be regarded not as traditional social relations but rather as innovations that developed in response to new needs' (*ibid.*, p.37). In accepting this conclusion, however, one must not repudiate entirely the views of those who emphasise the contribution of ancient habit to modern practices. Japan's distinctive historical experience had left her people with social attitudes which influenced the shape of the post-war system. The employment practices of the great business houses, some of which trace back their origins for several hundred years, cannot be disregarded in this connection. In the House of Mitsui these practices were systematically expressed in the Codes which defined in detail the rules for training and promotion and for the treatment of sick employees (Mitsui and Co.). There is some evidence that, on the eve of the Meiji era, practices that resembled the seniority wage system were to be found in some of the new factories.

Nevertheless, in most of the large plants in the Meiji and the Taisho (1912-26) eras. there was little sense of reciprocal obligation between management and workers. The provision of welfare facilities was rudimentary and the seniority wage system did not usually extend beyond the staff. Indeed, the conditions which then prevailed contained little promise of the intricate and elaborate system of today. Of this, the distinguishing feature is the preference for consensus rather than confrontation. All those employed in an enterprise have been persuaded (when the system works well) to regard themselves as members of a group or family. They differ in rank, on which great store is set in Japan, but they are all associates in a joint venture. As one British writer has put it: 'They occupy different rungs of the same ladder' (Clark, p.108). Or, in the words of a Japanese report on the enterprise union — such a union represents the interest of the workers in an enterprise but its administration and policy reflect an acknowledgement by its members that they are 'components of a communal body' (JI of L (1979), p.9). Were it not for this attitude, it would have been difficult to reconcile the cosy lifetime employment guarantee and the seniority system of wage payment with industrial efficiency.

If harmony in industrial relations has contributed much to Japan's economic success, rapid industrial expansion has helped to preserve the harmony. The growth in production was subject to interruption for only brief periods between 1950 and 1973, and so employers had little difficulty in honouring the lifetime commitment, especially as the labour force was mobile within each enterprise. At the same time, the seniority wage system has made a contribution to low-cost production and has stimulated structural change. This is because the most rapidly growing firms have been those that employ a high proportion of young, and therefore comparatively cheap, workers.

In the 25 years after 1955 average real wages rose by 300 per cent. The workers, therefore, were easily persuaded to co-operate with a system that was associated with a continuous improvement in the living standards. The conduct of wage negotiations within the enterprise brought home both to trade union leaders and to the rank and file the dependence of their incomes on productivity. Further, the fact that a substantial proportion of a worker's annual income was directly related to the profits earned by his firm helped to win his ready co-operation with management in the pursuit of efficiency.

The performance of Japan in industrial relations has not been a success without qualifications, for the benefits of the system have not been evenly distributed. In the first place, as we have seen already, the employees of small firms are weakly organised and, since the mortality among such firms is high, they cannot enjoy the same security of employment as those in large firms (Clark, pp.46-7). In the second place, even in the large firms, a proportion of the workers is excluded from many of the benefits enjoyed by the regular workers. This fringe of the un-privileged is composed of the 'temporary' workers (*rinjiko*). These fall into several groups. First there are those who are recruited as adults (rather than as school-leavers) and whose engagement, though ostensibly for a short period, may be indefinitely prolonged. Then, there are seasonal workers and, finally,'established' workers who, after retiring, are re-engaged by the same employer at a lower wage. There are no accurate figures by which the proportion of 'temporary' workers to total employment can be measured. Twelve per cent may be a reasonable estimate. The size of the fringe, however, varies widely from industry to industry and between firms in the same industry. The range in the chemical industry has been put between 11.4 per cent and 62.7 per cent (Okochi *et al.*, pp.403-4).

The 'temporary' workers are usually excluded from union membership, nor do they enjoy the benefit of lifetime employment and other privileges. Their presence in the workforce has been of considerable advantage to the employers in one respect. During recessions, a large firm is precluded by its lifetime commitment from discharging its regular workers, but it can cut its costs by getting rid of its 'temporary' employees, or by reducing its orders to sub-contractors. Many of these sub-contractors are small firms whose workers in bad times become unemployed or, more usually, are obliged to accept lower wages (see Table 3.7). The secular growth of Japanese industry and the shortage of young recruits that first made itself felt in the early 1960s obliged the employers to accord the privileges of their established labour force to an increased proportion of their workers. This trend was, however, reversed after 1973.

Table 3.7: Wage Differentials by Size of Firms in Manufacturing Industry (500 employees and over = 100)

Year	100—499 workers	30—99 workers	5—29 workers
1960	70.7	58.9	46.3
1970	81.4	69.6	61.8
1978	82.7	68.1	60.6

Source: M of L, *Monthly Labour Survey*. (Various periods. These figures are for annual cash earnings, including biannual bonuses.)

One must conclude that the benefits enjoyed by the regular workers, especially the high degree of job security accorded to them, have depended in some measure on the existence of a fringe of workers, whose employment has been insecure and whose wages have been at the mercy of market changes. The disabilities of the 'temporary' workers were not, of course, conspicuous during the long period of almost continuous industrial expansion, and it is this buoyancy in the labour market that has been the main factor in keeping down the rate of unemployment. That rate has been very low by Western standards. Between 1965 and 1979, which included the long depression after 1973, the *recorded* rate of unemployment (seasonally adjusted) never rose above 2.2 per cent and fell as low as 1.1 per cent. These figures, are, however, an unreliable guide to the level of economic activity because, in recessions, large numbers of workers are kept in employment, even if there are no jobs for them. If one were to take account of the employees so retained the unemployment rate might well be put at twice the recorded rate. On the other hand, there can be little doubt that the mobility of labour within firms and between occupations has been just as an important an influence in keeping down unemployment as it has been in maintaining a high rate of economic growth.

As already mentioned, the early post-war legislation established machinery for conciliation and arbitration in disputes. In the private sector the Commissions set up for these purposes were often called upon to act in the early post-war years, but the role they most commonly exercised was that of a mediator, or adjuster of differences, rather than of an arbitrator. From the description of the wage system already given, it can be seen that most of the issues that arose in that context were not such as could be dealt with by formal arbitration procedures. Much of the collective bargaining, moreover, has been focused on the formulation of rules of employment as required by the Labour Standards Act. In this process the Commissions have been active, but, on the whole, their importance in the private sector has diminished markedly during the last 20 years. On the other hand, in the public sector (including the public corporations) to which the Trade Union Act and the Labour Relations Adjustment Act do not apply, compulsory arbitration procedures have been frequently used. In this sector the rights of the workers to take industrial action have been restricted by law, and decisions about wages and conditions have been influenced by political as well as by economic factors. Even in this sphere, the Central Labour Relations Commission and the National Enterprise and Public Corporation Labour Relations Commission have, in the last 15 years, shown a disposition, when giving decisions on wages and other matters, simply to follow the pattern set by collective bargaining in private industry (ibid., pp.127-32 and 278n).

The Differential Structure

The Japanese worker's readiness to co-operate with his employer in the pursuit of efficiency can be attributed at least as much to the financial benefits that he has derived from the rise in industrial productivity as to inherited traditions that incline him to prefer consensus to confrontation. Throughout the post-war period a steep increase in real earnings accompanied the expansion in production (see Table 3.8). During the first two decades after the war output per man rose much faster than wages which, despite the urgent demand for labour for manning the new factories, were then held down by the ample supply of recruits from rural areas. In the early and middle 1960s, when that supply showed signs of exhaustion, productivity still kept ahead of wages because the huge investments in industrial equipment made in earlier years were then yielding their fruits. It was largely because of this relationship that Japan was able to keep inflation in check. After 1969 real wages for a period ran ahead of

Table 3.8: Industrial Production, Productivity, Wages and Employment in Manufacturing (1975 = 100)

Year	Production	Productivity	Real Wages	Employment
1955	13.2	18.3	32.8	41.2
1960	25.9	28.3	41.0	68.3
1965	44.9	40.9	49.3	92.0
1970	92.5	76.7	75.3	107.0
1973	117.0	104.6	98.9	106.0
1975	100.0	100.0	100.0	100.0
1979	133.1	(1978) 127.4	109.2	94.2

Sources: Ministry of Labour and Japan Productivity Centre.

productivity, because labour's bargaining power had grown through the increasing scarcity of recruits for industry. Consequently, cost-plus inflationary pressures were intensified. In 1973, however, the arrival of the depression put an end to industrial growth for nearly four years and held back wage increases.

The wages referred to are, of course, averages, and these are misleading unless one keeps in mind the wide diversity of wages between firms and within firms. It has already been shown that the responsibilities accepted by the large firms for their regular workers are not extended to 'temporary' workers or to those employed by their sub-contractors, many of whom are small. The wages paid to the latter are determined by a highly competitive market and the gap between them and the wages paid to the regular workers in large firms has been wide. These differences are symptomatic of the 'dual economy' or the 'differential industrial structure', as Professor Ohkawa prefers to call it (Ohkawa, pp.45-6). In 1974 the average monthly wage of employees in firms with 10-49 workers was only 60 per cent of that of employees in firms with 1,000 and over (JI of L, 1979-80c, p.13). The differences had tended to contract during the 1960s, but the trend was checked, and probably reversed, after the onset of the depression in 1973. One obvious cause of the disparities is the higher productivity of the workers in the large firms, the consequence in the main of superior equipment. Further, the average length of service is lower in the small firms than the large firms; and the large firms usually have the pick of the best workers. But the explanation is to be found mainly in the fragmentation of the labour market.

The differences apply to all the numerous constituents of which the total monthly or yearly wage is made up. According to the analysis conducted by the Ministry of Labour into the ratio of special cash payments during the year to contractual monthly earnings, that ratio has been consistently higher for large than for small or medium-sized firms with 5-9 employees (ibid., p.16). Another source of difference is education (see Table 3.6). Even sums payable on retirement vary both firms with 5-9 employees (*ibid.*, p.16). Another source of difference is education (see *Table 3.6*). Even sums payable on retirement vary both with the size of the firm and with the educational qualifications of the workers. Thus in 1975 the typical university graduate employed by a firm with 1,000 or more workers received on retirement 13 million yen, but only 7.4 million yen if employed by a firm with 30-99 workers (ibid., p.18).

These differentials deserve to be emphasised not only because of their social implications, but also because they present the entrepreneur, when organising production, with a range of choices denied to him in countries where greater uniformity exists (cf. Ohkawa, p.64). In industries or processes for which methods of production are not dictated by technical conditions, the Japanese manufacturer can choose between those that depend on capital-intensive, large-scale methods and those that can make use of labour-intensive, small-scale methods. For products for which the market is fickle or unstable, he can choose to organise production in such a way that he can adjust his costs quickly to changes in demand, while following different methods where flexibility is not called for. The widely recognised capacity of Japanese industry to adapt itself to change can be explained in part by the existence of these differentials.

Adaptation to Depression

For over a quarter of a century Japanese industry had enjoyed almost uninterrupted economic expansion. In 1973 this period came to an abrupt end. Production fell and remained low for several years, the demand for industrial labour declined, and the advance of real wages was halted. Even after recovery set in, during 1978, it was acknowledged that the period of rapid growth was over for good. Japan might hope to maintain during the 1980s an annual growth rate of 4-5 per cent (compared with 10-12 per cent in the later 1960s), but that rate would depend on her success in effecting far-reaching structural changes in the economy. Not only the textile and labour-intensive industries were in retreat before the advance of production in several developing countries, but even in some branches of engineering (e.g. shipbuilding) Japan's dominance could not be regarded as secure. Secondary industry as a whole was likely to yield place to some of the tertiary trades.

It was a testing time for the trade unions and the system of industrial relations. The question was asked whether the harmony that had prevailed for two decades could be preserved in the new conditions. Industrial firms adversely affected by the fall in demand were burdened by their lifetime-employment commitment to their workers. At the same time the rapidly changing age-composition of the population was accentuating their difficulties. The reduction in the number of school-leavers and the rise in the proportion of middle aged and elderly called in question the feasibility of maintaining the seniority wage system. The employers were assailed from two sides. The government was urging them to defer the compulsory retirement age from 55 to 60, while the younger members of the labour force, whose bargaining power had been enhanced by the shortage of recruits, found good reason to resent the seniority wage system. Thus the depression and the circumstances that accompanied it shook the foundations on which the country's industrial development had hitherto rested. Some changes had been in train for a decade. For example, many employers had long favoured widening the scope for 'merit payments', and, despite the resistance of the unions, these became increasingly common. In the steel industry and in a few others it has lately been decided to raise the compulsory retirement age, a change that is likely to increase costs. For some industries that suffered badly in the depression, there were derogations from the lifetime-employment commitment.

Yet, despite these modifications, most of the conventional practices associated with the system of industrial relations survived intact. Firms forced to contract did not in general abandon their obligations to their employees. Among the textile firms a partial solution was found in diversification and the transference of redundant textile operatives to new activities, e.g. chemical production. Part of the reduction in the labour force was achieved by a temporary ban on the recruitment of workers and by the encouragement of retirement by generous allowances. Some firms set up associated companies specifically for the purpose of providing jobs for their surplus workers. In the case of a large man-made fibres firm the activities of the new companies ranged from engineering and chemical manufacture to distribution and research. The shipbuilding firms, even in the period of the most rapid expansion, had acquired interests in other branches of engineering as a safeguard against a decline in their main business. When the demand

for ships slumped, they were able to find jobs for most of their
redundant workers in these other branches, or in companies associated
with them. The enterprise unions had no reason to resist this
reallocation of labour. Their relations with the employers made them
full conscious of a common interest in improving productivity and
maintaining profitability. They recognised that adaptability was the
key to success in a highly competitive economy and, since their
members' incomes were assured, they were well disposed towards labour
transference in the pursuit of continued progress. As Professor Okano
has pointed out, labour management *within* the firm in Japan performs
the role of the labour market, so that even if the market itself lacks
resilience, the allocation of labour over the economy is efficiently
carried out (Okano and Okabe). The close association of unions with
management also explains the former's realism when confronted by
changes in the economic climate. Before 1973 the unions' demands for
steadily rising real incomes were attuned to their belief in continued,
rapid industrial expansion. When the slump came, the unions'
immediate reaction was to resist the check to real wage increases, and
the number of strikes increased. But expectations were quickly
modified to accord with the worsened conditions and after 1974 the
number of workdays lost rapidly declined.

Conclusion

The experience of the depression, and the reactions of the employment
policies of firms and unions to it, have demonstrated Japan's skill in
adapting her institutions to changing circumstances. Over much of
industry the lifetime commitment and other characteristic features of
Japan's employment system have been modified without being
abandoned, just as the introduction of merit payments has occurred
without the renunciation of the conventional payments system. What
has not yet changed is the concept of the business enterprise as an
organism, or a group of men of differing ranks and functions but all
linked by reciprocal obligations.

Bibliography

Ayusawa, I., 'The Labour Problem in Japan', *Japan Quarterly* (Tokyo),
  1 (1), pp.99-111

Clark, R., *The Japanese Company* (Yale University Press, 1979)

DCI (Department of Commerce and Industry), *Factory Statistics* (Tokyo, 1938)

ILO (International Labour Office), *Industrial Labour in Japan* (Geneva, 1933)

JI of L (Japan Institute of Labour), *Japan Labour Statistics* (various) (Tokyo)

―――― 'Labour Unions and Labour-Management Relations', *Japanese Industrial Relations Series* (Tokyo, 1979)

―――― 'The Japanese Employment System', *Japanese Industrial Relations Series*, 1979-80a (Tokyo)

―――― 'Employment and Employment Policy', *Japanese Industrial Relations Series*, 1979-80b (Tokyo)

―――― 'Wages and Hours of Work', *Japanese Industrial Relations Series*, 1979-80c (Tokyo)

Levine, S.B., *Industrial Relations in Post-War Japan* (University of Illinois Press, Urbana, 1958)

M of L (Ministry of Labour), *Japan Labour Code* (Tokyo, 1953)

―――― *Japan Labour Year Book* (various) (Tokyo)

Mitsui and Co., *The 100 Year History of Mitsui and Co. Ltd., 1876-1976* (Tokyo, 1977)

Ohkawa, K., *Differential Structure and Agriculture: Essays on Dualistic Growth* (Kinokuniya, Tokyo, 1972)

Okano, Y. and Okabe, M., *Labour Productivity and Employment Problems in Japan* (Paper presented to Seminar on *Job Creation: Government or Markets* (Institute of Economic Affairs, London, December 1978)

Okochi, K., Karsh, B. and Levine, S.B., *Workers and Employers in Japan* (Princeton University Press, 1974)

PMO (Prime Minister's Office), *Labour Force Survey* (various) (Tokyo)

Reubens, E.P., 'Small-scale Industry in Japan', *Quarterly Journal of Economics* (August 1947)

Taira, K., 'The Character of the Japanese Labour Markets', *Economic Development and Cultural Change* (Chicago, January 1962a)

―――― 'The Dynamics of Industrial Relations in Early Japanese Development', *Labour Law Journal* (Chicago, July 1962b)

―――― 'The Inter-Sectoral Wage Differential in Japan, 1881-1959', *Journal of Farm Economics* (Chicago, May 1962c)

Uyeda, T., *The Small Industries of Japan* (Institute of Pacific Relations, New York, 1938)

4 SWEDEN

T.L. Johnston

Introduction

In this chapter we shall not be joining the funeral procession led by those chanting the mournful dirge to the effect that the Swedish collective bargaining model is dead, that Sweden has lost her Middle Way. Even is she had, that so-called middle road has served Sweden well. Our purpose is to set the labour movement and its contemporary situation in the wider context of industrial relations, past and present. We shall look first at the dimensions of the Swedish labour movement as it had evolved up to the Second World War; then take up the story of post-war development of white-collar unionism and of the public sector and trade unionism in it. We shall note how fully organised the Swedish labour relations scene has become in the process. We then have to examine the ways in which various union policies have been developed within this tightly structured framework; in doing so we probe the concept of solidarity and examine how this has been expressed in a broadening range of union programmes, from pay policy and collective bargaining to economic democracy and, possibly, in the direction of 'workers' control'. The past decade in Swedish collective bargaining has been one of the most innovative and stimulating of the numerous exciting phases through which the Swedish labour movement has passed in its hundred year history. Yet we have to look at this in context. We begin, therefore, with an overview of developments up to the Second World War.

Trade Union Growth

The Dominance of Blue Collar Unionism to 1944

Industrialisation came late to Sweden. When it did she was fortunate to enjoy the particular conjuncture of basic resources of timber and iron ore and an inventive cadre of technologists which enabled her quickly to establish a modern base of high-quality manufacturing industries. Dependence on export markets was and remains a dominant feature of the Swedish economy, and therefore of her industrial relations and the labour movement in it. In the early days the labour movement, founded almost exactly one hundred years ago, drew

97

much of its zest from intellectuals and its radical doctrine from
Denmark and Germany. By the time the Confederation of Swedish
Trade Unions – popularly known as 'LO', the term subsequently used
throughout this chapter – was formed in 1898, however, a pragmatic
and reformist mantle was already settling comfortably on the trade
unions. The broad division of labour between LO, the industrial wing,
and the Social Democratic Party, the political wing, founded in
1889, had been established. As we shall see later, the trade union
movement of blue-collar workers manifested in LO has for many years
been pursuing a policy of solidarity. This has of course to be defined,
and redefined. The point to notice here is that it would be a mistake to
assume that working-class solidarity is something that it has proved
easy to absorb and practise just because of the early and sustained close
alliance between the LO and the Social Democratic Party. Equally,
solidarity in working-class dress has not always had the same
connotations to white-collar unions which have come into prominence
since the Second World War.

Even if the LO had had colourful ambitions regarding the
transformation of society in accordance with some kind of socialist
creed – and its Rules and Objects do still contain the reference to
promoting political, social and economic democracy – LO very
quickly learned about the hard grit of industrial negotiations from
the employers. Private industry established the Swedish Employers'
Confederation (SAF) in 1902, as a countervailing power to LO. By
the time the first decade of this century had ended the two sides,
LO and SAF, had been through some monumental jousts with each
other. Yet these encounters did set ground rules for the industrial
relations scene. SAF succeeded in establishing its management
prerogative stance, the right to hire and fire, in its famous Clause
23 (later 32). This has now become outmoded as a consequence of
the 1976 Act on the Joint Regulation of Working Life. LO for its
part had made its key point concerning the right to organise. These
respective objectives formed the heart of the famous December
Compromise of 1906 between LO and SAF. By 1909 the interaction
of the two theses had worked through to an equilibrium which the
employers found satisfactory in the matter of bargaining muscle, but
which had left LO weak and exhausted after the major stoppage of
1909. For many years thereafter LO was on the defensive.

As early as this two important themes had already made their mark.
First, the parties had developed very explicit negotiating procedures,
even if LO was proving to be the weaker party. Second, LO learned

from its position of weakness that it simply could not hold the line on (say) restrictive practices and control over jobs. It accepted that it had to match its pattern of organisation to the rapid tempo of industrial development in an internationally dependent Swedish economy. Some of the remarkably practical, indeed almost philosophical argument in favour of industrial and occupational mobility on the part of workers goes back a long way in the thinking and planning of LO. Industrial unionism became a leading tenet, and as early as 1912 a clear organisation plan for LO unions based on organisation by industry had been crystallised. This early manifestation of flexibility and the need to adapt has carried right through the subsequent history of industrial relations thinking and organisation on the union side. The dictum that labour should adjust to the changing needs of the economy was no doubt thrust on LO by the aggression of SAF in the early days; but, having accepted it, LO has built a broad industrial and manpower strategy on that foundation (Anderman; Johnston, 1963). It is also one of the reasons why Sweden has been the prime practitioner of active manpower policies.

The 1930s were important in weaving some additional strands in the fabric of the labour movement, which have also carried forward to the contemporary scene. First, there was the incipient growth of white-collar unionism. With the benefit of hindsight it can be argued that LO committed a colossal blunder when it did not seek to accommodate white-collar organisations within it. In part the explanation lay in the wide range of political interests and philosophies which white-collar workers espoused, and to which LO could not be expected to be sympathetic. In principle, the white-collar unions still see themselves as politically non-aligned, something which is alien to LO, with its historic roots in social democracy. In part also, LO simply did not anticipate the changes in the occupational structure which were in train, and which were to gather momentum after the Second World War, not least as a consequence of the growth in public activity. SAF had also played its part in suggesting that white-collar workers were different, for in 1910 SAF made it clear that it was opposed to supervisors being members of the same unions as the blue-collar workers they supervised. When legislation was passed in 1936 to facilitate the right to organise LO did not see the legislation as necessary for its own affiliates; that battle had been fought, and resolved in the 1906 Compromise with SAF. There is no doubt, however, that the 1936 enactment did give an enormous filip to white-collar unionism as will be seen in the next section.

Nevertheless, there is some justification for LO's neglect of this curious new animal, the white-collar union member, in the 1930s. LO was preoccupied with the heady task of changing from a defensive organisation, operating in a bourgeois political environment, to a positive and thrusting union movement, eager to work with the new Social Democratic government which came to power in 1932. It was not all champagne, or even beer and circuses. The history of industrial relations in Sweden in the 1920s had been a stormy one, and in the early days of the new regime there were serious industrial disputes which posed a threat to developing a social democratic society. It was the Social Democratic government which knocked the heads of unions and employers together, and insisted on the more orderly conduct of industrial relations, not least with a view to protecting 'neutral third parties' in industrial disputes.

The outcome was the famous Basic Agreement between LO and SAF, signed at Saltsjöbaden in 1938. Its importance can hardly be overestimated, for it established the very crucial proposition that the state would stay out of the industrial relations ring provided that the parties demonstrated they could keep the peace. The Basic Agreement contained procedural codes on a variety of matters — negotiating procedures, limitations on coercive action so that third parties were not impeded, the handling of emergency disputes, and notice of layoffs and termination of employment. In addition to these important rules of the game, however, the Basic Agreement was significant in three other respects. First, the Social Democratic government made it clear to the unions that they had to behave responsibly, not least when a friendly government was in power. This has been of immense importance subsequently for the way in which LO developed and nursed its priorities. Second, the Agreement likewise put pressure on the employers to think broadly about economic and social priorities. They saw this point, and took it. Third, and not least, the Agreement was a prime example of what can be termed a *private social contract*, between LO and SAF. Although the Basic Agreement preceded the era of full employment and the search for national wages policies, by bringing LO and SAF together it set the scene for some kind of continuing dialogue between these two social partners. Much of the post-war experience of wage bargaining has represented a continuing effort to set some kind of privately agreed central contractual framework for the course which pay developments should follow.

There was then, by 1938, a clearly articulated model for the industrial relations system in Sweden of which LO formed part. This model was the product of sometimes bitter industrial conflict, but by that year it had settled down into a highway code operated by established organisations on both sides, and with a trade union movement accustomed to adapting to structural change. The transition to the post-war era of full employment was then an easy one. The idea of the Basic Agreement proved transferable to other sectors as white-collar unionism spread (SAF concluded a Basic Agreement with the Union of Clerical and Technical Employees in Industry – SIF – in 1957), and a Basic Agreement for the public service (government officials) was concluded at the time these officials acquired full collective bargaining rights in 1965. What has *not* proved easy since the Second World War has been the adjustment to an industrial relations environment in which LO was not the sole central trade union organisation. The spread of white collar unionism has posed new problems and demanded more sophisticated solutions.

Trade Union Structure

Manual Trade Unionism Since the Second World War

It is scarcely necessary here to recount the growth in LO membership since its founding in 1898. (Bain and Elsheikh; Johnston, 1962.) We can confine ourselves to the main post-war features. By turning to Figure 4.1 (p.111), the reader will obtain an immediate overview of all the various union groupings that have emerged since the Second World War.

In 1945 LO membership was 1,107,000, of whom 17 per cent were women. By 1979 the membership had almost doubled, growing steadily to 2,089,000, 39 per cent of the membership being female. The number of unions affiliated to LO was at its peak in the 1940s, with 46 unions in membership. Since then there has been a steady reduction, to 25 unions, reflecting the changes in technology and structure of the economy to which LO has always been willing to adjust in a pragmatic way, in the light of its organisation plan. This is reviewed regularly. Of the 25 LO unions in 1979, only six had a membership over 100,000 (Table 4.1).

The six unions in Table 4.1 account for nearly three-quarters of the LO membership. Table 4.2 shows the size distribution of the member unions, the main concentration being in the size group 10,000 to 50,000 members, with 13 unions. Thus LO is not an organisation of very large unions.

It is unlikely that there will be major changes in size, for instance via

Table 4.1: Trade Unions with over 100,000 Members, 1979

Municipal Workers' Union	486,000
Metal Workers' Union	452,000
State Employees' Union	193,000
Building Workers' Union	155,000
Commercial Employees' Union	152,000
Factory Workers' Union	102,000

Source: LO, *Annual Report.*

Table 4.2: LO Member Unions by size, 1979

Membership	No. of unions
Less than 10,000	3
Between 10,000 and 50,000	13
Between 50,000 and 100,000	3
More than 100,000	6
	—
	25
	—

Source: LO, *Annual Report.*

mergers, in the near future. In all probability the smallest union, that for Chimney Sweeps (with 1,350 members), will merge with a union such as the Municipal Workers' Union. Most of the large consolidating union mergers have already occurred, in printing, general manufacturing and, not least, in government employment. The State Employees' Union (193,000 members) was formally constituted in 1970, replacing an earlier and looser form of cartel arrangement, and covering blue-collar workers in government-owned enterprises, railways, postal and telecommunications services, waterfalls and roads, and the prison service. In part, this merger was a response to the centralisation of bargaining on the employer's side which followed the passage of legislation in 1965 granting full collective bargaining rights to public employees.

The most important change in LO union membership, and therefore in power and influence within LO, has occurred through the growth of the Municipal Workers' Union. It now has a stronger poll position, with a larger membership than the Metal Workers' Union, traditionally the

key union in LO because of the dominance of a heavily exporting
manufacturing industry in the Swedish economy. This is but one
manifestation of the 'two sector' model of Swedish industrial relations
and bargaining which has stemmed from the mushrooming of public
activity in central and, in particular, local government services. We
return to this below.

Since 1960 there has been a very major change in the structure of
LO unions concerning branches. In 1960 there were about 8,000,
mainly geographically based, branches in the LO family. Partly through
union mergers, but also as a consequence of a deliberate policy of
rationalisation of the administration of the unions, the number of
branches had declined sharply, to 2,448 in 1970 and 1,629 in 1979.
The arguments in favour of this process of creating larger branches
were essentially grounded in efficiency and economy. Full-time officials
can be employed to service larger branches, and it is claimed that the
larger branches do service members better than the previous small
branch run by a part-time official. Some criticism on the other side
has suggested that the rationalisation of branch structure was one
factor in the sprouting of unofficial strikes in the late 1960s. The
evidence for this is not very strong, and the causes of unofficial action
seem to be rooted more in problems arising from centralised wage
bargaining and from the fashion of doing one's own thing. Certainly,
there is no great desire to return to more localised branches. In recent
years the importance of shop floor participation is being emphasised
as part of the progress towards industrial democracy. To that extent
the larger branch can act as a filter between the individual plants
and a national union, disseminating ideas and information. The LO
unions do in any case retain a very firm plant anchorage for their
activities, even when branches have become larger units.

In terms of its constitution and governmental powers, LO has not
experienced dramatic changes since the war. The really major
reorganisation of the government of the LO unions occurred in 1941,
largely in response to the recognition that the unions had to be
equipped to keep their own house in order, particularly when the
Social Democratic Party was in power. Since 1941 LO has maintained
the 'four absolutes' introduced in that year – (a) the policy of open
door unionism through the right to join, (b) the right to transfer
membership and (c) the obligation on an individual member to do so
in the context of the LO plan of organisation and, the most dramatic
of the absolutes, (d) the right of veto for the national executives of
unions in collective bargaining. These absolutes gave LO and its

affiliates very clear powers (Johnston, 1962, ch.1). There have been some minor changes since then, but typically, as with the conduct of central negotiations, the changes in the rules have simply reflected the practice of centralised bargaining that had become established. Since 1961 the secretariat (or central executive) of LO has taken more direct powers to resolve inter-union disputes itself, instead of allowing them to be settled by arbitration. The number of inter-union disputes increased for a spell in the 1970s, as a consequence of changes in the labour market, in the structure of firms, in materials worked upon, and in technology and equipment; but in 1979 there were only two inter-union disputes. The LO plan of organisation does of course provide a very explicit framework within which inter-union disputes can be adjudicated. There is none of the *ad hoc* approach typical of the inter-union dispute machinery which the British TUC operates.

Within the blue-collar trade union movement, LO has not had to contend with major dissidents. The syndicalists continue as a small and rather romantic group. In the 1970s the Achilles' heel concerned the small breakaway Harbour Workers' Union which has sought to establish an independent base from the LO-affiliated Transport Workers' Union. This maverick group is reputed to have caused as much trouble as the whole LO-SAF strike/lockout confrontation in the spring of 1980. SAF refused to recognise the Harbour Workers, and has stuck on good grounds of solidarity to the position which LO adopted, namely that there was no basis for rival unionism within the LO family. The Transport Workers' Union had exclusive official jurisdiction.

With these minor irritations and occasional family squabbles, LO has continued its mastery of the blue-collar trade union movement in Sweden since the Second World War. The areas of uncertainty and difficulty have come from a different quarter, that of the growing white-collar trade union movement.

White-Collar Unionism, and Inter-Union Relations

LO is still Big Brother in Swedish trade unionism. But two important federations of white-collar workers have to be included in any reckoning of the union scene in Sweden. The Central Organisation of Salaried Employees (TCO) had an active membership of 936,000 at the beginning of 1980, and the recently (in 1975) merged SACO/SR group, covering professionally qualified persons and senior civil servants, has some 220,000 members.

TCO – the Central Organisation of Salaried Employees. When TCO was formed in 1944, from a merging of two smaller groups in private and public employment, it had a combined membership of 180,000. It has increased its membership more than five-fold, to 936,000. Over half its membership (529,000) is female. TCO is predominantly an umbrella organisation for white-collar workers, concerning itself with broad national policy issues on matters ranging from labour law to public policies on energy and research, and leaving the 22 affiliated unions to conduct their salary and other negotiations concerning terms and conditions. Three TCO unions had a membership in 1979 in excess of 100,000 (Table 4.3); Table 4.4 shows TCO member unions by size.

Table 4.3: TCO Trade Unions with over 100,000 Members, 1979

Union of Clerical and Technical Employees in Industry (SIF)	273,000
Union of Municipal Employees	135,000
Civil Servants' Union	121,000

Source: TCO, *Annual Report.*

Table 4.4: TCO Member Unions by Size, 1979

Membership	No. of unions
Less than 10,000	9
Between 10,000 and 50,000	6
Between 50,000 and 100,000	4
More than 100,000	3
	22

Source: TCO, *Annual Report.*

The most useful grouping of TCO unions is to consider them by sector. The private sector accounts for 47.5 per cent of TCO membership, and 13 unions, of which by far the largest is the Union of Clerical and Technical Employees in Industry, have interests there. As a group they form the largest segment of PTK – the Private Salaried Staffs' Cartel, discussed in more detail below.

In central government, where 28.5 per cent of the membership of TCO is to be found, TCO-S, the State Salaried Staff Section, with 12 member unions involved, has developed from a loose cartel arrangement in the

1950s into a comprehensive negotiating body for its member unions in central government employment. Again, the enactment of the 1965 legislation granting collective bargaining rights to civil servants provided a great impetus to this concentration of negotiating power in the Section rather than the individual unions.

In local government, with 24 per cent of the TCO membership, 7 unions co-operate in TCO-K, the Municipalities Staff Section, which has a similar though less centralised function to that of TCO-S.

These sectoral groupings go a long way towards systematising what would otherwise by a very heterogeneous mass of white-collar groupings within TCO. The arrangements have also helped to facilitate collaboration with LO groups. This is particularly true of the rapport which has developed in recent years between the LO State Employees' Union and TCO-S, both in planning negotiations and actually conducting them with the central government's employer, the National Collective Bargaining Office (*Statens avtalsverk*). Collaboration between LO and TCO on the local authority front is less fully developed. In the private sector, the TCO unions dominate PTK, and collaboration between it and LO has increased in recent years, without ever becoming a matter of course, at least in pay negotiations.

Since it was established in 1944 TCO has accordingly grown and become a settled focal point for white-collar unions in the three main sectors, and they have found it increasingly in their interests to work together under the broad TCO umbrella. However, TCO has had its Achilles' heel over the years – the Foremen and Supervisors' Union (SALF), which has had a fickle relationship with TCO. In 1980 it resigned from TCO, for the second time. SALF has members in all three sectors, though the largest element of its membership of 74,000 is to be found in private industry. It is the strongly centralised bargaining in central government, to which, as we have seen, TCO-S is an adherent, with powers to conclude agreements, that has proved a recurring problem to SALF. It would prefer to conduct its own negotiations with central government, but neither the employer side nor the TCO-S bargainers are prepared to allow it to manoeuvre outside the tight structure which the cartel groupings facilitate. SALF has long pursued what is known as the cork principle in its pay strategy, that its members should float on top of the pay system generated for those they supervise. The tight system has increasingly found it difficult to accommodate mavericks.

'Across the board' collaboration between LO and TCO has grown in recent years, from the rather sporadic sparring about pay which

sometimes occurred in the 1950s and 1960s to the collaboration
between them which developed in the early 1970s, at the time when a
Royal Commission was working on the theme of democracy in industry.
The work of this Commission led to the 1976 Act on the Joint
Regulation of Working Life. However, the remarkable thing about the
final legislative proposal was that it was based not on the majority
report but on the reservation put forward by the LO and TCO
representatives in the Commission (Schmidt, p.226). This provides
a graphic illustration of the way in which employees, whether blue
or white collar, can achieve an agreed view on some key matters in
collective bargaining.

This is less true, however, of collaboration between LO and TCO
(as a whole or through PTK) in matters of pay. Although TCO has a
long tail of low-paid employees, and can therefore sympathise with
much of LO's preaching about the needs of low-paid persons, TCO
also covers a very broad spectrum of occupational skills and therefore
of pay hierarchies throughout the economy. In this respect TCO unions
straddle the occupational and pay structure more comprehensively
than either LO, with its blue-collar emphasis, or the other white-
collar grouping, SACO/SR.

*SACO/SR – the Association of Professional Employees and Civil
Servants.* SR had an honourable history as a small specialist federation
covering senior government employees. SACO, the Confederation of
Professional Associations, was set up in 1947 as a pressure group for
highly qualified manpower. In its time SACO acquired a reputation as
being militant and not afraid to rock the LO-TCO and LO-SAF boats
by going its own way, for example in 1966 and again in 1970. SR
and SACO joined forces in 1975, forming a federation of 26 affiliated
unions, with a membership in 1979 of 220,000, as against a
combined membership in 1970 of 100,000. Membership growth has
been rapid. The organising datum is higher education, and SACO/SR
is proud to espouse the 'craft' principle, organising horizontally for
specialist highly qualified groups. About three-quarters of the
membership is in the public sector, covering such categories of central
government employees as teachers, senior civil servants, and officers
in the armed forces. About a fifth are engaged in the private sector, as
qualified engineers, economists, some being self-employed as doctors,
lawyers, dentists, etc. All 26 affiliated groups have negotiating interests
in the central government sector.

SACO long pursued a pay policy which was anathema to LO,

stressing the significance for highly qualified manpower of lifetime earnings, the need to take account of repayment of study loans in assessing the pay of qualified persons, and the importance of distinguishing gross pay from net (after tax) pay in a society with a steeply progressive direct tax structure. SACO/SR and TCO-S do not really collaborate in pay negotiations with central government, because of this special and 'élitist' pay philosophy which SACO/SR has pursued for the highly qualified occupations covered by the member associations.

The distinctive stance of SACO/SR can also be exemplified in another way. In the course of the bargaining for pay increases in 1979/80, a powerful bargaining grouping, nicknamed The Gang of Four, was formed for the state and local authority sector. The four groups comprised TCO-S, TCO-K, and the two LO groups covering central government employment (the State Employees' Union) and local government employment (the Municipal Workers' Union). In aggregate these groups had some 1,170,000 members, nearly as many as the numbers involved in the traditional leading sector, LO-SAF in private industry. The Gang of Four did not, however, include SACO/SR as a fifth accomplice. Again, the point is that SACO/SR seeks to go its own occupational way, whereas the collaboration between LO and TCO groupings can range across a wide common territory of lower-paid occupations.

Mention has already been made of a final clustering of unions which cuts across Federation frontiers. PTK – the Private Salaried Staffs' Cartel – was formed in 1973 at the TCO Congress of that year, and consisted initially of the large Union of Clerical and Technical Employees in Industry, the Foremen and Supervisors' Union, and the white-collar union for commercial employees. It now has 21 affiliated unions, consisting of the founder members drawn from TCO plus other TCO unions, *and* 14 of the SACO/SR affiliates with interests in private employment, the largest SACO/SR group being the civil engineers, with 17,000 members. SAF is the negotiating counterpart for PTK. The Cartel is a bargaining body, concerned with pay, terms and conditions, and workplace democracy issues; but it stays away from wider policy issues which occupy TCO and SACO/SR as central groupings. PTK is not entitled to conclude binding agreements on behalf of its affiliates, but can arrive at central recommendations which set the framework for subsequent agreements arrived at by the participating groups.

There has been substantial co-operation between PTK and LO on the theme of co-determination. From the beginning of the endeavours to introduce and implement the Act on the Joint Regulation of Working Life, LO and the white-collar unions in the private sector have tried to work in harness, as a 'collective'. A central, and also local, council for LO and PTK was established in 1977 to co-ordinate policies on the various labour laws introduced in the 1970s, particularly the Joint Regulation Act. On pay rounds, collaboration has been patchy. LO and PTK co-operated in negotiations in 1976-7 (for the first time since 1956), but efforts to agree a common stance for 1980 broke down early in that year. Again, there are substantial occupational and pay stresses as between LO and a union such as SIF – the Union of Clerical and Technical Employees in Industry – which covers many senior and well-paid white-collar workers, and endeavours to mix collective or tariff pay arrangements with substantial elbowroom for individual salary differentiation. SIF is very much the classic economic trade union. The more PTK establishes a set working relationship on pay questions, however, the more difficult it will prove for the SACO/SR adherents of PTK to go along with consensus-making. Behind the façade of PTK there is also the fairly healthy suspicion that SIF is so large in its own right, with more than half (273,000) of the 535,000 members covered by PTK, that it can decide at any time to go its own way if it chooses to do so.

What are we to make of this ferment of union growth, particularly among white-collar workers, since the Second World War? First, it is clear that the growth of white-collar unions has been accompanied by substantial experimentation regarding the most appropriate groupings for negotiations. Even in the past few years experimentation with groupings such as PTK, the collaboration in the civil service sector between LO and TCO unions, and the merging of SACO and SR suggest that there is dynamism and reappraisal of strategies and interests on a continuing basis. This element of change involves some uncertainty about the precise nature of the coalitions from one year to the next. Possibly that is a healthier type of pluralism in industrial relations than Sweden would have experienced if LO had in the 1930s taken all white-collar unions into its fold. The labour movement would have been much more monolithic, and possibly more susceptible to government intervention, than is the case with the present evolving mix of interest groups.

Many of the differences between the groups of unions stem from genuine differences of interpretation concerning the concept of 'low pay', or the much-debated principle of equal pay for work of equal value. The different pay systems in different sectors also cause stresses and strains. Other differences stem from attitudes towards recompense through the pay packet for the costs of prolonged and expensive occupational training.

Two features do, however, stand out in the growth of white-collar unionism since the war. First, the growth of the public sector has provided an enormous boost for unionism, aided as this growth has been by a deliberate policy of promoting, through the 1965 legislation, a collective bargaining model for public servants which in essentials is similar to that in private industry (*Jägerskiöld*). The public sector has been the main source of employment growth in recent years, a phenomenon which is expected to continue (Ministry of Labour). Such growth, past and prospective, has precipitated much anxiety on the part of private industry about the efficient use of resources in an open economy, and about the role of the private, as against the public, sector as the 'legitimate' wage leader for the total economy – see the Policy section below.

The second point is that white-collar unionism has made big strides towards matching LO's penetration of its membership potential. The aggregate figures for union membership in Sweden are given in Table 4.5. As a crude organisation percentage this amounts to some 80 per cent of the total work force of some 4.3m persons. When it is remembered, however, that a growing proportion of the labour force is opting for part-time employment, and that women constitute a large minority (about 45 per cent) of the total labour force, the organisational penetration is clearly extremely high. It is well known that LO has achieved over 90 per cent, and TCO claims over 80 per cent. It is no less true now than it was 20 years ago that the Swedish unions have marketed themselves most successfully, and that without any artificial aids such as 'the closed shop'.

Table 4.5: Aggregate Membership Figures, 1979

LO	2,089,000
TCO	936,000
SACO/SR	220,000
Foremen's Union (ind.)	74,000
	3,319,000

By way of summing up the complex pattern of union groupings in Sweden, and also as a lead-in to the consideration of the major policy issues which have concerned Swedish unions in recent years, Figure 4.1 contains a schematic expression of inter-union relations.

Figure 4.1: Interplay Among Main Swedish Union Groupings

Groups	Main areas of interface
Within LO (central manual worker organisation of 25 trade unions; total membership in 1979, 2,089,000)	problem of private (open economy) sector, and growing public sector, in pay policy
Between LO and TCO (larger white-collar worker central organisation with 22 affiliates; total membership in 1979, 936,000)	(a) no continuing top-level dialogue on pay, since TCO does not itself negotiate (b) strong collaboration on non-wage matters, such as co-determination
Between parts of LO and parts of TCO	(a) strong in public sector — the Gang of Four (two LO and two TCO central and local government unions) (b) strong in private sector (with PTK — Private Sector Salaried Staffs' Cartel) on co-determination (c) sporadic in private sector on pay rounds
Within TCO	(a) strong on co-determination (b) weak on inter-sectoral pay bargaining (c) recurring problem with Foremen and Supervisors' Union (presently outside TCO)
SACO/SR (smaller white-collar central organisation with 26 affiliates; total membership in 1979, 220,000)	(a) strong internal agreement on occupational skills criterion (b) weak collaboration with other groups, such as TCO, though some involvement with PTK on negotiations

Note: The reader is reminded that the private Swedish Employers' Confederation is known throughout the text as SAF.

Trade Union Policy

Introduction

The main themes which have dominated Swedish collective bargaining in recent years are:

(a) the concept of solidarity
(b) the shape of centrally negotiated pay arrangements
(c) the pressure for greater industrial democracy
(d) the unresolved problem of employee investment funds.

Solidarity as a Pay Principle

For over 40 years LO has been explicitly wedded to a policy for pay which is grounded in the emotive and rather elusive idea of 'solidarity' (LO, 1953; Meidner, 1974; Meidner and Öhman, 1972; Turvey). From rather crude beginnings, where the emphasis was simply on narrowing pay differentials and assisting the 'poorer-paid' groups within LO, the emphasis has gradually widened out to comprehend a wider vista. This has included the whole question of the distribution of income, particularly wages and salaries, throughout the total labour market, and not simply within the LO collective; solidarity has also assumed more subtle forms, with regard to the growing interest in the quality of working life as an expression of equity and equal treatment of people in employment.

For many years LO's efforts at squeezing pay differentials did not appear to make much progress, but in the past decade there is substantial evidence statistically to support the thesis that LO's steady pressure, via the design of pay bargaining, to bring about a narrowing of pay hierarchies is producing results. Table 4.6 indicates how pay differentials have narrowed in industry within the last 20 years.

In the matter of women's pay relative to men's, LO has also succeeded in narrowing the gap since SAF and it agreed in 1960 to the elimination of women's clauses from collective agreements. In 1960 women's average pay in industry was 70 per cent that of men; in 1979 it had risen to 91.5 per cent. There has also been a substantial narrowing of the spread in the national pay structure, though, with high marginal rates of direct taxation, it is not easy to make meaningful comparisons of net income positions after tax (the issue which SACO/SR has always considered to be important).

The really intriguing point about the wages policy of solidarity, however, concerns the *consequences* it has had for other parts of

Table 4.6: Pay Spread, SAF-LO Sector, since 1959

| Year | Mean deviation of agreements from overall industrial average | | Total range or spread |
	Above average pay	Below average pay	
1959	+16.7	−12.9	29.6
1961	+16.8	−12.4	29.2
1963	+15.5	−11.4	26.9
1965	+15.3	−10.6	25.9
1968	+13.6	−9.5	23.1
1970	+11.2	−8.8	20.0
1973	+8.3	−7.9	16.2
1974	+7.4	−7.3	14.7
1976	+6.6	−6.5	13.1
1978	+6.0	−6.7	12.7

Source: LO, *Annual Reports.*

economic policy. A few of these will be examined later, but the overall list looks something like this:

(1) Any 'scientific' applications of solidarity/equity require some tool such as job analysis and evaluation to assist the allocation process. LO has long been aware of this. The efforts to find some kind of comprehensive job description system for the economy and an agreed set of job evaluation criteria have, however, been half-hearted, and have now been largely abandoned, in favour of the crude horsetrading in the course of pay rounds.

(2) Pursuit of solidarity on the part of LO has forced it successively to seek to steer the distribution of pay by means of increasingly complex central agreements. While it was SAF that initially, in the mid-1950s, pressed for co-ordinated central bargaining as a means of avoiding whip-sawing, LO has come to rely very heavily on the profile of pay agreements to assist its cause.

(3) From the start, LO recognised in its pay policy of solidarity that forcing up low wages (in effect establishing a minimum wage) would mean displacement of labour. Hence LO's espousal of an active labour market policy (Johnston, 1963; LO, 1953). A vast battery of labour market policy measures has been mounted to assist redeployment. This has had some remarkable successes. Yet there is sustained evidence of shortages of skilled workers in engineering and construction.

(4) LO also accepted that a protectionist attitude to jobs was self-defeating. Twenty years ago it urged its members to accept redeployment, provided labour market policy helped people to retrain and relocate. In recent years there has, however, been far greater interest in internal labour markets, in seeking to promote adjustments within companies.

The obverse of this has been the growing interest in co-determination as one means of promoting and demonstrating solidarity among employees.

(5) Increasingly, LO has come to recognise that the tool of solidarity in pay policy may not in itself suffice to achieve the redistribution of income that is desired. Since 1974 there has in fact been an explicit recognition that pay bargaining had to take place in the context of some known government tax package, particularly for direct tax rates and for the tax burdens on employers; it is now standard practice for the government to inform the negotiating parties of its fiscal strategy before they begin their wage round. However, while LO has recognised that it cannot achieve its income distribution objectives solely via the pay policy weapon, it has also looked further ahead, and discerned another consequence of its pay policy of solidarity.

(6) In its 1951 pronouncement (LO, 1953), LO recognised that one consequence of basing pay policy on equity rather than ability-to-pay was that profitable companies would enjoy large retained 'excess profits' which could otherwise have been extracted as pay increases if capacity-to-pay had been allowed its head. This, LO recognised, has implications not only for the distribution of income but also for the whole question of the ownership of wealth and property. Hence its more recent concern for worker sharing through the device of employee investment funds. This is discussed more fully below.

(7) Wage drift, the phenomenon which the Swedish trade union economists popularised if they did not invent it, was from the beginning a continual bugbear *within* the LO collective in promoting equity; it has continued to provide acrimonious ground for argument *between* LO and other, white-collar, groups, particularly those in the public sector. LO becomes very upset when public sector white-collar unions sometimes seek and obtain compensation for the wage drift which only a small proportion of LO members obtain through their flexible pay systems.

In total, therefore, solidarity in pay has proved to be a tail which has wagged a very considerable dog. This can be seen in the make-up of central pay bargains.

The Shape of Centrally Negotiated Pay Arrangements

After the sporadic experimentation with centralised SAF-LO bargaining in the early 1950s, largely as a consequence of the Korean War, there has since 1956 been an uninterrupted sequence of central pay negotiations. This has varied over the 25-year period, for example in

the use made of mediation facilities, reliance on cost-of-living
protection clauses, the duration of the agreements (one to three years),
the degree of explicit collaboration between LO and other groups,
such as PTK, the resort to coercive action (with SACO proving an
irritant in 1966 and 1970), the degree of brinkmanship employed, and
the absence of any comprehensive clash until the sensational lockout-
strike interface in April-May 1980. There is enough good red meat
in the history of central bargaining to make for a surfeit of collective
bargaining case history. Yet three things stand out in this saga. First,
the pragmatic way in which efforts are made by particular pressure
groups to change the national pay structure in their favour makes for
uncertainty in each pay round. The consequences of a previous
agreement as well as the economic prospects for the private and public
sector influence the approach to and the make-up of each round. As
we have seen, there is enough variety in the objectives of particular
groups to incite them to take initiatives. Second, the problems of wage
drift, and of differing types of pay system, have encouraged a
'compensation mentality', and the centrally structured agreements have
become ever more complex in their endeavours to estimate in advance
what their consequences will be, and in some instances to obtain
compensation in advance for these consequences. The agreements, both
private and public, seek to strike a balance among (a) general pay
increases, (b) kitties or pots which particular bargaining groups can
allocate themselves, (c) preferential treatment for particular groups or
individuals, (d) guarantees with regard to earnings, (e) compensation
for such phenomena as wage drift and incremental drift, and (f) cost-
of-living escalator clauses. Thirdly, as already indicated, this whole wage
round drama is also increasingly conducted against a backcloth of fiscal
policy in general, and direct tax rates in particular. Ironically, in
recent years its consequences in terms of real improvement in standards
have been negative, for real income has declined during the recession.

We have already noted how the growth in the public sector
activity, in public sector unionism, and in the collective bargaining
rights of public employees, have increasingly made SAF uneasy about
the role of the public sector as pay leader. Some ten years ago a
consensus was reached on the overall framework for pay bargaining
which utilised the notion of a corridor for pay development, the
corridor being determined by the increase in productivity of the
competing (internationally exposed) sector of the economy plus
the change (rise) in world market prices for products sold in international markets (Edgren *et al.*). This model seemed promising for

a world of stable growth, prices and exchange rates; but it has appeared less relevant since the dislocations in the world economy following the price increases of 1973.

Nevertheless, SAF is determined to fight the pervasive notion that the public sector can act as wage leader in the highly-pressurised pay rounds. It was much aggrieved in 1980 when the Gang of Four appeared to extract more from their high-pressure bargaining than SAF thought LO was willing to accept for the competing, private industry sector. At its Congress in the autumn of 1980 SAF nailed firmly to the mast the thesis that the competing sector of the economy must still be the bell-wether for what happens in shaping a pay round. It also endorsed Principles for Fair Pay which stressed the need for productivity and for remuneration to reward effort (SAF). This battle between private and public is by no means resolved, all the same. The recent report of the Commission on Employment Policy saw the public sector as the one likely source of additional job generation for the growing Swedish labour force (Ministry of Labour).

One can sum up the experience of pay policy in the following way. The sensational lockout-strikes of 1980 appeared to the uninitiated to be the demise of the Swedish collective bargaining model. Nothing could be further from the truth. As we have suggested, there has been a continual search for ways of achieving complex and controversial objectives, such as pay solidarity; there has been determined and sustained effort on the part of strong white-collar groups to resist being swamped by LO's egalitarian ideas; in any wage round there are sufficient uncertainties and conflicting objectives to ensure genuine horsetrading and bargaining brinkmanship; the surprising thing, therefore, is that conflict is so infrequent, not that it occasionally occurs. The obvious explanation for the general level of peacekeeping is of course that the consequences of actions by particular groups wash through the tightly-structured institutional system. This typically lends stability, while retaining some uncertainty.

The Pressure for Greater Industrial Democracy

The decade of the 1970s saw a heavy bombardment of industrial relations legislation in Sweden — the Security of Employment Act 1974, the Promotion of Employment Act of the same year, legislation giving enhanced status to shop stewards, amendment of the workers' Protection Act, legislation providing for minority employee representation on company boards, concerning the working environment, an Act of 1979 concerning equality between men and women at work and, the keystone of the whole legislative arch, the 1976 Act on the Joint Regulation of Working Life.

Until the late 1960s, LO adopted a very sceptical stance towards such esoteric matters as 'co-determination' in its wider sense (see the West German chapter), and appeared quite content to advance the cause of industrial democracy through the gradual extension of the consultative machinery for Works Councils which LO and SAF had established by central agreement in 1946. There is no doubt, however, about the change in the level of ambition which began to take shape around 1970. Various explanations have been offered for the change of gear – a more radical outlook on the part of the Social Democratic Party, concern about the disadvantaged and about the environment, resentment against the severe dislocations caused by the structural rationalisation of the economy (which LO had helped to occur), resentment also against the SACO strike action in 1966, the general contagion of the 1968 troubles in France, and concern for the causes of the unofficial strikes in 1969-70 (Korpi). Yet the Social Democrats and LO did not have a monopoly of radical thinking at that time. The Liberal Party was making similar noises, and employer groups such as SAF also began to experiment with the organisation of work and job reform (Jenkins).

The 1971 quinquennial Congress of LO proved a landmark in this ferment, for the Congress marked out a radical programme for industrial democracy which was shortly afterwards echoed by the appointment of the Royal Commission already referred to (LO, 1971). When the Act on the Joint Regulation of Working Life was passed in 1976 it therefore represented the culmination of a sustained period of questioning and analysis concerning the balance of power in Swedish industrial relations. As we have already noticed, the Act as promulgated incorporated the main themes upon which LO and TCO had agreed (Schmidt).

The provisions of the Act substantially broaden the area of negotiable matters on which the employer has a primary duty to negotiate, require employers to provide a regular flow of information, and introduce the core concept of participation agreements. The Act also gives unions 'priority of interpretation' with regard to the interpretation of such participation agreements and to disputes about an employee's obligations at work. The traditional right and prerogative of management is substantially reversed by these provisions.

The Act was nevertheless a framework only, and the expectation is that collective agreements concluded between the parties will clothe

the legislation in realistic and relevant arrangements. LO and SAF agreed to a low-key introduction of the provisions of the Act, since they were embarking upon new territory together. It was also the intention that they should conclude a new Central Agreement. As we have already pointed out, LO and PTK have been able to agree a common line in their thinking about how the Act should be complemented by a central agreement, and they have put more than one joint proposal to SAF for an agreement. SAF too has proposed various versions of an agreement. Yet the parties have not yet concluded an agreement. The main bones of contention have concerned arbitration as an alternative to the Labour Court, the level of fines that may be imposed, and the prior right of interpretation which the Act allocates to employees. Since the change in the political constellation in 1976, it is not possible for LO to put pressure on SAF via the legislature to conclude an agreement or amend the Act, and SAF appears content to take a slow and cautious approach to concluding an agreement. With that in mind, it is difficult to evaluate the impact which the 1976 Act has so far made, though some of the initial evaluations have expressed disappointment with the outturn so far. It is too early to judge.

The 1976 Act applies in principle across the whole labour market, and central agreements have been concluded for the public sector, the co-operative movement, and for banking and insurance. Again, there is the clear impression that the public sector in recent years has sometimes gone ahead of the private sector in industrial relations matters. SAF would argue that it is easier for public sector employers to concede than for the exposed private, industrial sector to give in to employee demands.

Employee Investment Funds

From the start of its sustained campaign to equalise wages, LO has recognised that its policy of pay solidarity might enable more profitable firms to escape with excess profits. After various flirtations with the problem, such as siphoning these excess profits off into sector funds or, as in 1974, into environmental improvement funds (in addition to the conventional Swedish investment fund used as a counter-cyclical instrument), LO grasped this nettle also at its 1971 Congress. The outcome of its interest was the report which it considered at its 1976 Congress (Meidner, 1978; Öhman).

Although the general thesis of the proposals for employee investment funds had become reasonably familiar through discussion

in other countries, such as Denmark and Germany, this was the first
occasion on which such a proposal had been specifically advanced
as a serious proposition in Sweden. The report argued for the
establishment of employee-controlled collective funds to which profits
would be allocated, and in due course the majority ownership of
shares in companies covered by the scheme could pass into the hands
of the funds. Not only was this seen as a method of equalising the
ownership of property and wealth, and promoting democracy in
industry through the leverage on decision-making which the control
over the funds would provide, it was also seen as a means of providing
a new source of capital to meet the investment requirements of
Swedish industry.

The original LO scheme has been substantially modified in subsequent
discussion with the Social Democratic Party, and alternative schemes have
been propounded, ranging from private profit-sharing to individual
savings schemes financed from wages. Everyone is agreed that new
sources of risk capital for Swedish industry are highly desirable. What
is not agreed is the method for achieving this. Critics see in the LO
approach a deliberate takeover bid for the control of industry, and
are therefore concerned to ensure that any funds which are set up have
safeguards against collectivisation of ownership. The whole debate
has passed into the hands of a Royal Commission, which is highly
unlikely to reach an agreed view about the problem. Yet there is no
denying that the LO initiative introduced a new dimension into
discussion about the legitimate content of economic and industrial
democracy.

This section can be summarised by repeating that the adoption by
LO of a policy of solidarity in pay has had numerous and unanticipated
ramifications. While it did not initiate the arrangements for central
and co-ordinated bargaining, this type of bargaining has certainly been
used by LO to promote its philosophy; at the same time LO has
recognised that workers displaced by a policy aimed at raising minimum
wages require an active labour market policy; more recently it has come
round to the view that disparities in income and wealth cannot be
resolved only by pay policy, but require some additional mechanism,
such as employee investment funds. Solidarity has also found new
manifestations, in the form of the efforts to promote through
legislation greater democracy at the place of work. Other union groups
have been happy to support this initiative, while taking a less radical
attitude towards employee investment funds, and a decidedly
jaundiced view of LO's efforts to swing the whole wage negotiating

process behind its wage policy of solidarity. For its part, SAF has been willing to see a more positive philosophy permeating plant industrial relations, has declared its stout opposition to employee investment funds which savour of collectivism, and is ever eager to ensure in the central pay negotiations that equity does not triumph perpetually over the requirements of productivity-based remuneration.

Conclusion

Sweden remains an extremely progressive country in terms of its industrial relations innovation. The 1976 Act on the Joint Regulation of Working Life represents a major shift in power, though it is too early to judge how this will work out on the shop floor once the legislation is clothed, in private industry, in agreed procedures. The earlier 1965 Act which promoted collective bargaining in public employment was equally innovative. It has had major consequences in the field of white-collar unionism, and also in the balance of bargaining initiatives. Is the poll position to be occupied by the private or public sector? That is the great unresolved question of pay bargaining.

In that bargaining itself, the parties continue to wrestle with the adjustment of relative positions which originate in pressure group bargaining rather than some agreed national job evaluation for a 'just national pay structure'. In their wrestling, the parties continue to be inventive in seeking to combine equity with efficiency. The LO principle of pay solidarity has achieved some statistical success, but it has also led LO into some new and ambitious thinking about the appropriate distribution of wealth and income in society. Perhaps the pay system is expected to achieve too much as the regulator of equity. As we noted, the link between pay and fiscal strategy is now more clearly recognised as a relevant element in designing a pay round.

Although the institutional structure on the trade union side has now become heavily saturated with powerful groupings, the evidence adduced here suggests that there is no danger of the system ossifying. There are enough special interest groups with varying aspirations to ensure that collective bargaining will continue, and continue to throw up fresh ideas and practices. Paradoxically, heavily organised labour markets may be under greater pressure to innovate than those in which there is more slack and greater room for manoeuvre. Swedish groups have to work hard to make their way, to shift pay scales in their favour, and retain the support of their memberships.

Perhaps heavy collectivisation of partially competing unions in labour markets provides a spur rather than a soporific influence?

Bibliography

Introduction

Publications cited have been restricted to those available in English. The literature in Swedish is voluminous.

For a useful general background survey of the Swedish system, see Forsebäck, L., *Industrial Relations and Employment in Sweden*, 2nd ed. (Swedish Institute, Stockholm, 1980).

Economic and Industrial Democracy, an international journal, first published in 1980, is a useful new addition to the Scandinavian literature in English.

Anderman, S., *Trade Unions and Technological Change* (Allen & Unwin, London, 1967)

Bain, G.S. and Elsheikh, F., *Union Growth and the Business Cycle* (Blackwell, Oxford, 1976)

Edgren, G., Faxén, K.O. and Odhur, C.E., *Wage Formation and the Economy* (Allen & Unwin, London, 1973)

Jägerskiöld, S., *Collective Bargaining Rights of State Officials in Sweden* (University of Michigan, Ann Arbor, 1971)

Jenkins, D., *Job Reform in Sweden* (SAF, Stockholm, 1975)

Johnston, T.L., *Collective Bargaining in Sweden* (Allen & Unwin, London, 1962)

—— (ed. and trans.), *Economic Expansion and Structural Change* (Allen & Unwin, London, 1963)

Korpi, W., *The Working Class in Welfare Capitalism* (Routledge & Kegan Paul, London, 1978)

LO, *Trade Unions and Full Employment* (LO, Stockholm, 1953). (An abbreviated version in English of the report *Fackföreningsrörelsen och den fulla sysselsättningen* presented to the LO Congress in September 1951.)

—— *Industrial Democracy* (LO, Stockholm, 1972). (English version of the Programme adopted at the 1971 Congress of LO.)

Meidner, R., *Co-ordination and Solidarity. An Approach to Wages Policy* (Prisma, Stockholm, 1974)

—— *Employee Investment Funds. An Approach to Collective Capital Formation* (Allen & Unwin, 1978)

Meidner, R. and Öhman, B., *Fifteen Years of Wage-Policy* (LO, Stockholm, 1972)

Ministry of Labour (Stockholm), *Policy for Employment for Everybody* (Stockholm, 1979). (A summary of the final report of the Swedish Government Commission on long-term employment policy, May 1979.)

Öhman, B., 'Wage-earner Funds. Background, Problems and Possibilities — A Summary', *Economic and Industrial Democracy, 1* (3) (August 1980) (Sage Publications, London)

SAF, *Fair Pay, A Pay Policy Programme* (Stockholm, 1979)

Schmidt, F., *Law and Industrial Relations in Sweden* (Almqvist & Wiksell Int., Stockholm, 1977)

Turvey, R., *Wages Policy under Full Employment* (Hodge, London, 1952)

5 THE UNITED KINGDOM

Eric Owen Smith

Introduction

Accounts of the long-term growth of British trade unionism are replete with phrases which illustrate the complexity and turbulent history of the world's first trade union movement. Such phrases have an aphoristic quality for the informed observer but they may initially appear esoteric or emotional to the newcomer. Some examples are: the Tolpuddle Martyrs; the Derby turn-out; the Sheffield outrages; the Junta; Tonypandy; the Triple Alliance; Black Friday; the General Strike; the Mond-Turner talks; the Bridlington agreements; the ETU affair; and the Pentonville five. All these events have been, and will continue to be, the subject of research and commentaries. As in other chapters, the principal objective is to whet the intellectual appetite of readers so that they will want to discover more. (Cronin; Crouch; Pelling; Webbs.)

The complexity of trade union growth in Britain is further illustrated by the fact that there have been a number of highly significant court cases which have involved the trade unions. Examples are: Taff Vale; Osborne and Rookes *v* Barnard. Moreover, attempts have been made by British governments to define the legal position of trade unions in the 1820s, 1870s, then during and after the two world wars, and yet again in the 1970s. (Owen Smith; Pelling.)

The movement itself has passed through distinctive periods of growth. In this analysis, mention must be made of, first, the craft unions which emerged in the 1850s, followed by, secondly, the general unions of unskilled workers which emerged towards the end of the nineteenth century. Thirdly, some intermittent attempts – both successful and unsuccessful – to form industrial unions and increase inter-union co-operation were made between the First and the end of the Second World War. Fourthly, since the end of the Second World War there has been a growing tendency for white-collar workers to join trade unions. These waves in trade union growth or consolidation were often accompanied by waves in strike activity. If a somewhat arbitrary and approximate measure of such peaks in strike activity is employed, then there are seven notable waves: 1889-92; 1910-13; 1918-23; 1926; 1957-62; 1968-72; and 1979. (Cronin, p.48; DE *Gazette*, August 1980; Morris; Table 5.1.)

Trade Union Growth

c.1900–1926

Trade union expansion, confidence, militancy and success characterised
the two decades prior to the First World War (Flanders, p.7). Next,
union leaders contained a threatened rank and file revolt against the
reduction in real wages which resulted from their policy of co-operating
with the government in the prosecution of the First World War. They
achieved this by integrating the unofficial workers' representatives'
(shop stewards') movement which arose at the time into the official
trade union movement (Clegg and Adams, p.16; Flanders, pp.8-9).
However, the next two waves of militancy culminated in the collapse
of the Triple Alliance of Railway, Transport and Mineworkers in 1921,
followed by the abject failure of the General Strike called by the
Trade Union Congress (TUC – the central trade union organisation in
Britain) in 1926. These two events marked the end of militancy until
1957 (Flanders, p.10). On both occasions virtually the whole trade
union movement had supported the miners' attempts to prevent
reductions in money wages. Also on both occasions the miners were
left to continue the dispute alone but they ultimately suffered heavy
defeats at the hands of the pit owners and government (ibid.).

1927–1957

The Trade Union and Trade Disputes Act of 1927 severely curtailed
trade union power (ibid.; Pelling, p.187). Moreover, employers and trade
unions drew closer together in the late 1920s and early 1930s, a trend
preceded by the so-called Mond-Turner talks. Both parties were
confronted with falling prices and contracting markets (Clegg and Adams,
pp.8-9; Flanders, p.10; Pelling, p.188). This change in attitude among
the leadership of both sides of industry was followed, from 1933
onwards, by rising prices, declining unemployment and a revival of
the downward trend in trade union membership which had begun in
1920 (Clegg and Adams, p.11). Trade union density (the percentage
of the labour force organised in trade unions) had grown from 10 per
cent in 1892 to 20 per cent in 1912. It reached 30 per cent by 1917
and 45 per cent by 1920. Thereafter it fell back to 23 per cent by
1933, subsequently climbing again to 30 per cent by 1938 and 40 per
cent by 1943 (Sayers Bain and Price, 1980, Table 2.1). Later
developments in trade union density will be analysed in the next
sub-section. At this stage it is important to note that the new attitudes
of the parties had been moulded in depression, and although their shape

remained intact during the recovery, it was unlikely that the pattern of the 1930s could be regarded as permanent (Clegg and Adams, p.11).

In the 1940s, there were, however, other factors which created a favourable bargaining atmosphere; in terms of real wage movements, the contrast between the two world wars could not have been more impressive (ibid., p.14). During the Second World War average earnings increased more rapidly than wage rates which in turn increased more rapidly than prices (ibid.). There was another difference: the most important single individual involved in sponsoring the Mond-Turner talks on the TUC side (Ernest Bevin of the powerful Transport and General Workers Union – TGWU) became Minister of Labour in the wartime coalition (ibid.; Pelling, pp.188-9). It was agreed that strikes and lockouts should be made illegal and that there would be compulsory references to unsettled disputes to the National Arbitration Tribunal, all of which was embodied in Order No. 1305 (Clegg and Adams, p.14). In a sense, these latter features of war policy did not differ from the First World War, when compulsory arbitration had also operated and labour leaders had participated in the government (Pelling, pp.153, 155, 212; Wrigley, passim). However, an annual average of 5.3 million working days were lost through strike action in the First World War, compared to an average of 1.8 million in the full years of the Second World War – a direct reflection of the aggressive relationship between rank and file union members and government during the First World War, a period when real wages were falling (Clegg and Adams, p.5; Pelling, pp.155-6). While it is true to say that the average number of strikes was greater in the Second World War (1,491 compared to 814), the general atmosphere was one of co-operation as opposed to confrontation (Flanders, pp.64-5; Table 5.1). There was little attempt to enforce the law against striking and in any case the average stoppage involved roughly 300 employees and lasted about four days (Table 5.1).

The new spirit which evolved during the 1930s and during the Second World War continued to blossom in the immediate post-war period. Both the wartime coalition government and the TUC had advocated the doctrine of full employment for the post-war period – a policy goal which was largely achieved for the first two decades following the war (Crouch, p.20; Flanders, p.44). The post-war Labour government also introduced substantial gains that could not have been achieved by industrial action (Flanders, p.88). These gains included the repeal of the Trade Disputes Act, which enabled civil service trade unions to reaffiliate to the TUC if they so wished. It also reintroduced

Table 5.1: Trends in Strike Action

Period	Average number of stoppages per year (S)	Average number of workers involved per year (WI)	Average number of working days lost per year (WDL)	WDL/WI. (Duration: i.e. average number of WDL per striker per year)	WI/S. (Size: i.e. average number of strikers per strike per year)
1893[1]	599[1]	634,000[1]	30,439,000[1]	48[1]	1,058[1]
1894–1903	687	217,000	5,984,000	28	316
1904–1913	626	473,000	9,319,000	20	756
1914–1918	814	632,000	5,292,000	8	776
1919–1921	1,241	2,108,000	49,053,000	23	1,699
1922–1932[2]	479[2]	395,000[2]	7,631,000[2]	19[2]	852[2]
1933–1939	735	295,000	1,694,000	6	401
1940–1944	1,491	499,000	1,816,000	4	335
1945–1954	1,791	545,000	2,073,000	4	304
1955–1964	2,521	1,116,000	3,889,000	3	443
1965–1974	2,633	1,386,000	9,016,000	7	526
1975–1979[3]	2,310	1,639,000	11,648,000	7	709

[1] Yearly totals.

[2] Excluding 1926, the year of the General Strike and coalmining dispute, when over 162 million days were lost.

[3] Note *five*-year period.

Notes:
(i) 1893-1979 S and WI *beginning* in each year. 1893-1913 WDL *in progress* in each year. 1914-1979 WDL *beginning* in each year.
(ii) Strike statistics compiled by the Department of Employment relate only to disputes over the terms and conditions of employment. Not all disputes are reported to the Department. These statistics do not distinguish between official and unofficial stoppages, although the *Gazette* nowadays contains separate data on these. Small stoppages involving fewer than ten workers and those lasting less than one day are excluded from the statistics except any in which the aggregate number of working days lost exceeded 100. The figures also exclude any loss of time, e.g. through shortage of materials, which may be caused at other establishments by the stoppages which are included in the statistics. The figures include, however, time lost by workers laid off at establishments where stoppages occurred but who were not themselves parties to the disputes.
(iii) The size of the employed population has displayed a large increase, and the proportion of the labour force organised in trade unions has varied, during the period covered by Table 5.1. A number of trends and generalisations are not affected by these factors, however.

Sources: Calculated from:
(i) 1893-1913: Department of Employment and Productivity, *British Labour Statistics: Historical Abstract 1886-1968*, HMSO, 1971, Table 197. (ii) 1916-1964: Royal Commission on Trade Unions and Employers' Associations, *Written Evidence of the Ministry of Labour*, HMSO, 1965, First Memorandum, para. 122.
(iii) 1965-1979: Department of Employment *Gazette*, August 1980, pp.874 and 932.

the principle by which those trade unions affiliated to the Labour
Party would require each member to pay a political levy to that party
unless they contracted-out in writing (Pelling, p.222). Further reforms
were made to the social security system. Price control, rationing and
food subsidies were continued at a time when physical shortages of
materials and food, as well as improving the balance of payments,
dominated government policy; a considerable programme of
nationalisation was also undertaken (Flanders, p.88; Pelling, p.222;
Shonfield, p.89). Order No.1305 was kept on the statute book. All
these measures were reciprocated on the part of the trade unions by a
growing voluntary acceptance of wage restraint (Flanders, p.88). This
was particularly pronounced between January 1948 and September
1950 when wage rates rose by only 6 per cent but retail prices rose
by 12 per cent (Clegg and Adams, p.19).

By the time the Conservatives were returned to office in 1951 there
were already signs of trade union disenchantment with wage restraint,
although the TUC announced that as it had become an established
party to be consulted on industrial and economic matters, close
contact would be maintained with the processes of government and
administration (ibid., p.20; Pelling, p.234). However, Order No.1305
had been radically modified by the outgoing Labour government,
probably in keeping with the growing political conviction that the state
should generally pursue a more limited role (Shonfield, pp.91-2, 99
and 101). The National Arbitration Tribunal had been maintained under
the title of the Industrial Disputes Tribunal, whose awards were still
legally enforceable. However, the ban on strikes and lockouts had
been removed (Clegg and Adams, pp.20-21; McCarthy and Ellis,
pp.126-7). Moreover, the urge to return to a pre-1914 system where
market forces imposed adjustments in living standards was fostered
in the early 1950s (Shonfield, p.101). Trade union leaders were
pushed more and more on to the defensive against public opinion, the
courts, the government and the employers (Pelling, p.244). Even their
own members reacted against the preoccupation of full-time trade
union officials with the problems of full employment. Their neglect of
plant-level problems created a power vacuum into which the shop
stewards stepped (Shonfield, p.116). This polarisation of power
downwards was a most significant development (Kahn-Freund, p.84).
It was to prove a more permanent feature than the similar movement
during the First World War.

1957 to date

Two events began the process of rupturing the post-war consensus. First, in 1958 a prolonged strike by the TGWU busmen in London ended in failure because the government refused to intervene and other trade union leaders refused to support Frank Cousins, the somewhat politically ambivalent leader of the TGWU at the time (Pelling, pp.244-5). There was considerable evidence that public opinion supported the government and blamed the union for the disruption (Crouch, pp.38-9). Secondly, in accord with a tougher attitude on the part of the government, the Minister of Labour (Iain Macleod) announced that he was allowing the Industrial Disputes Tribunal to go out of existence (Pelling, p.245). Macleod, for his part, thought the Tribunal's awards were inflationary, although there was no evidence to support this view (McCarthy and Ellis, p.127).

Even as an ideal, the belief in market forces and free collective bargaining did not last for long. In practice governments had been legislatively involved since the first trade unions were formed. However, the break with the principle of non-intervention gathered momentum during the 1960s and 1970s (Bosworth and Wilson; Dawkins; Owen Smith; Shonfield, p.113). There were three policy areas which were affected by a mounting volume of legislation: attempts to alter supply and demand schedules in the labour market, the implementation of incomes policies and changing the law governing collective bargaining. Such legislation was aimed at ameliorating structural rigidities in the labour market, reducing the uneconomic use of manpower, modifying the worsening problem of wage inflation, curbing the alleged abuse of trade union power and decreasing the number of strikes. This latter policy problem changed during the course of the 1960s and 1970s, since the number of strikes reached something of a plateau while the number of working days lost and workers involved both displayed dramatic increases (Table 5.1; DE *Gazette*, September 1980, p.994). This may have been partly caused by the re-emergence of the national official strike as union leaders sought to regain the initiative from workplace representatives. The question of strikes and other issues involved in trade union power will be analysed in the Policy section below.

Both employers and successive governments added further volatile elements to the problems of the 1960s and 1970s. Indeed, even before the gradual rupturing of the post-war consensus, a majority of organised employers seemed to have come to the conclusion by 1956 that there was even greater danger than industrial conflict —

continuous inflation (Clegg and Adams, p.143). But the employers alone were not strong enough to bring about wage restraint, for the government indirectly controlled the nationalised sector (ibid., pp.144-5). However, in 1957 the engineering employers in particular were prepared to confront the unions on the mistaken premise that the government would support them (ibid., pp.145 and 151).

By the time the Labour government of 1964 was elected, industry seemed impressed by the new government's commitment to planning. The employers were in any case in the process of merging both their central bargaining and trade organisations to form the Confederation of British Industry, a move conducive to a greater planning effort (Crouch, p.51). The nationalised industries were allowed to affiliate to the new body. When the Conservatives were returned to office in 1970, however, employers were again perturbed by the worsening strike and wage inflation position. Once again the Conservatives disillusioned them, this time by a dogmatic approach to legislation which resulted in small anti-union employers suing employees of other companies (Owen Smith, pp.126-7). Towards the end of the 1970s, a number of employers confronted the unions.

Successive governments in these two decades were caught up in the dilemma posed by a longer-term feature of trade union growth. This dilemma arises from the court rulings on the degree of trade union immunity from the Common Law, a right which basically enables trade unions to function without being sued for restraining trade. In 1964 the Courts virtually nullified the protection given to unions by the 1906 Trade Disputes Act (Rookes *v* Barnard). For the fifth time in a century, therefore, a Royal Commission (the Donovan Commission) was set up to recommend ways out of the legal *impasse* and also to offer suggestions for the more general reform of collective bargaining. When the Commission reported in 1968, however, it was itself divided on the issue of legally controlling trade union power. Indeed, it was demonstrated that the bargaining strength of work groups at the local level may be a more important policy issue than trade union power at the national level. Employers too have tended to decentralise their collective bargaining. As a result single-employer bargains in private manufacturing industry set the pace for manual wage settlements which multi-employer bargainers follow. Although employers achieved a rationalisation of payments systems during the 1970s the reform of the bargaining structure was a policy issue. (Brown in Blackaby, pp.130-1, 139-40, 145-6; Owen Smith.)

Hence a Labour government recommended in 1969 a mixture of

voluntary reform and legal control in the White Paper *In Place of Strife*.
Trade union opposition effectively resulted in the government
withdrawing its proposals on condition that the trade unions
implemented their own reforms. In 1971, however, the Conservatives
introduced their much more draconian Industrial Relations Act. When
representatives of work groups (shop stewards) were adversely
affected by this Act – including the imprisonment of five dockers –
the government was obliged effectively to place the Act on ice (Owen
Smith, pp.124-7). The Labour government of 1974-9 repealed the
IR Act and enacted its own Trade Union and Labour Relations Act
and Employment Protection Act. Some features of the EP Act were,
in turn, repealed by the Conservatives' Employment Act 1980. In
September of the same year, the then leader of the Labour Party (James
Callaghan) promised the TUC that a future Labour government would
repeal the Employment Act in return for an effective trade union code
of self discipline (*The Times*, 3 Sept. 1980, p.1). He was seeking a way
to end the 'legislative see-saw'.

On the other hand, although there were some changes in the titles
and functions of the various institutions set up by the statutes
mentioned in the last paragraph, there was an important element of
continuity. First, the Department of Employment was the relevant
government department which drew up the legislation. A Secretary of
State – a minister of cabinet rank – was its political head. Secondly,
the Industrial Tribunals with an appeals mechanism to a special branch
of the High Court (Employment Appeals Tribunal) became an integral
part of the industrial relations system. They heard appeals against
alleged injustices committed by employers. Thirdly, the Certification
Officer listed trade unions, examined their accounts and certified,
where appropriate, that they were independent of employers' influence.
By no means all the listed trade unions received Certificates of
Independence. Employers' associations were also listed by the
Certification Officer and he investigated complaints by trade union
members about the conduct of amalgamation ballots and breaches of
political fund rules. (Only half of the trade unionists affiliated to the
TUC are also affiliated to the Labour Party. There is also an active
and vigilant Federation of Conservative Trade Unionists.) Under the
Employment Act, the Secretary of State is empowered to make
regulations which enable the Certification Officer to administer secret
trade union ballots, a subject which will be taken up again in the
Policy section. Finally, the demand for the independent conciliation,
mediation and arbitration services of the Advisory, Conciliation and

Arbitration Service (ACAS) increased dramatically during the decade (Kessler). ACAS also made valuable contributions to the Codes of Industrial Relations Practice issued during the 1970s (Owen Smith, pp.123, 128, 130-2).

A final variable – that of trade union density – added a further dimension to the growing complexity and confrontation which has characterised recent trade union growth. This density ratio had fallen from 45.2 per cent in 1948 to 43.7 per cent in 1967, thus reflecting the fact that the decline in manual union membership was more rapid than the increase in white-collar unionisation (Sayers Bain and Price, 1980, Table 2.1). One of the most significant post-Donovan developments, however, was the sudden upsurge in the density ratio of trade unionisation. Both legislation and changing attitudes on both sides of industry increased trade union recognition. By 1978 the density ratio had reached 54 per cent. Two features of this growth should be stressed. First, the rate of growth in white-collar unionisation outstripped the steady rate of growth in white-collar employment. Hence by 1974, 36 per cent of all union members were white-collar employees compared with 26 per cent ten years earlier. Secondly, the manual labour force fell by 1.6 million between 1964 and 1974 and although manual union membership also declined (by a smaller amount), manual union density rose from 52.9 per cent to 57.8 per cent over the decade – a level equalled only once before, in 1920 at the height of the short-lived post-First World War boom in union membership (Price and Sayers Bain, p.345).

These dramatic changes reflected the change in the composition of the labour force, that is the substitution of more highly qualified personnel. For example, the proportion of white-collar workers in British manufacturing industry rose from 8 per cent in 1907 to 25 per cent in 1966. White-collar membership rose 80 per cent in the period 1948-70, whereas manual union membership rose 0.8 per cent in the same period. Female membership of both types of union rose much faster than male membership. This was all in spite of the fact that white-collar workers and females in general have been historically reluctant to join trade unions (Sayers Bain and Price, 1972). This upsurge in middle-class militancy can also be gauged from the fact that an increasing number of white-collar unions have somewhat reluctantly affiliated to the TUC. Although the total number of affiliates fell from 172 in 1964 to 112 in 1978, the number of white-collar affiliates increased (Tables 5.3, 5.4 and 5.5 below). Most of the TUC's very large trade unions have a white-collar membership .

A totally different policy scenario thus emerged in recent years: strike breaking became more difficult for two reasons. First, in terms of the availability and skill level of alternative military labour (Kessler, p.16). Secondly, because alternative middle-class volunteers no longer exist – they are themselves active union members. Having isolated these two factors, the analysis can now proceed to the structure and policy sections.

Trade Union Structure

The combined effects of trade union growth and amalgamations have produced a complex union structure. Hence unions which *began* as purely craft organisations have gradually admitted *other categories* of workers. By far the best example of this (*first*) type of union is the Amalgamated Union of Engineering Workers (AUEW) which was founded as a craft union in 1851 and only gradually extended its rank to include semi-skilled males (1927), junior workers (1937 and 1940) and women (1943). It took the decision to affiliate to the Confederation of Shipbuilding and Engineering Unions (CSEU) as late as 1946. In 1967 it amalgamated with the foundry workers' union to form its foundry section. In 1971 further amalgamations took place with the draughtsmen's union and the construction workers' union to form another two sections. The first of these latter two sections became the white-collar section of the union (TASS), while the second became its construction section. All four sections have a total membership of 1.5 million members. They are all affiliated to the TUC and the CSEU. Bargaining in the engineering industry is dominated by the AUEW: 40 per cent of the CSEU's affiliated membership (2.5m) belongs to this one union (CSEU *Report*, 1978, p.3). The growth pattern of the electricians' union (EETPTU) has been very similar to that of the AUEW.

There are, *secondly*, two very large unions – the Transport and General Workers Union (TGWU) and the General and Municipal Workers Union (GMWU) – which have *not confined* their recruitment or amalgamation to any particular industry, although both unions nevertheless have understandable concentrations of membership among non-rail transport and manual municipal workers, respectively. The TGWU has also succeeded in expanding its membership in the motor vehicle industry at the expense of the AUEW. Two of its eleven trade groups ('Industrial Unions') plus its white-collar section are all affiliated to the CSEU. Both the TGWU and GMWU, along with the National Union of Public Employees and the Confederation of Health Service Employees, organise hospital workers, although the latter two unions have larger memberships in this sector. All four unions carry equal representation on the ancillary staff negotiating body at the present time.

A *third* category of union is completely *open* to all employees in a *particular* industry, but these are not usually industrial unions. For example, if the largest rail union, the National Union of Railwaymen, is defined as an industrial union, one immediately has to account for the two smaller unions which also organise railway workers. These are the Associated Society of Locomotive Engineers, which organises foot-platemen, and the exclusively white-collar union, the Transport and Salaried Staffs Association. ASLEF has remained independent in the belief that it will maintain its members' wage differentials over other railway workers. The inter-union conflict emanating from such a belief has frequently manifested itself.

The steel industry also has one large union and several minority groups of workers who may be members of large unions such as the AUEW. Once again, these groups have segregated themselves principally to defend wage interests. *Entry* into these smaller organisations tends therefore to be more *closely controlled* by the unions concerned. Skilled groups of workers are usually organised in this *fourth* category of 'union'.

Two unions in printing, one large and one small, hold a near monopoly of skilled print work. There are two further unions – again one much larger than the other – for other manual workers, while the white-collar journalists again have their own organisation. So much inter-union strife has been caused of late by technological change and the militancy of newspaper owners that a drastic rationalisation plan to create an industrial union has been put forward by the TUC. In fact, only one major industry – mining – has an industrial union. This is because several unions ceded organisational rights to the National Union of Mineworkers when the industry was nationalised following the Second World War (Meyers, p.11). Even here, however, there is some competition between the NUM and the Colliery Overmen when it comes to the organisation of white-collar workers.

A *fifth*, and final, group of unions are those involved in the *exclusive* recruitment of white-collar workers, some of which have already been mentioned above. These unions either recruit in a particular 'industry' – for example, teaching and the civil service –

or are more general in character. Two good examples of this latter
category (along with TASS) are the Association of Supervisory,
Technical and Managerial Staffs (ASTMS) and the Association of
Professional, Executive, Clerical and Computer Staffs (APEX), both
of which have for many years been affiliated to both the CSEU and
the TUC.

All the civil service unions, from those organising top civil servants
to those organising clerical workers, are now affiliated to the TUC,
something which the repeal of the Trade Disputes Act back in 1946
had made legally possible. All the major teaching unions are also now
affiliated to the TUC. In both cases, this process took well over a
decade to run its full course. It caused a great deal of controversy
within many of the organisations concerned. This controversy
stemmed from the fact that a number of TUC affiliates are also
affiliated to the Labour Party. It had also affected the local government
officers (NALGO) when they began the affiliation trend in 1964.
Nevertheless, both the teaching and the civil service trade unions
represent memberships in the TUC almost double that of the mining
group of unions.

It is at the same time interesting to note that within both the
civil service and teaching, multi-unionism derives from a preference
by the more highly qualified workers to maintain their own separate
organisation. For example, within teaching, the largest union is
the predominantly female National Union of Teachers. However,
another sizeable union (Association of Schoolmasters and Union of
Women Teachers) has traditionally tended to organise what in the days
of excess demand for most kinds of teachers were known as 'orthodox
career teachers', as opposed to either females who intended leaving
the profession on marrying or educational reformists. However, the
significant difference between these two unions has been over the
salary differential between longer serving teachers and those just
entering the profession. In other words the ASM/UWT has opposed
any narrowing of differentials which would affect the life-time pay
expectations of teachers. Lectures in colleges and universities each
have their own trade union, although the former have conducted
their wage negotiations in tandem with the schoolteachers and, as a
result, have gained from this latter group's militancy in recent years.
The small organisations representing head and some ex-grammar-
school teachers are not affiliated to the TUC.

Inter-union competition has been generated not just by the question
of wage differentials but also by the recruitment opportunities generated

by the rapid expansion of white-collar unionism. For example, it may appear that there are 23 unions affiliated to the CSEU. Quite apart from the relative insignificance of some of the smaller unions, however, each of the four major manual unions (AUEW, EETPTU, TGWU and GMWU) has its own white-collar section affiliated. In addition there are two exclusively white-collar unions (ASTMS and APEX).

Some unions have been created, while other unions have changed their title, in order to unionise unorganised white-collar workers. Such a trend can be illustrated by a series of recognition issues which occurred in the engineering industry during the 1970s. Throughout this decade the United Kingdom Association of Professional Engineers (UKAPE), a body opposed to TUC affiliation, until it eventually merged with the EETPTU in 1979, sought negotiating rights in the industry. Matters were further complicated in the second half of the decade by the decision of the Electrical Power Engineers' Association, a TUC affiliate, to change its name to the Engineers' and Managers' Association (EMA) and commence recruitment activities which would allow it to extend beyond its traditional area of organising staff employees in the electricity supply industry. As seen above, all existing unions in the engineering industry belong to the TUC and are therefore subject to the TUC's Bridlington Agreement. This would result in their being brought before the TUC Disputes Committee if they recruited dissident members of another TUC union. UKAPE by its very nature was not bound by these rules. For that matter they did not deter EMA either because both organisations attempted to recruit staff at plants where TASS was recognised.

TASS tends to be a militant and independent minded organisation — even to the extent of trying to prevent the merging of the various sections of its parent organisation (AUEW) into one large unit. When TASS complained to the TUC, EMA was ordered to stop its recruitment campaign and to withdraw a recognition reference which it had lodged with ACAS. EMA litigated against both the TUC and ACAS, although by 1980 it had decided to comply with the TUC instruction and apply for affiliation to the CSEU. In the same year ACAS was cleared by the House of Lords for not having proceeded with the EMA reference while the TUC Disputes Committee was handling the case.

Similarly, UKAPE eventually decided to amalgamate with the EETPTU, a TUC affiliate. Moreover, UKAPE's litigation against ACAS also went as far as (the final) House of Lords appeal. On this occasion the ACAS decision that UKAPE should not be recognised was challenged. As with the EMA case the Lords overturned earlier judgements against ACAS and found that ACAS had exercised its discretion wisely in the sense that there was a threat of industrial strife if UKAPE was recognised. In fact ACAS had followed precedents created earlier in the decade when its predecessor (the Commission on Industrial Relations) and the IR Act's National Industrial Relations Court had both refused to uphold UKAPE's recognition claims – on the grounds that it would result in further fragmentation of the bargaining structure if further small unions were recognised.

It would, therefore, be wrong to assume that a large number of small trade unions is the principal cause of inter-union rivalry. The growth of white-collar unionism, a spur to amalgamate for numerical strength, and the defence of wage differentials, sometimes stemming from the attitudes of *work groups* as expressed through their workplace representatives, are much more important dynamic factors. Indeed, *intra* union disputes arise from perceived wage structure anomalies. In any case, the dramatic decrease in the number of TUC trade unions (from 172 in 1964 to 112 in 1978) can be seen in Table 5.3. A further historical perspective may be obtained from note (ii) in Table 5.3. Moreover, as can be seen from Tables 5.2, 5.3 and 5.4 the large trade unions dominate the collective bargaining scene: the 26 trade unions with over 100,000 members affiliated to the TUC represented 10 million members, which is 85 per cent of the total TUC affiliated membership (Table 5.3) and 77 per cent of the 13 million trade union members in the Department of Employment's and Certification Officer's data (Table 5.2). Finally, total TUC affiliated membership is 92 per cent of the DE and CO data. Further elucidation of these data is contained in the footnotes to Tables 5.2, 5.3 and 5.4.

The extent to which the TUC membership and power structure have reflected changes in the structure of the labour force is demonstrated in the contents of, and notes to, Table 5.5. The decline of the staple industries and the rise of professional trade unionism is particularly evident from Table 5.5. For example, the decline in employment in mining, the railways, textiles, clothing and agriculture has been reflected by the decline in trade union membership in these industries. In some cases the number of trade unions has also declined. On the other hand, the expansion of unionism among public sector white-collar workers is equally evident. Moreover, an entirely new trade union group had been created to accommodate the expansion of technological white-collar membership (group 6). Public sector unionism as a whole had reached a density of 83 per cent by the mid-1970s (Price and Sayers Bain, Table 2). In manufacturing the equivalent figure was 62 per cent

Table 5.2: Comparison of the Data on Trade Unions (all as at 31 December 1978)

	Number of unions	Number of members
Trade Union Congress	112	12,128,078
Department of Employment	462	13,112,000
Certification Officer	485	13,053,596[1]

[1] Based on the 455 unions which had submitted returns — i.e. 422 listed and 30 unlisted unions which submitted returns by 31 December 1979 plus 3 listed unions which submitted returns after this date. In addition to the 425 listed unions which had submitted returns, there were 60 which failed to do so (= 485).

The TUC lists its affiliates only; the DE lists trade unions with headquarters in both Great Britain and Northern Ireland, whereas the CO omits Northern Ireland; the CO includes each section of certain trade unions as separate entities, the TUC (generally) and the DE (always) treat them as one organisation. The DE included 207 trade unions with under 499 members compared to only 11 affiliated to the TUC. The CO includes in his list numerous small staff associations, many of which do not hold Certificates of Independence. In 1979, the CO also listed 191 employers' associations and received returns from a further 186 unlisted ones.

Sources: TUC *Statistical Statement*, 1979, p.12. DE, *Gazette*, December 1979, pp.1241-2. CO, *Annual Report*, 1979, paras 1.5; 3.21-3.25 and Appendix 4.

Table 5.3: Distribution of TUC Affiliated Unions by Size of Membership (31 December 1964 and 1978)

		Number of Unions		Membership (000's)		Percentage of TUC membership	
		1964	1978	1964	1978	1964	1978
Over	100,000	17	26	6,351	10,291	72.42	84.85
50,000 –	99,999	17	14	1,180	957	13.46	7.89
10,000 –	49,999	43	30	1,019	771	11.60	6.36
5,000 –	9,999	13	9	85	59	0.97	0.49
1,000 –	4,999	52	17	127	44	1.44	0.36
500 –	999	6	5	4	4	0.05	0.03
Under	499	24	11	5	2	0.06	0.02
Totals		172	112	8,771	12,128	100.00%	100.00%

Notes:
(i) See Table 5.4 for a further analysis of the 'Over 100,000' group.
(ii) The Department of Employment annual analysis of trade union membership contains a large number of small trade unions, normally not affiliated to the TUC. This necessitates annual revision of data, usually in an upwards direction. In 1978, for example, there were 207 unions included with memberships of under 499 (*Gazette*, December 1979, p.1242). Recently, however, the DE data have been adjusted in the light of data published by the Certification Officer. Total membership covered was nevertheless only 1 million more than TUC coverage. This has historically always tended to be the case, but the difference in the total number of unions has been larger: 1893, 1,279 (DE) against 179 (TUC); 1918, 1,264 against 266; 1945, 781 against 192; and 1960, 664 against 183. Note also that the average for the TUC was 205 unions compared to 112 in 1978. (DEP, *British Labour Statistics 1868-1968*, HMSO, London, 1971, Table 196; TUC *Report* 1978, pp.743-5; Table 5.2.)
Sources: Calculated from TUC *Report*, 1965, pp.18-61 and TUC *Statistical Statement*, 1979.

Table 5.4: Certification Officer's Data (31 December 1978)

Unions each with 100,000 members or more:	Number of members
Transport & General Workers Union	2,072,818
Amalgamated Union of Engineering Workers	
Constructional Section	35,235
Engineering Section	1,199,465
Foundry Section	58,728
Technical Administrative and Supervisory Section	200,954
National Union of General & Municipal Workers	964,836
National & Local Government Officers Association	729,405
National Union of Public Employees	712,392
Association of Scientific, Technical & Managerial Staffs	471,000
Union of Shop Distributive & Allied Workers	462,178
Electrical, Electronic, Telecommunication & Plumbing Union	438,269
National Union of Mineworkers	371,470
Union of Construction Allied Trades & Technicians	325,245
National Union of Teachers	293,378
Civil & Public Services Association	224,780
Confederation of Health Service Employees	215,246
Society of Graphical and Allied Trades 1975	201,665
Union of Post Office Workers	197,157
National Union of Railwaymen	171,411
Association of Professional, Executive, Clerical & Computer Staff Staff (APEX)	152,543
National Association of Schoolmasters/Union of Women Teachers	140,701
Royal College of Nursing	134,389
Amalgamated Society of Boilermakers, Shipwrights, Blacksmiths and Structural Workers	131,099
Banking, Insurance and Finance Union	126,343
Post Office Engineering Union	121,404
National Union of Tailors & Garment Workers	116,095
Iron and Steel Trades Confederation	113,432
National Graphical Association	109,904
Society of Civil and Public Servants	106,903
Total of above unions with 100,000 members or more	10,598,445
Total of 366 other listed unions with less than 100,000 members	2,448,063
Total of listed unions	13,046,508
Total of 29 other unlisted unions which submitted returns	7,088
TOTAL of all unions for 1978	13,053,596

Note:
Only the Royal College of Nursing among the unions with over 100,000 members is not affiliated to the TUC. If the white-collar section of the AUEW is counted as a separate entity (as in the TUC data) there are therefore 26 unions with over 100,000 members affiliated to the TUC (see also Table 5.3).

Source: CO *Annual Report*, 1979, Appendix 4.

Table 5.5: Trade Groups of Unions Affiliated to the TUC (as at 31 December 1964 and 1978)

Trade group	No. of unions 1964	No. of unions 1978	Membership 1964	Membership 1978
1. Mining and Quarrying	3	3	513,007	291,330
2. Railways	3	3	386,786	277,217
3. Transport (other than Railways)	10	6	1,547,986	2,190,051
4. Shipbuilding	3	1	120,309	131,051
5. Engineering, Founding and Vehicle Building	19	10	1,387,561	1,434,219
6. Technical Engineering and Scientific	–	4	–	728,582
7. Electricity	3	1	334,385	420,000
8. Iron and Steel and Minor Metal Trades	15	9	217,951	141,753
9. Building, Woodworking & Furnishing	16	4	525,363	409,745
10. Printing and Paper	9	6	364,293	426,315
11. ⌈Cotton	6	} 15	93,048) }	} 121,043
⌊Textiles (other than Cotton)	22		87,681)	
12. ⌈Clothing	7	} 6	165,429) }	} 261,904
⌊Leather and Boot and Shoe	5		97,505)	
13. Glass, Ceramics, Chemicals, Food, Drink, Tobacco, Brush Making and Distribution	14	9	475,246	616,747
14. Agriculture	1	1	135,000	85,000
15. Public Employees	8	11	695,829	2,259,243
16. Civil Servants and Post Office	9	12	520,842	947,382
17. Professional, Clerical & Entertainment	15	10	311,571	421,660
18. General Workers	4	1	791,220	964,836
Totals	172	112	8,771,012	12,128,078

Notes:
(i) In 1968, Congress (see *Report*, pp.143-4) approved the following changes to the General Council (the body elected by the Annual Congress to carry out executive functions):
   (a) that the representation from Mining and Quarrying (Group 1) should be reduced from 3 seats to 2 seats;
   (b) that representation from Railways (Group 2) should be reduced from 3 seats to 2 seats;
   (c) that Cotton (Group 10) and Textiles – other than Cotton (Group 11) – should be merged to form a new group with 1 seat;
   (d) that Clothing (Group 12) and Leather, Boot and Shoe (Group 13) should be merged to form a new group with 1 seat;
   (e) that a new 'Technical Engineering and Scientific' group should be formed with 1 seat on the Council . . . (increased to 2 seats, 1974: *Report*, p.30);
   (f) that representation from Groups 3, 5, 15 and 17 be increased by one seat each.
In 1969 (see *Report*, p.130) two unions with the bulk of their membership in engineering were allowed to transfer from Group 8 to Group 5.
Group 15 was increased to 2 seats in 1970: *Report*, p.175.
In 1977 the number of seats held by Groups 3, 15 and 16 was increased by one each (*Report*, p.27).
(ii) The General Council has 41 seats with 2 seats reserved for women, although the size and principle of female representation has been debated at Congress (1975 *Report*, pp.37-9 and 377; 1976 *Report*, pp.66 and 440-1). This debate developed into a reappraisal of the whole structure of the General Council (1977 *Report*, pp.27, 32 and 385). The proposed amended structure would have given automatic representation to the large unions but allowed, in one proposal, unions with under 100,000 members to elect, by proportional representation, representatives from among themselves. This motion was lost by 6.5m to 5.2m votes (1978 *Report*, pp.29 and 464-71). A similar scheme was put forward at the 1979 Congress and remitted 'on the basis of clear assurances' for the General Council to make proposals to the 1980 Congress (1979 *Report*, pp.431-3).
(iii) The General Council in turn elects several committees from among its membership, including an 'inner cabinet' called the Finance and General Purposes Committee.
Sources: TUC *Report*, 1965, p.62, and *Statistical Statement*, 1979, p.12.

(73 per cent manual; 32 per cent white collar); there was a 23 per cent density in agriculture and 12 per cent in private sector services (ibid.). This means that over 90 per cent of the labour force was organised in mining, the railways, sea, airport and inland water transport, the public utilities and national government. Engineering, printing, the Post Office, education and local government were between 70 per cent and 85 per cent organised. Construction and agriculture were 27 per cent and 22 per cent organised, respectively, whereas distribution had the figure of only 11 per cent (ibid., Table 3).

The changing structure of British trade unions, therefore, has reflected the various factors influencing trade union growth. Industries which have a tradition of high trade union density, however, remain highly organised. In addition, there has been a dramatic expansion in trade unionisation generally. The effects of this expansion on trade union policy, and the reactions of both government and employers, can now be analysed.

Trade Union Policy

Introduction

The relative wage advantage of trade unionisation is gained by means of collective bargaining. On the trade union side power may be expressed through various forms of collective action: work-to-rules, overtime bans and strikes. Fairly reliable data are available only for the latter and they were presented on a time-series basis in *Table 5.1* above. Whether Britain's relative strike record is a major economic problem is a subject far too involved to be debated here, because differing hypotheses have been advanced and many caveats have to be entered (DE *Gazette*, February 1976, January 1978 and September 1980; Owen Smith, pp.135-6; Smith *et al.*). In any case, how can one be sure that strikes are not a symptom of relatively low investment, productivity and real wages rather than their cause?

Further, an undue emphasis on strike action may lead one to overlook the dramatic increase in voluntary third-party involvement in industrial disputes which has recently taken place (ACAS, *Annual Reports*). Hunter is surely correct in stressing that the potential saving to the economy of an effective conciliation and arbitration service is very large indeed (Hunter, p.241). Relatively little publicity has also been given to the now established areas in which secret ballots frequently take place. In this sense the proposals in the Employment Act 1980 were uncontroversial since secret postal ballots have become gradually more widespread. For example, two 'moderate' candidates for the AUEW presidency and general secretaryship received large majorities as a result of the introduction of postal ballots, although in the Seamen's Union moderate candidates were not helped by such a system. Moreover, offers of pay increases in electricity supply and the Post Office which had been accepted by union executives were rejected in ballots. In mining there were over 20 ballots in the 1970s alone, including an 81 per cent vote in support of the executive's call for strike action in 1974 but only 49 per cent in 1979. The percentage voting 'Yes' following the pay offer at the end of the 1972 mining strike was no less than 96.5 per cent (Hughes and Moore, p.150). The independent Electoral Reform Society organised the ballots on behalf of the NUM.

An analysis of the features which *underlie* strikes will more fully illustrate the guiding principles of trade union policy. Moreover, trade unionists have supplemented the means of *picketing* and governments have reacted. Recent trends in both underlying factors and picketing are therefore analysed in the first sub-section. In the second sub-section, an examination of another controversial area in trade union policy — the closed shop — is made. Finally, attention is focused on the relatively weak financial position of British trade unions.

Picketing

Trade unions operate within a confused framework of labour law. They have no precisely defined rights to strike or picket. Matters are made unusually complex by Britain's unwritten constitution and the existence of an ancient system of common law. This made it historically necessary to attempt definition of the degree of *immunity* from liability when trade unionists technically commit a civil wrong by temporarily breaking employment and commercial contracts during a trade dispute. In addition, a battery of criminal laws could be invoked against pickets. These latter laws apply to such alleged offences as obstructing the highway or the police, causing a breach of the peace by displaying material or using abusive words, and making undue noise. The police — who have considerable discretionary powers to determine whether picketing is peaceful — hold inconsistent views, while the courts seem even more divided in their views on what constitutes trade union law.

Hence the Employment Act 1980 contained the Conservative government's reaction to developments during the 1970s, when mass picketing and the picketing of parties not directly involved in a trade dispute had taken place, so-called 'secondary picketing'. The Act and one of its two accompanying Codes of Practice required picketing to be limited to small numbers, usually not exceeding six persons. (Picketing, *Code of Practice*, para. 31.) This did not affect the discretion of the police to limit numbers (ibid., para. 28). Immunity was removed

where picketing was not confined to the pickets' own place of work, or
to a first customer or first supplier of the employer in dispute, or to an
associated employer to whom work had been transferred because of the
dispute (ibid., Annex). An official of the picketing employees' union
may be included among the small number of pickets and either he or
his appointed deputy is required to supervise the pickets and issue them
with means of identification (ibid., paras 16 and 32-4; DE *Gazette*,
August 1980, pp.849-53).

In terms of trade union policy, however, the picketing to which the
government had reacted was used during the 1970s in a number of
bargaining issues. As in the early 1920s, the miners attracted the
support of other workers during their strikes of 1972 and 1974. As
in the early 1920s, there had again been relative and an absolute
decline in their earnings (Hughes and Moore, ch.2; Morris, p.125). In
relative terms, miners' average earnings fell from 7 per cent more than
male average earnings in manufacturing in 1967, to 93 per cent of
manufacturing in 1971 (Hughes and Moore, pp.24-5). Absolutely,
miners also suffered a decline in real living standards, not just through
rising prices but also because they entered earnings ranges carrying
greater tax liability (ibid., pp.27-9). This latter phenomenon had
become a growing problem, particularly for the lower paid: the tax
threshold for a married man with two children fell from national
average earnings level for the decade following the Second World War
to a little over half that level in 1971-2 — the so-called 'poverty-trap'
(ibid., pp.92-3). In the case of coalmining, another similarity with
the early 1920s was the decline in the demand for coal. On the other
hand, there had been a marked shift to a more capital-intensive
technology and marked productivity improvement (ibid., pp.38-9
and 154). In a sense this gave the miners greater bargaining power since
the sophisticated underground machinery required the permanent
attention of their members.

Other workers supported the miners in 1972 when the movement of
coal and coke came virtually to a standstill. The eventual pay settlement
was to put miners' earnings slightly over those in manufacturing. Perhaps
the most spectacular event during the strike was the mass picket of the
Saltley coke depot in Birmingham. The General Secretary of the NUM
was later to tell a Court of Inquiry:

Our pickets have done something more than hasten the course of
this dispute. They have acted as ambassadors of the mining
community in every city and port of this country. We have enjoyed

in practical form, and with steadily growing effectiveness, the solidarity and support of the organised workers of this country. Instead of remaining isolated and alone beside our pits, we have built the unity of action and understanding that has been the immense positive feature of this strike. It is that and that alone that has forced the Government from the dictatorship that it had been imposing not just on miners but on all the workers of this country.

Those picket lines have been the one way of shortening this dispute and moving from Government dictation to a just settlement. When the industrial workers of Birmingham marched in their thousands to join our picket line they showed we do not stand alone, and that the purpose of our picket lines is understood by the working people of this country (ibid., p.10).

Although the miners were much more circumspect in their use of picketing during the 1974 dispute, they succeeded in forcing a general election which resulted in the Conservatives (and their Incomes Policy) being defeated. The outcome of the 1972 and 1974 disputes was therefore the precise opposite of the wage cuts resulting from the 1921 and 1926 confrontations. Towards the end of the 1970s British miners, like their European colleagues, were able to record an increase in relative pay (Saunders in Blackaby, pp.194-5 and 208). The extent of their relative gain was exceptional, however (ibid., p.203).

However, the debt structure of the nationalised industries, whereby they are required to make interest payments to governments and restrain prices irrespective of the state of demand for their product, have caused great difficulties (Hughes and Moore, ch.5). This same rigidity was also a major element in both the Post Office strike of 1971 and the steel strike of 1980. In this latter case an offer of 2 per cent was made by the British Steel Corporation on the grounds that it was all that it could afford. The commercial reality was that the BSC was making modest losses but paying huge 'dividends' to the government, the party which had encouraged the large capital investment programmes of the 1970s (*The Times*, 17 Dec. 1979, p.13). Moreover, the 'going rate' of pay increases at the time was nearer 20 per cent. After a strike lasting 13 weeks, during which there was mass picketing, the involvement of ACAS and a Court of Inquiry, a resumption of work was made for an increase of 16 per cent.

Successive governments had gradually deemed it more and more necessary to exercise (whether overtly or covertly) control over the general level of pay settlements. This control may perhaps be exercised most effectively over the public sector with the result that different groups of workers in this sector fall behind the general level of pay settlements. In the 1970s, these groups were, in turn, workers in the local authorities, the Post Office, electricity supply, mining, the public services and steel. In desperation, the Labour government set up an independent Pay Comparability Commission just before losing office in 1979, but this was disbanded by the Conservatives. Manual wages in the public sector taken as a whole surged ahead of the private sector during the 1970s — in complete contrast to the 1950s and 1960s (Brown in Blackaby, p.146). By November 1980 the Conservatives had announced a 6 per cent pay ceiling for the forthcoming local authority workers' pay round. This pressure on the pay structure has to be distinguished from, first, the narrowing of pay differentials between skilled and unskilled workers which took place during successive periods of formal incomes policies. Secondly, there was another kind of pressure during incomes policy off periods, when the size, dispersion and frequency of pay settlements tended to increase. Incomes policies have therefore tended to favour less skilled employees. (Dawkins; Metcalf; Owen Smith and Dawkins.) This was in direct contrast to fiscal policy which had created the poverty-trap described above. It also contrasted to the high levels of unemployment later created by monetary policies.

As well as being of crucial significance in the coal and steel strikes, the dynamics of the pay structure, that is comparisons between different groups of employees at a time of economic stagnation, can be related to another three disputes where picketing caused considerable controversy. These are the two nationwide stoppages in the public services and road transport sectors, plus the local Isle of Grain power station dispute. Both of the national stoppages took place during the winter of 1979 and both were called by relatively low-paid groups against the recommended Incomes Policy limit of a 5 per cent pay rise — less than the rate of inflation. Striking transport workers attempted to control the movement of goods by road. Public service workers in hospitals and schools also took militant action, a logical extension of the threats and actual militant action staged by the medical and teaching professions earlier in the decade. In both cases control over work groups by the unions concerned was often lost, but the desired economic effects were the shortages similar to those created by the miners and electricity supply workers. Similar tactics to the miners — highly mobile groups of pickets ('flying pickets'), secondary pickets and sympathetic action by other trade unionists —

were used. But the violence and arrests on picket lines tended to increase, while the direct and more tangible hardships to young and old caused by the public service workers aroused an unprecedented degree of hostility. Transport workers blockaded certain areas and required drivers passing picket lines to hold special dispensation. As a result, the TUC drew up guidelines for pickets.

There was also violence on the picket lines at the Isle of Grain. In this case, however, the dispute lasted over a year (1979-80) and involved a group of employees ('laggers') organised by the GMWU. Although the laggers serve an apprenticeship, it was considered at the Isle of Grain that they were placed too high in the wages structure. An attempted rationalisation brought the GMWU laggers out on a prolonged strike. When the Generating Board threatened the closure of this power station site (Europe's largest), both the construction and engineering sections of the AUEW, together with the Electricians' Union, agreed to train laggers and send them through the picket line. This was when the violence erupted in May 1980.

An inevitable inter-union dimension was consequently introduced by competing work groups. The action taken by the AUEW and electricians resulted in the TUC insisting that the GMWU laggers be reinstated, although there was reluctance to press the issue to the extent of suspending the three unions from Congress. Such a situation would have been even more serious than the David and Goliath case which had involved the National Association of Licensed House Managers (13,000 members) and the TGWU (2 million members). The NALHM applied for affiliation to the TUC in 1974 and June 1975 (TUC 1975 *Report*, p.37, and 1976, p.65). Three other affiliated unions, including the TGWU, objected and the NALHM's application was turned down. However, the NALHM successfully applied later in 1975 when it gave assurances that it would confine recruitment to licensing house managers. Later, TGWU beer delivery draymen refused to recognise the NALHM membership card of the manager of the Fox and Goose Public House, Ansells Limited, Birmingham, but were ordered to do so by the TUC. When the TGWU draymen refused to implement this award their union faced suspension from the TUC (1977 *Report*, pp.4 and 390-4). During the Congress debate the TGWU's white-collar section was accused of poaching 100 (0.77 per cent) NALHM members, the equivalent in percentage terms of 154,000 TGWU members. Amid confusion there was a narrow vote in favour of the suspension of the TGWU followed by another vote against suspension. The conflict was resolved in 1977 when the General

Council of the TUC were informed that beer deliveries to the Fox and Goose had been resumed in October of that year (1978 *Report*, p.54).

In passing to a final case of mass picketing — that staged at the Grunwick processing laboratories during 1977 — yet another dimension in trade union policy may be illustrated. This is the problem of gaining recognition from small employers who feel themselves excluded from the important new centralised institutions of large employers, trade unions and consultation with government (Crouch, p.115). Indeed, employers' associations nowadays act principally as lobby organisations rather than bargainers (Brown in Blackaby, p.140). This polarisation of power upwards — away from the formal machinery — is as important as polarisation downwards to workplace representatives (Kahn-Freund, p.84). But in the Grunwick case, both the employer and the union (APEX) were caught up in organisations which represented opposing political philosophies. The employer was advised by the militant National Association of Freedom, while the union's Strike Committee, somewhat to the embarrassment of its General Secretary, staged an equally militant campaign which involved mass picketing. ACAS was also embroiled, since it had responsibilities in the field of trade union recognition at the time. Matters were made even more complex by the fact that a large group of Asian employees joined APEX after their dismissal and simultaneously sought reinstatement and union representation (Crouch, p.113). ACAS was refused access to those employees who were not dismissed. Reliance was therefore placed on a poll of the strikers alone which, of course, produced a vote in favour of recognition. The ballot was challenged in the courts, who found in favour of Grunwick. A court injunction was also granted against the postal union's blacking of Grunwick mail. By 1978 the pickets had abandoned what had become a hopeless task.

Hence many of the militant developments in the 1970s reflected deep-seated economic trends. This in turn created problems for the institutions involved, ultimately resulting in two controversial Codes of Practice — a topic to be taken up again later. Grunwick epitomised the polarisation of political reactions; this is seen in a wider spectrum in the debate surrounding the closed shop, to which the analysis now turns.

The Closed Shop

Closed shops, or union membership agreements (UMAs), have a long history. An authority on labour law (Professor Kahn-Freund) quite rightly saw market and job control as one of the two *centrally*

important characteristics of British labour relations, the other
characteristic being that in many sectors of British industry important
trade union decisions are made usually at the workplace by the
membership itself rather than by elected representatives. Professor
Kahn-Freund lucidly defined market and job control as the traditional
union policy designed not only to regulate terms of employment but
also access to jobs and supply in the labour markets (Kahn-Freund,
p.3).

It is crucial to note that Kahn-Freund was a practising lawyer in
Germany before becoming a refugee from the Nazis. He became a
naturalised British citizen and served on the Donovan Commission
(*The Times*, Obituary, 16 Nov. 1979, p.vii). Surely he was correct
to claim that as an immigrant he had the advantage of having to
learn what was inherent in British institutions (Kahn-Freund, p.2)?
Early trade unions in Britain were imbued with the spirit of the
crafts, confining access to work to members (ibid., p.42). But this
is only part of general history: *these characteristically British job
divisions are a pervasive element in the social structure of the country*
(ibid., pp.48-9). There is a careful and rigid division of professional
and commercial activities (ibid., p.48). Unlike professions such as
medicine and the law, however, workers have not been able to
practise legal entry control (McCarthy and Ellis, p.65). Confining
jobs to union members evolved with trade unionism, but total
compulsion was not necessarily practised by trade unions and
management generally had no sympathy with free-riders (Weekes,
pp.213 and 216). Some trade unions ran the gauntlet of TUC
opposition by registering under the Conservatives' Industrial Relations
Act 1971 so that UMAs could be maintained and extended.
Some unions were temporarily expelled for doing so. Significantly
this Act was partially discredited by cases involving two eccentric
individuals who consciously allowed their union membership to
lapse (Owen Smith, pp.125-6).

It was an ironic quirk of history which transformed closed shops
into an important legal issue. Once employees became legally
protected from unfair dismissal under the various statutes of the 1970s,
employers were legally vulnerable if they dismissed a person who
refused to comply with a closed shop. In addition, the Conservatives
reluctantly recognised closed shops since they were opposed to the
principle underlying them (DE *Gazette*, August 1980, p.853). On the
one hand, this opposition was based on the belief that having required
to join a union as a condition of obtaining or holding a job runs

contrary to British traditions of personal liberty (ibid.). On the other hand, closed shops were a fact of industrial life and there were employers and trade unions who believed that such agreements could help create stability (ibid.). The same logic had led to exceptions being made when the Industrial Relations Act legalised the right not to join a trade union (Owen Smith, pp.136-7).

There are two basic kinds of closed shops. By a pre-entry closed shop the union seeks to control the supply of labour by restricting entry to the union and by insisting that jobs be offered only to individuals who are already union members. In a post-entry closed shop the employer is given recruitment autonomy but new appointees must join the appropriate union as a condition of employment. There are about 5.2 million workers affected by closed shop agreements, that is about 23 per cent of the labour force (Gennard *et al.*, 1980a, p.17). By far the largest proportion (84 per cent of the 5.2 million) are in post-entry closed shops (ibid., pp.19-20). The dominant single industry in terms of pre-entry closed shop is paper, printing and publishing (ibid., p.20). Industries with the highest proportion of employees in closed shops are: mining (87 per cent), the public utilities (80 per cent), printing (66 per cent), shipbuilding (57 per cent), transport (56 per cent), coal and petroleum products (55 per cent) and metal manufacture (50 per cent) (ibid., pp.17-18). Generally speaking closed shop agreements have spread, but three circumstances have been identified where high-density unionism has not accompanied such a spread (ibid., p.21). First, where demand for a closed shop has been resisted by managements in the non-industrial part of the civil service, certain parts of the health service, textiles and journalism. Secondly, there has been no demand for closed shops among higher grade civil servants, in education, or among Post Office engineers. Thirdly, in a relatively small number of cases closed shop agreements have been rescinded by management.

As the closed shop spread during the 1970s, so negotiators concluded increasingly sophisticated post-entry closed shop agreements which precisely defined the obligations and rights of employees where union membership existed as a condition of employment (Gennard *et al.*, 1979, p.1092). Religious objection has been widely accepted as grounds for not joining a union and the rights of existing non-members were similarly protected (ibid., pp.1090-1). Another post-Donovan development was the increasing supervision of UMAs by the TUC, including detailed guidance on union rules concerning the admission and disciplining of members (Gennard *et al.*, 1980b, p.592;

TUC *Reports*, various). However, all these developments were
undermined by the publicity accorded to a number of cases, notably
the unscrupulous recruitment method used by one of the smaller print
unions (SLADE). Moreover, closed shops, which are arrived at by
collective agreement, of course, were increasingly seen as an attack on
individual liberty.

Hence the Employment Act 1980 and its accompanying Code of
Practice on closed shops extended the grounds on which it would be
unfair to dismiss an employee for not becoming a trade union member.
These grounds were, first, in the event of an employee holding *any*
deeply held personal conviction; secondly, any existing non-union
members were protected if a closed shop were introduced; thirdly, if
any future closed shop agreement were concluded which had not been
approved by at least 80 per cent of all affected employees voting in
a secret ballot, individual employees who refused to join a trade
union could not be fairly dismissed. Such aggrieved employees could
appeal to an Industrial Tribunal. For the first time, the employer
could require any trade union representative whom he alleges to have
exerted pressure over non-union membership to become a party to
the proceedings (Closed Shop, *Code of Practice*, para. 11). The
Tribunal could then order that person to recompense the employer for
any sum up to the total amount of any compensation awarded by the
Tribunal.

Industrial Tribunals are also empowered under the Act to hear
allegations by individuals who claim that they have been unreasonably
expelled from, or refused, union membership. No action may be taken
against such an employee until all proceedings, including those
provided by the TUC, have been completed (ibid., paras 14 and 53).
All new closed shop agreements have to be clearly drafted and
approved by at least 80 per cent of the affected employees. Both new
and existing agreements are now subject to review (ibid., paras 35
and 42).

It is, of course, far too early to comment on the effect of these
provisions on the much longer-term phenomena outlined in the last
two sub-sections — that is the factors *underlying* strike action, picketing
and the closed shop. However, the Codes of Practice on picketing and
the closed shop represent attempts to tackle the two most difficult
aspects of collective bargaining. Opposition to various aspects of the
draft Codes was voiced by the trade unions, employers, the police and
MPs. Even the constitutional propriety of the amended Codes laid
before Parliament was questioned because it was not clear whether

their contents were advice or law. The Secretary of State's alleged
precipitate action in not leaving ACAS and the parties themselves
to draw up the Codes was also condemned, as was the extension of their
use from industrial tribunals to the courts (*Hansard*, 13 Nov. 1980,
cols 647-764).

The Financial Positions of British Trade Unions: A Policy Constraint

At the end of 1938 total union reserves stood at £20 million, and by
the end of 1955 at £76.5 million. Unadjusted for inflation, reserves
per member were about £4.10 in 1938 and about £9.00 in 1956. In
real terms (that is at 1938 prices), however the figure for 1956 had
declined to £3.60 (Clegg and Adams, p.116). By 1975 the total funds
of trade unions had risen to £190.2 million and trade union membership
to 11.6 million (CO, *Annual Report* 1976, Appendix 4). This gave an
unadjusted figure of £16.40 per member, but the retail price index
(1958 = 100) had risen from 93.6 in 1956 to 278.7 in 1975
(= 197.8 per cent). By 1978 the total funds were £270 million and
membership 13 million (CO, *Annual Report* 1979, Appendix 4).
Although this meant a per member figure of £20.77, the RPI had
risen by 46.2 per cent (Table 5.6). Even if the £16.40 per member in
1975 had shown a realistic growth in real terms, therefore, the figures
by 1978 should have grown by a factor of at least 0.46 to keep pace
with inflation (£16.40 plus £7.54 = £23.94). A similar position
emerges if one compares the change in members' contributions as a
proportion of the basic weekly wage. This figure fell from 1.5 per cent
in 1939 to about 0.75 per cent in 1960 (Pelling, p.255). As a percentage
of earnings, the average weekly contribution in 1975 and 1978 was in
the order of 0.3 per cent (Table 5.6). This compares to between 1 and
2 per cent in the Federal Republic of Germany (Cullingford, p.60;
Jühe, pp.81 and 117 – Chapter 7 bibliography).

On this basis alone, the inevitable conclusion emerges that British
trade unionists receive union services on the cheap. In addition,
however, it is apparent from Table 5.6 that expenditure on dispute
benefit has increased. Indeed, the AUEW was forced to delay agreed
salary rises to its officials in 1980 because of financial difficulties
(*The Times*, 23 June 1980, p.11). Moreover, the Conservative
government announced in 1980 that in assessing the payment of
supplementary benefits to strikers' families, the assumption would be
made that the striker had provided £12 per week himself, whether
in strike pay or in some other way. (The *full* amount of a striker's
tax refund would also in future be taken into account – *The Times*,

Table 5.6: Trade Union Finances (1975-1978)

Year	Income		Expenditure				Total % change in dispute benefits – over previous year	Average annual earnings – all industries and services: manual & non-manual	Retail price index 1974 = 100
	Average annual contribution per member	Total income per member per annum	Average annual dispute benefit per member	Average annual total benefit per member	Administrative costs per member	Total expenditure per member per year			
1975	£8.65	£10.44	29p	£1.43	£6.82	£9.07	–	£3078.4	134.8
1976	£10.74	£12.49	17p	£1.51	£7.76	£10.30	–39%	£3640.0	157.1
1977	£11.92	£13.91	34p	£1.73	£8.78	£11.55	+110%	£3993.6	182.0
1978	£13.09	£15.14	70p	£2.24	£9.86	£13.52	+114%	£4518.8	197.1
% change 1978/1975	51.3%	45.0%	141.4%	56.6%	44.6%	49.1%	–	46.8%	46.2%

Sources: Earnings and RPI data: calculated from Department of Employment *Gazette*, August 1980, pp.920 and 928.
All other data: Certification Officer, *Annual Reports*, 1976-1979 inclusive.

27 March 1980, p.6.) The government contended that the miners had not paid dispute benefit in 1972 and 1974, nor did the firemen during their dispute in 1977. Two of the steel unions had also not paid strike pay in 1980. An average supplementary benefit payment of £17.40 per week had been made in 1979, while in the steel strike the sum rose to £22 (*The Times*, 16 April 1980). In response to the government's action the TGWU increased its strike pay from £6 to £9 per week and basic contributions from 25p to 38p per week (*The Times*, 28 June 1980, p.2). Similarly, the AUEW increased its disputes benefit from £9 to £12 per week, together with an increase in weekly contributions for skilled members from 45p to 50p (*The Times*, 23 June 1980, p.1). (Average weekly earnings in engineering in 1979 were about £95 – DE *Gazette*, August 1980, p.918.) Strike pay in West Germany, for a monthly contribution of £5, is between £40 and £45 per week.

Conclusion

Both government policies and the unions' internal financial situation could conceivably undermine trade union bargaining power. However, the dynamics of the wages structure, already identified as a key factor in trade union structure, will not necessarily be halted by stringent collective bargaining laws and monetary policies. The spread of trade unionism and the willingness of almost every work group, including professional ones, to indulge in various forms of militant action also makes future trends uncertain.

Bibliography

Advisory, Conciliation and Arbitration Service, *Annual Reports* (various) (London)

Blackaby, F.T. (ed.), *The Future of Pay Bargaining* (Heinemann, London, 1980)

Bosworth, D.L. and Wilson, R.A. in P. Maunder (ed.), *The British Economy in the 1970s* (Heinemann Educational, London, 1980)

Certification Officer, *Annual Reports* (various) (London)

Clegg, H.A. and Adams, R., *The Employers' Challenge* (Basil Blackwell, Oxford, 1957)

Cronin, J.E., *Industrial Conflict in Modern Britain* (Croom Helm, London, 1979)

Crouch, C., *The Politics of Industrial Relations* (Fontana, Glasgow, 1979)

Dawkins, P.J. and P. Maunder (ed.), *The British Economy in the 1970s* (Heinemann Educational, London, 1980)

Department of Employment, *Gazette* (various)

Flanders, A. in W. Galenson (ed.), *Comparative Labor Movements* (Prentice-Hall, New York, 1952)

Gennard, J. *et al.*, 'The Content of British Closed Shop Agreements', Department of Employment, *Gazette* (November 1979), pp.1088-92.

Gennard, J. *et al.*, 'The Extent of Closed Shop Arrangements in British Industry', Department of Employment, *Gazette* (January 1980a), pp.16-22

Gennard, J. *et al.*, 'Throwing the Book: Trade Union Rules on Admission, Discipline and Expulsion', Department of Employment, *Gazette* (June 1980b), pp.591-601

Hughes, J. and Moore, R. (Editors for the National Union of Mineworkers), *A Special Case?* (Penguin Books, Harmondsworth, 1972)

Hunter, L.C., 'Economic Issues in Conciliation and Arbitration', *British Journal of Industrial Relations, XV* (2) (1977), pp.226-45

Kahn-Freund, O., *Labour Relations* (Oxford UP, 1979)

Kessler, S., 'The prevention and settlement of collective labour disputes in the United Kingdom', *Industrial Relations Journal, 11* (1) (1980), pp.5-31

Knowles, K.G.J.C., *Strikes – A Study in Industrial Conflict* (Basil Blackwell, Oxford, 1952)

Lockyer, J., *Industrial Arbitration in Great Britain* (Institute of Personnel Management, London, 1979)

McCarthy, W.E.J. and Ellis, N.D., *Management by Agreement* (Hutchinson, London, 1973)

Metcalf, D., 'Unions, Incomes Policy and Relative Wages', *British Journal of Industrial Relations, XV* (2) (1977), pp.157-75

Meyers, F., *European Coal Mining Unions: Structure and Function* (Institute of Industrial Relations, University of California, Los Angeles, 1961)

Morris, M., *The General Strike* (Penguin Books, Harmondsworth, 1976)

Owen Smith, E. and Dawkins, P.J., 'Incomes Policy – the Macro and Micro Implications', *Loughborough Papers on Recent Developments in Economic Policy and Thought*, No. 10 (1978)

Owen Smith, E. in P. Maunder (ed.), *The British Economy in the 1970s* (Heinemann Educational, London, 1980)

Pelling, H., *A History of British Trade Unionism* (first edition) (Penguin Books, Harmondsworth, 1963)

Price, R. and Sayers Bain, G., 'Union Growth Revisited: 1948-1974 in Perspective', *British Journal of Industrial Relations, XIV* (3) (1976), pp.335-55

Sayers Bain, G. and Price, R., 'Union Growth and Employment Trends', *British Journal of Industrial Relations, X* (3) (1972), pp.366-81

Sayers Bain, G. and Price R., *Profiles of Union Growth: A Comparative Statistical Portrait of Eight Countries* (Blackwell, Oxford, 1980)

Shonfield, A., *Modern Capitalism* (Oxford UP, London, New York, 1965)

Smith, C.T.B. *et al.*, 'Strikes in Britain', Department of Employment *Manpower Paper*, No.15 (London, 1978)

Trades Union Congress, *Reports* (various) (London)

Webb, S. and B., *The History of Trade Unions 1666-1920* (2nd ed.) (Longmans Green, London, 1920)

Weekes, B., 'Law and the Practice of the Closed Shop', *Industrial Law Journal, 5* (4) (1976), pp.211-22

Wrigley, C., *The Government and Industrial Relations 1910-1921* (Department of Economics, Loughborough University, 1979)

6 THE UNITED STATES OF AMERICA

Andrew W.J. Thomson

Introduction

In examining the growth of trade unionism in the United States, it is of course essential to understand the institutional, economic and political background of developments. It is therefore proposed to link the section on trade union growth with an inevitably cursory review of the history of the labour movement in the United States, and to split this into three sections: one dealing with the early period up to the 1930s, which were a watershed in American labour history; a second dealing with the period from the 1930s until 1970, which was a period of growth and consolidation; and the third dealing with the decade 1970-1980, which has been a period of stagnation and retrenchment. Any reader wanting an immediate statistical review of union growth should turn to Table 6.1.

Trade Union Growth

The Beginnings to the 1930s

The origins of American trade unions can be traced to the end of the eighteenth century with the appearance of a few skilled craftsmen's organisations in the large cities. At this stage they were composed of journeymen who expected to become masters in their own right, and combination was as much to raise prices against the public as to raise wages against the employers. Such organisations, like all unions until the late nineteenth century, were ephemeral, and they also suffered attacks by the common law for being combinations in restraint of trade, the most famous of such cases being the Philadelphia Cordwainers case of 1806.

In this early period there was no organisation of unskilled workers, but by the 1820s these latter were becoming involved in the workingmen's political groupings which sought improvements by legislative means. There also emerged a set of policy alternatives which faced the nascent union movement, which could essentially be divided into three. There was a division between political means and economic or collective bargaining means, and within the former there was a division betwen the utopian reformist groups and somewhat later the

155

adoption of socialist objectives.

Taking the utopian reformists first, these groupings emerged at intervals throughout the century, with Robert Owen playing a considerable part with his attempts to set up new types of community organisation such as New Harmony in Indiana. However they reached their zenith with the emergence of the Knights of Labor in 1869 and its rise to major national significance by 1886. The Knights rejected the wage system and essentially wanted a return to a Rousseauvian ideal of small-scale independent craftsmen, farmers, merchants and producers' co-operatives. Their organisation was avowedly all-inclusive and thus not geared to collective bargaining or strikes, although many of the locals were in fact single craft-based. In 1886, almost by mistake, the Knights won a major strike victory over the Wabash Railroad, and hundreds of thousands of workers flocked to the standard, hoping to improve their own conditions. In the single year of 1886 membership grew from 100,000 to 700,000, but the ramshackle organisation could not handle these numbers, especially insofar as most joined merely to obtain immediate economic benefits and wanted support for strikes. Disillusion set in and the Knights declined as fast as they had grown, and with their decline there disappeared the concept of a simplistic economic structure in which large-scale industrialism could be held at bay. The development of worker organisation in parallel to industrial organisation and the widening of the market has been brilliantly charted by John R. Commons in an article in 1909 which must still stand as the best article ever written in the field of industrial relations.

The alternative philosophy to the Knights was represented by the craft unions which began to achieve some degree of permanence by the 1850s. They were much narrower in focus, concerned primarily with collective bargaining, and were exclusive in occupational organisation. They had no national organisation until 1881, which in 1886 became the American Federation of Labor. There were several attempts to link the national unions with the Knights, and indeed there was quite a lot of overlapping membership. The AFL itself in its early days was split between those who were opportunist and pragmatic, accepting the wage system, and seeking improvements as and when they could be achieved by collective bargaining, and those who espoused a European type of socialism, recognising the inevitability of large-scale organisation, but seeking the overthrow of capitalism and private property. The socialist group were influential for many years within the AFL, but they never achieved dominance, and the major influences for the present day came from

the 'business unionism' side of the AFL. In passing, however, we
should also note that there were some distinctively American forms of
anarchic socialism, notably illustrated by the Industrial Workers of
the World, the 'Wobblies', who engaged in various acts of sabotage and
had others unjustifiably ascribed to them. This latter strain, together
with a degree of corruption and violence within the craft unions of the
AFL, helped to give the union movement a bad name.

By 1900 the union movement had less than a million members,
representing less than five per cent of non-agricultural employment, but
a period of growth then ensued with membership rising to two million
by 1910 and five million by 1920. However, this latter figure,
representing 16 per cent of non-agricultural employment, was something
of an illusion, since it was largely based on a temporary acceptance of
unionism during the abnormal circumstances of the First World War.
More generally even the mainstream unions of the AFL found
recognition and successful bargaining an uphill struggle, since American
employers were generally much more antagonistic than elsewhere,
especially in manufacturing industry, and the law continued to be used
to prevent both organisation and successful industrial action. Moreover,
the structure and organisation of the unions was not geared to the
organisation of manufacturing. All these aspects are worth an additional
explanation.

American employers were much more individualistic and less
oriented to association with other employers than their European
counterparts. This is both a reason why it has been so difficult for
American unions to achieve recognition and why American collective
bargaining has developed on such a decentralised basis. In Europe,
there was always an incentive for employers' associations to enter
into collective bargaining provided that the whole or most of the
product market could be covered, because the price of labour could
thereby be taken out of competition. But if, as in America, there was
little disposition to join associations, which would in any case have
been rendered more difficult by the sheer size of the country and the
page of development in the pre-First World War period, each
employer who recognized unions was likely to be at a labour cost
disadvantage *vis-à-vis* his competitors. Had the unions managed to
achieve widespread organisation in manufacturing, it is likely that
employers' organisations would have grown up in response, and
bargaining would have been much more centralised and unions more
accepted into the fabric of American life. But this did not happen, and
widespread organisation had to wait until the late 1930s, by which time

American manufacturing was itself organised into sufficiently large company units for them to be self-sufficient for bargaining purposes, and not to require association bargaining.

That American unions did not achieve early recognition was also partly due to the other factor mentioned above, the role of law. The common law, as in the Cordwainers case of 1806, saw unions as conspiracies in restraint of trade, and although unions came to achieve legal acceptance as entities, as in Britain the means which they used and the ends to which they used them were severely curtailed. Indeed American unions fared much worse than those in Britain because they could not summon sufficient political power to achieve legislative change. Three aspects of law in particular were disadvantageous to the growth of unions. One was the use of injunctions to prevent an employer's business from being irreparably damaged by industrial action. The second was the use of the 'yellow dog' contract by which employers could require of their new employees that they would not join unions; any union organiser seeking to organise such employees could then be charged with inducement of breach of contract. The third was the use, or rather misuse, of antitrust legislation to control unions. The Sherman Act of 1890 was a populist piece of legislation passed to help control the burgeoning and aggressive big business of the period; there is no evidence whatsoever that it was intended to apply to unions, yet it was predominantly against unions that the Act was effectively used, and the passage of the Clayton Act in 1914 to remedy the situation made matters if anything worse. There can be little doubt that without a different legal structure to that which existed before the 1930s the American unionism could never have become a significant movement.

The third main problem of the American labour movement before the 1930s was that the AFL was organisationally and philosophically dominated by a craft mentality which found no place for the unskilled or semi-skilled worker. Moreover, the craft unions were bitterly jealous of their own jurisdictions, and conflicts were frequently as much between unions as between unions and employers. The new assembly-based industries of the twentieth century were just not compatible with the craft consciousness of the traditional AFL, and this was a further important reason why the AFL made little headway. Indeed apart from construction and printing and a few enclaves elsewhere in coal, railroads and local service industries, the AFL was in a desperate state in the early 1930s, with weak leadership, an already outdated structure, and faced with legal and employer antagonism to unionism as an anti-American institution. It was, however, parodixically, the great Depression of the 1930s, which had initially created even more difficulties for the unions, which was responsible for a new social, political and legal climate in which unionism could flourish, and to this we now turn.

From the 1930s to 1970

The New Deal was the creator of the modern American labour movement, but it is worth noting in passing that a significant step forward was taken in 1932 by the passage of the Norris La Guardia Act, which outlawed the yellow dog contract. The first step towards the general encouragement of unions was taken by the Roosevelt administration in Section 7(a) of the National Industrial Recovery Act of 1933, which protected the rights of workers to join unions. (The railway unions had managed to obtain legislation favourable to themselves in 1926.) Roosevelt had no real idea of how to stimulate industrial recovery, but he saw the desirability of social and industrial experiments, and one of these was the sponsoring of unions based on the controversial theory that under-consumption required higher wages to create higher demand. However, the NIRA was declared unconstitutional by the Supreme Court in 1935, and as a replacement, Congress passed the most favourable piece of legislation ever enacted for labour in America, the Wagner Act. This specifically stated that the federal government encouraged the practice of collective bargaining and created unfair labour practices to prevent employers interfering with employee rights and to make them 'bargain in good faith'. Perhaps even more importantly, it set up the National Labor Relations Board (NLRB) to administer the Act and to determine issues of recognition through representation elections based on the certification of one single union as the representative of all employees in a designated bargaining unit.

This system of recognition did however beg a question of enormous significance for the development of American collective bargaining, namely what should be the basis of the appropriate bargaining unit. The AFL at this time was still craft-based, and it wanted units which were based on occupational interests. However the NIRA had set off a reaction both within the union movement and spontaneously amongst workers in manufacturing. A small group of unions favouring an industrial principle of organisation, led by John L. Lewis of the Mineworkers, broke away from the AFL to form the Congress of Industrial Organizations in 1935. The CIO immediately capitalised on the spontaneous growth of union feeling in manufacturing and chartered such industrial unions as the United Steelworkers and the United Automobile Workers. In spite of the Wagner Act, which was validated by the Supreme Court in 1937, many large employers, including the big car, rubber and steel companies, refused recognition, and around 1937 there were some of the most celebrated and often bloody strikes of American labour history. Most resulted in recognition for the CIO unions, and the CIO rapidly grew to a similar size of the AFL. This was a period, perhaps the only period, when labour took the initiative with the backing of government and to a considerable extent public opinion also, and created for themselves a new economic and political order. The president of the CIO, John L. Lewis, became the most visible public figure after Roosevelt himself. The measure of growth during this period was that union membership tripled between 1933 and 1939.

The AFL was forced to respond to the CIO challenge by becoming much more aggressive in its organising and changing its structure away from a craft base to become much more eclectic. Thus important AFL unions such as the Machinists could only grow in manufacturing by becoming craft-industrial unions, seeking to organise related workers wherever its key skill workers had jobs, but not happy for the skilled workers to be swamped by the unskilled. There were thus many situations where rival AFL and CIO unions were competing in the same plant, but not always desirous of the same group of workers. This was where the battles over the appropriate bargaining unit arose, and it was a problem which the NLRB resolved by holding what were in effect two elections, one based on a craft unit and one based on a more inclusive industrial unit. If the craft workers voted for the craft union, it would be certified for the craft union only, but if they voted for the industrial unit, they would become part of the larger industrial unit. This did not prevent continued disagreement, with the AFL unions claiming that the NLRB favoured industrial units, and the CIO unions claiming that the presence of a craft unit upset the principle of industrial unionism and weakened any industrial group. The Board has continued to find this issue one of the most difficult, for even after the official AFL-CIO merger in 1955, unions have competed for any given group, and the bargaining unit decision has greatly influenced the outcome.

The Second World War was another period of advance for the American labour movement, with membership reaching some 36 per cent of non-agricultural employment by 1945, even though many of its leaders thought that the compromises they had to make slowed down the organising momentum of the immediate prewar period. But labour was given an important place in the war effort and a tripartite National War Labor Board was established to deal with disputes. This was a period of consolidation and working together with management, and from this time also dates the developments of a sophisticated system of grievance procedures culminating in third-party arbitration, which has become one of the hallmarks of the American collective bargaining system.

In many respects, the end of the war marked the end of the golden age of American trade unionism. After the war there was an outbreak of strikes as workers gave up their wartime compromise, and public opinion, which had backed the unions against the dominant power of big business, now saw the unions as becoming too dominant in their turn. With the onset of the Cold War, there was also a reaction against Communist influence in some of the CIO unions, and the outcome was the Taft-Hartley Act of 1947. This was seen as union-busting legislation, but its main intention was to balance the employer unfair labour practices with union unfair labour practices, especially activities seen as detrimental to employees, but including some aspects of collective action such as the secondary boycott.

The more recent developments in the American labour movement can be mentioned more briefly, since they become involved in more detailed discussion later in the chapter. In 1955 the AFL and CIO merged, since the AFL unions in particular had lost most of their craft distinctiveness and competition between the two federations was not only taking up much of their organising energy, but was seen as wasteful and harmful to their public image.

A further feature of public image which was significant at this period was the issue of corruption. Labour in America had always been subject to the influence of racketeering as gangster or Mafia groups had seized control of locals, but between 1955 and 1960 there was a series of Congressional hearings under Senator McClellan which disclosed a widespread and unsavoury state of affairs. As George Meany, the AFL-CIO president, noted in 1957: 'We thought we knew a few things about trade union corruption, but we didn't know the half of it, one-tenth of it, or the one-hundredth part of it.' One outcome was the Landrum-Griffin Act of 1959, which set out certain standards of internal practice for trade unions. Another was the expulsion of several unions from the new Federation, notably the Teamsters and the Longshoremen; however, the expected decline of these unions did not occur, and the Teamsters became a dangerous independent, challenging many other unions in strategic areas. Indeed one of the worrying features for the Federation was its own weakness, for the Mineworkers had left the CIO a decade earlier and the Auto Workers, dissatisfied with the complacency of the Federation, were to leave a decade later.

Three further aspects need a brief mention. One was the rising significance of the public sector as a source of union organisation from the early 1960s. A second was the increasing difficulty of organisation in the developing areas of industry, in the white-collar occupations in the South, and amongst women, and growing self-confidence amongst employers that unionism could be rebuffed. The third feature was the increasing political weakness of the labour movement. These are, however, matters which bring us into the last decade.

The Decade 1970-1980

It is now time to examine the extent of American union organisation in more detail, and in particular the problems of the present and future. Table 6.1A shows historical growth of union membership from the first date, 1880, at which it is sensible to give actual numbers, up to 1976, which are unfortunately the most recent data available. Table 6.1B includes in membership those bodies which do not·call themselves unions but nevertheless engage in bargaining activities; most are professional bodies and by far the largest is the National Education Association, the main organisation for teachers. This division incidentally indicates that there are considerable problems about the precise measurement and boundaries of labour movement membership or indeed collective bargaining coverage, but these are issues which cannot concern us here.

What does concern us is the indication from the table that the peak point of organisation by density came immediately after the Second World War, and that one third of that percentage had been lost by 1976. However, actual membership continued to rise after 1945, if not as fast as the total labour force, and since the non-union organisations only began to bargain in the mid-1960s or so, the total members involved in bargaining grew quite substantially. But even this growth has now been reversed with an absolute decline in numbers in both parts of the table between 1974 and 1976. This may be a temporary aberration, but it is a very worrying development for the labour market in the context of a continued rapid growth of the labour force.

Table 6.2 takes the argument a stage further by showing the major sectoral breakdowns of membership. As can be seen, the major growth

Table 6.1A: Union Membership as a Percentage of Non-agricultural Employment, Selected Years, 1880-1976

Year	Thousands	Percent of non-agricultural employment	Year	Thousands	Percent of non-agricultural employment
1880	200.0	2.3	1945	14,796	35.8
1890	372.0	2.7	1956	17,490	33.4
1900	865.5	4.8	1966	17,940	28.1
1910	2,140.5	8.4	1968	18,916	27.8
1920	5,047.8	16.3	1970	19,381	27.4
1930	3,392.8	8.8	1972	19,435	26.4
1933	2,857	11.5	1974	20,199	25.8
1939	8,980	28.9	1976	19,432	24.3

Table 6.1B: Membership in Bargaining Organisations as a Percentage of Non-agricultural Employment, Selected Years, 1968-1976

Year	Thousands	Percent of non-agricultural employment
1968	20,721	30.5
1970	21,248	30.0
1972	21,657	29.4
1974	22,809	29.1
1976	22,463	28.3

Source: US Bureau of Labor Statistics, *Handbook of Labor Statistics,* various issues.

Table 6.2A: Union Membership by Industrial Sector, 1956-1976 ('000s)

Year	Manufacturing Members	Manufacturing % organised	Private Non-manufacturing Members	Private Non-manufacturing % organised	Government Members	Government % organised
1956	8,839	51.3	8,350	29.9	915	12.6
1970	9,173	47.4	9,198	23.6	2,318	18.5
1972	8,920	46.7	9,458	22.9	2,460	18.4
1974	9,144	45.6	9,520	21.5	2,920	20.5
1976	8,463	44.6	9,533	20.9	3,009	20.1

Table 6.2B: Membership in Bargaining Organisations by Industrial Sector, Selected Years, 1970-1976

Year	Manufacturing Members	Manufacturing % organised	Private Non-manufacturing Members	Private Non-manufacturing % organised	Government Members	Government % organised
1970	9,173	47.4	9,305	23.9	4,080	32.5
1972	8,920	46.7	9,619	23.3	4,520	33.9
1974	9,144	45.6	9,705	22.0	5,345	37.7
1976	8,463	44.6	9,721	21.3	5,853	39.2

Source: US Bureau of Labor Statistics, *Handbook of Labor Statistics,* various issues.

in the period 1960-1980 has come in the governmental sector, much of it through associations rather than unions as such. Even now the governmental sector is not nearly as heavily unionised as in most other countries, and it must still represent the major potential area for growth in the labour movement. One of the traditional explanations for the poor organising performance of US labour is that the structure of the labour force is moving away from labour's heartland, manufacturing; this is true, but as the table shows, there is a declining density even in manufacturing. What has happened is that the geographical and occupational labour force structures have changed in manufacturing away from the north-east to the south, away from urban to rural areas, away from men to women and especially away from blue-collar to white-collar occupations. Table 6.3 indicates the occupational densities of union membership, and the weakness in the white-collar groupings is evident. Many of those who are organised come from the government sector. The geographical skew in union density is also very considerable. Five states, New York, Michigan, West Virginia, Pennsylvania and Washington, have more than 40 per cent of their labour force organised, while Mississippi and North and South Carolina have less than 15 per cent. Six states, in fact, account for more than half the total union membership. On a sex basis, women had only half the degree of unionisation of men, 14 per cent as opposed to 28 per cent in 1975. Finally non-whites are more likely than whites to be members of unions, at 27 per cent versus 22 per cent, again in 1975. Both women and non-whites have been increasing their degree of unionisation in recent years.

The implications of a falling union density are serious in a number of ways, but most of all economically, and especially where wages are a significant part of competitive markets. As Roomkin and Juris (1978) have put it: 'Because bargaining power is still strongly related to union penetration and union penetration is declining, we expect to see significant changes in the industrial relations systems in manufacturing and construction.' The main reasons for falling penetration are probably still much the same as those already described in the pre-Wagner Act, namely employer attitudes, law, and union structure, but before proceeding to these in their modern guise we shall look briefly at unorganised worker attitudes towards unions.

Kochan (1979), using the 1977 Quality of Employment Survey, found that some 33 per cent of the non-union labour force would be willing to vote for unionisation if given the opportunity. Two-thirds of non-white workers in the sample indicated a preference for

Table 6.3: Occupational Penetration of Union Members, 1975

	Per cent in unions
Blue-collar Workers	40.5
Craft workers	41.4
Operatives	43.6
Non-farm labourers	31.0
Service workers	13.1
White-collar Workers	12.1
Professional and technical	14.1
Managerial and administrative	6.5
Clerical	15.9
Salesworkers	4.4
All Occupations	22.3

Source: Bureau of Labor Statistics, quoted in Kochan. It should be noted that the figures are from a different survey, one of individuals, than for Tables 6.1 and 6.2, which were based on information from unions and associations.

unionisation, by far the strongest positive variables discovered. At the other end of the scale managerial and administrative workers were far less supportive of unionism than the average. But no other significant variables appeared, whether age, education, sex, or industry. The factors that seemed to induce people towards unionisation were job-related conditions, not broadly-based ideological or social principles. The indications are therefore that there is a willingness to join unions if the circumstances were right. But translating this into actual membership is clearly difficult. Why?

There have been various discussions of this issue (Kochan, 1980, ch.5) involving a number of different variables, but we will only be able to look at the three mentioned above. Employers have become much more confident than in the immediate post-war period that they can defeat unions in elections, not least by avoiding the job-related conditions which create a willingness to unionise. This is especially concerned with geographical change, since companies expanding to the South usually hope thereby to avoid unionisation. They offer attractive wages, benefits and working conditions, and establish selection procedures and training programmes to avoid unionism. Such efforts are not always successful, but not through lack of trying to anticipate employee needs and offering as much as the union could expect to get. There has been a growth in anti-union consultancy companies, and many unionised companies are questioning whether their investment in union goodwill pays dividends.

Employer resistance is also reflected in legal developments. The number of elections won by unions has declined from around 80 per cent in the early years to under 50 per cent in recent years, the number of successful decertification elections has risen rapidly from 300 in 1970 to 849 in 1979 and the numbers of unfair labour practices for illegal discharge for union activity rose by 250 per cent between 1961 and 1976. Moreover, there was an increase in procrastinating tactics before elections to weaken the union drive, and as a result the AFL-CIO has sought a legislative restructuring of the procedures for elections for much of the decade. The issue came to a head in 1978, when the Carter administration backed a bill to this effect, but it was talked out in Congress. The net result of these developments is that favourable legislation is unlikely to be adequate to sustain union organising drives.

The third issue is union structure, which to some extent prejudges the next section, so suffice it to say here that the present union structure is not conducive to encouraging white-collar workers to organise in what are overwhelmingly blue-collar unions. Yet some 29 per cent of unorganised white-collar workers wanted union representation in the 1977 survey. Even in blue-collar areas organising drives are expensive, and since most union members are interested only in their own bargaining unit, it is difficult to persuade them to spend money on organising people who are not going to affect their own conditions. But it is not just the union structure but the bargaining structure which makes members parochial, and there is little chance of changing that. We therefore leave the question of union growth with some severe question marks about the growth potential of the American movement, although by the same token it should not be thought to be in danger of imminent collapse.

Trade Union Structure

The three key levels of union organisation are the local, the national and the federation, although there are also some intermediate bodies. Figure 6.1 indicates the structure of the AFL-CIO, and Table 6.4 lists those unions with more than 100,000 members. Those unions marked 'Ind.' and all the associations are not part of the AFL-CIO, but even though the two biggest unions are thus outside the federation, it does comprise some 78 per cent of union membership and 108 of the 210 bargaining organisations in the list compiled by the Bureau of Labor Statistics. Mergers between unions are reasonably frequent,

Figure 6.1: The Structure of the AFL-CIO

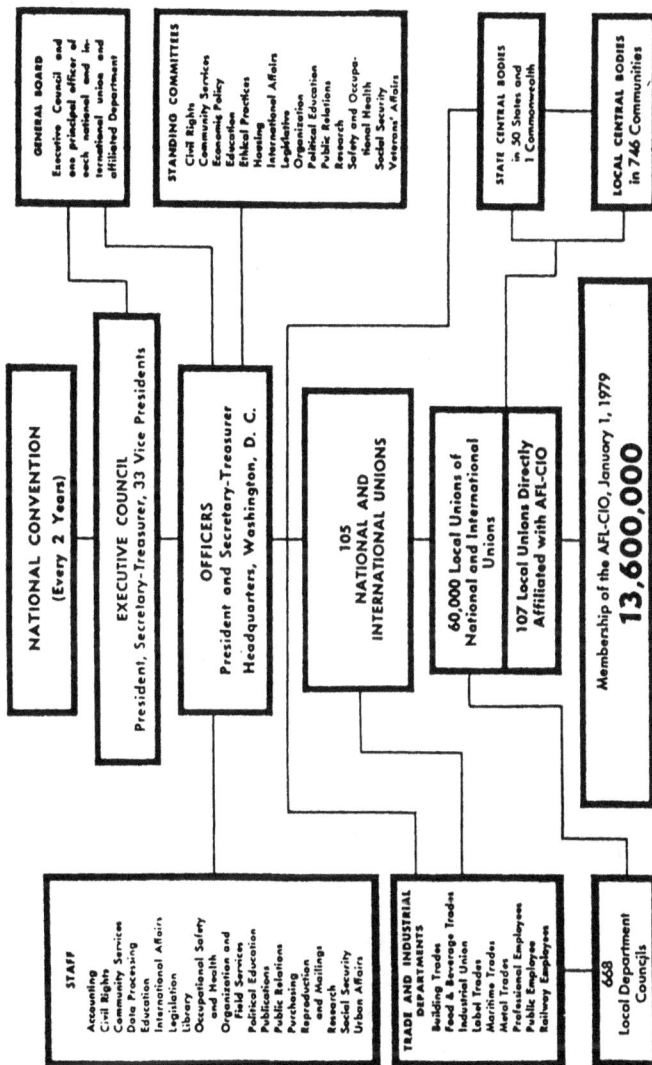

GENERAL BOARD
Executive Council and one principal officer of each national and international union and affiliated Department

STANDING COMMITTEES
Civil Rights
Community Services
Economic Policy
Education
Ethical Practices
Housing
International Affairs
Legislative
Organization
Political Education
Public Relations
Research
Safety and Occupational Health
Social Security
Veterans' Affairs

STATE CENTRAL BODIES
in 50 States and 1 Commonwealth

LOCAL CENTRAL BODIES
in 745 Communities

NATIONAL CONVENTION
(Every 2 Years)

EXECUTIVE COUNCIL
President, Secretary-Treasurer, 33 Vice Presidents

OFFICERS
President and Secretary-Treasurer
Headquarters, Washington, D. C.

105 NATIONAL AND INTERNATIONAL UNIONS

60,000 Local Unions of National and International Unions

107 Local Unions Directly Affiliated with AFL-CIO

Membership of the AFL-CIO, January 1, 1979
13,600,000

STAFF
Accounting
Civil Rights
Community Services
Data Processing
Education
International Affairs
Legislation
Library
Occupational Safety and Health
Organization and Field Service
Political Education
Publications
Public Relations
Purchasing
Reproduction and Mailings
Research
Social Security
Urban Affairs

TRADE AND INDUSTRIAL DEPARTMENTS
Building Trades
Food & Beverage Trades
Industrial Union
Label Trades
Maritime Trades
Metal Trades
Professional Employees
Public Employee
Railway Employees

668 Local Department Councils

Source: Directory of National Unions and Employee Associations, 1975; US Department of Labor BLS Bulletin (1977), p.2.

Table 6.4: National Unions and Employee Associations reporting 100,000 members or more, 1974

Organisation	Members	Organisation	Members
Unions:		Unions:	
Teamsters (Ind.)	1,973,000	Rubber	191,000
Automobile workers (Ind.)	1,545,000	Iron workers	182,000
Steelworkers	1,300,000	Retail, wholesale	180,000
Electrical (IBEW)	991,000	Oil, chemical	177,000
Machinists	943,000	Firefighters	172,000
Carpenters	820,000	Textile workers	167,000
Retail clerks	651,000	Electrical (UE) (Ind.)	163,000
Labourers	650,000	Sheet metal	161,000
State, county	648,000	Transport workers	150,000
Service employees	550,000	Bricklayers	148,000
Meat cutters	525,000	Transit union	140,000
Communications workers	499,000	Boilermakers	138,000
Hotel	452,000	Bakery	134,000
Teachers	444,000	Printing and graphic	129,000
Operating engineers	415,000	Maintenance of way	119,000
Ladies' garment	405,000	Typographical	111,000
Clothing workers	350,000	Woodworkers	108,000
Musicians	330,000	Government (NACE) (Ind.)	—
Paperworkers	301,000	Graphic arts	100,000
Government (AFGE)	300,000	Federal employees	
Electrical (IUE)	298,000	(NFFE) (Ind.)	100,000
Postal workers	249,000	Associations:	
Transportation union	238,000	Education association	1,470,000
Railway clerks	235,000	Civil service (NYS)	207,000
Letter carriers	232,000	Nurses association	196,000
Plumbers	228,000	Police	147,000
Mineworkers (Ind.)	220,000	California	106,000
Painters	211,000		

Source: Directory of National Unions and Employee Associations, 1975, p.65.

although not to the extent hoped for by the 1955 merger of the two federations; between 1955 and 1977 there were some 53 such mergers.

The local union in America is generally more powerful and better organised than its counterparts elsewhere, as is commensurate with a decentralised system of bargaining. There are two basic types of local:

those based on single plants, which are common in large-scale
manufacturing industry, and those which are geographically based,
drawing in workers from several employers, and frequently craft-based.
Both types are governed by elected officials, usually a president,
secretary-treasurer and executive committee, and there will also in
most cases be a negotiating committee, a finance committee and shop
stewards who are the union representatives in sub-divisions of the
local's jurisdiction. It should be noted that the shop stewards are more
closely integrated into the official union structure than is the case in
Britain and have relatively less independent power.

In the plant-based locals, officials are not normally paid or full time,
although this may happen in some of the larger locals. In the more
dispersed union local, however, there is usually a full-time business
agent who is in practice more important than the president, especially
in the building trades where jobs are relatively transient. Moreover,
because of the more scattered nature of the dispersed local's
membership, participation tends to be more limited, again giving
more power to the business agent. For routine matters, participation
is very limited, with 10 per cent attendance being unusual, but there
is normally a high turnout for important issues such as the election
of officers, the taking of a strike vote, or the ratification of a contract.

Although the local is a powerful body by European standards,
it is subject to formal controls by the national, and these controls
have tended to increase over the years, not least because bargaining
has tended to centralise somewhat. The local is chartered by the
national, and the national's constitutional power over it often extends
to approving collective agreements, sanctioning local strikes,
supervising local elections and disciplinary proceedings, and inspecting
financial records. Varying amounts of subscriptions are sent to the
national, more in industrial unions than craft unions, but there is
usually effective financial control over strikes, since American
workers only take official strike action if they are paid. The national
also has a degree of control with its use of political patronage for
jobs higher in the union hierarchy for ambitious local officers, and
in the last resort the national can establish a trusteeship over the
local and put in its own representatives as officials.

The national union is the basic unit of American trade unionism and
the strongest single entity in the system. It is controlled by the national
convention, but by no means all unions hold annual conventions. In
most unions the convention elects the national officers, although there
are some in which this is done by a vote of the total membership. The

convention also has the final say in policy issues, changes in the
constitution, and is the highest tribunal for internal disciplinary
proceedings. Nevertheless, most conventions can be manipulated by
the officers and the executive committee, who are responsible for
policy and administration between conventions; clearly the longer
the period between conventions the greater is the power of these
officials.

It is far from easy to challenge the incumbent officials, but there
have been sufficient examples of this being done successfully for
there not to be complete security of office. In any case there is an
argument in favour of strong leadership of unions, as the Mineworkers
illustrated by their internal difficulties under a weak president in the
late 1970s. Nevertheless the question of union democracy at the
national level is one which has caused a good deal of concern in the US,
and was in large part the subject of the 1959 Landrum-Griffin Act.
There is some degree of factionalism in most unions, although the
Typographical Union, which has an explicit two-party system, is
probably unique in the world.

One of the most notable features of the American union movement
is that the central federation, the AFL-CIO, is very weak by comparison
with the national unions. Not only do the latter preserve their autonomy
very jealously, but there is a significant proportion of the total union
membership outside the federation anyway, and the federation can
only perform a limited number of services for its affiliates in a
decentralised bargaining system. There is little sense of ideological
solidarity in the American movement, and relatively little decision-
making which needs to be done centrally in a system which is based
on collective bargaining, and relatively little political clout to be
exercised on behalf of the unions.

Nevertheless, the AFL-CIO has as its major function the task of
representing the movement on matters of common concern, and with
the increased intrusion of the state into matters affecting industrial
relations, it has become more significant within the movement in the
last 15 years or so. It also has three other primary functions. One is
to resolve disputes between member unions, especially over
jurisdictional questions; this was indeed one of the major attractions
of a federation for the early craft unions. The second is to maintain
standards of behaviour within the labour movement, but as we have
already noted, although the powers of expulsion have been used, they
have not been as effective as the federation had hoped, and too many
expulsions would obviously weaken the federation itself. The third is

to provide a point of co-ordination for union activities, of which the
two main ones are probably political education and organising. It is
in this last area that the federation has been perhaps most heavily
criticised, given the lack of union penetration into key areas of the
economy, and it was in fact one of the main reasons for the UAW
leaving it in 1968, just as it was one of the great hopes of the AFL-CIO
merger.

As well as the central AFL-CIO, Figure 6.1 shows that there are
various subordinate bodies. In Washington there are of course standing
committees and staff groupings, but more importantly the industrial
departments, which act to co-ordinate the activities of unions within
a given sector. These latter have somewhat increased their role in
collective bargaining and structural questions in recent years, a function
which has traditionally been withheld from the federation. Outside
Washington there are state central bodies in all the 50 states, carrying
out the considerable amount of political activity required at this
level, since many labour issues are state rather than federal matters in
the US. Finally, there are the local central bodies, usually called city
centrals, equivalent to the trades councils in Britain.

Trade Union Policy

In a book published in 1920, after his death, Hoxie identified five
different types of trade unions and trade union policies in the United
States. These were business unionism, uplift unionism, revolutionary
unionism, predatory unionism, and dependent unionism. These five
types have been present to a greater or lesser extent throughout most
of American trade union history, although revolutionary unionism
has been extinct for some two decades, but in this section we will deal
with business unionism only, since it was then and is now by far the
most dominant form of trade unionism in America. Moreover Hoxie's
description of business unionism fits as well now as it did at that time:

> It is essentially trade conscious, rather than class conscious. That is
> to say it expresses the viewpoint and interests of the workers in the
> craft or industry rather than those of the working class as a whole.
> It aims chiefly at more, here and now, for the organized workers
> of the craft or industry, in terms mainly of higher wages, shorter
> hours, and better working conditions, regardless for the most part
> of the welfare of the workers outside the particular organic group,

and regardless in general of political and social considerations, except insofar as these bear directly upon its own economic ends. It is conservative in the sense that it professes belief in natural rights and accepts as inevitable, if not as just, the existing capitalistic organization and the wage system, as well as existing property rights and the binding force of contract. It regards unionism mainly as a bargaining institution that seeks its ends chiefly through collective bargaining, supported by such methods as experience from time to time indicates to be effective in sustaining and increasing its bargaining power . . . In method business unionism is prevailingly temporate and economic. It favours voluntary arbitration, deprecates strikes, and avoids political action, but it will refuse arbitration, and will resort to strikes and politics when such actions seems best calculated to support its bargaining efforts and to increase its bargaining power (pp.45-6).

Several features may be identified from the above statement. Union orientation in America is very heavily towards collective bargaining, this bargaining tends to have a degree of parochialism attached to it, there is relatively low attention to politics as a means of achieving ends, and the unions generally accept the existence of capitalism and the social and economic order. Furthermore they emphasise the strength of the American system from the union point of view, namely at the day-to-day levels, reflecting the strength of institutional structure, the comprehensiveness and codification of the system at the level of localised collective bargaining, the professionalism of the actors, and the relatively closely defined links between levels and organisation on both sides. By the same token they point to some of the weaknesses of the system at the higher levels, such as the lack of any coherent philosophy within the union movement, the apparent complacency about questions of union structure and level of organisation, and far from least, the loss of political power and credibility of unionism within American society, and consequentially the fact that there are few issues of significance being channelled through the industrial relations system. In other words the system is not in any major way an agent of social change. Instead it remains a means of setting the terms and conditions of employment for an increasingly narrow group of American workers, creating no social dynamic as it does so, and posing no challenge to the established order. Much of this orientation has to do with two features, namely the decentralised system of collective bargaining, and the lack of any labour or socialist party in American politics.

Taking the issue of decentralised collective bargaining first, it is arguable that it was employers in American industrial relations history rather than unions who created the system of decentralisation, but there is also no doubt that it was convenient for the unions which existed, since they would have found it very difficult indeed to achieve an adequate degree of organisation to enforce industry-wide bargaining. There is moreover a good deal of evidence that union members want the existing parochial state of union orientation to continue. The 1977 Quality of Employment Survey emphasised the handling of grievances and wages, fringes and job security as the main priorities of union members. Their main complaint, in fact, was that unions were not sufficiently responsive to these demands, especially in terms of the unions' internal administration and communications. The issues with the lowest priority were increasing the amount of say that workers have on the job, or in running the employer's business. There was, however, some indication that an expansion of union activity in areas such as health and safety might be appreciated. Nevertheless the overall finding was that there were no changes in the fairly narrowly defined orientation of union memberships in comparison to the past. Nor is it easy to see that there has been any change in the national leadership on these matters. To be sure there has been a considerable turnover in the old guard of American union leadership, but the new leaders have no identifiably different perspectives to the older ones.

Of all the differences between the European and American systems of industrial relations perhaps most immediately noticeable is the political and cultural context in which they operate. The United States has never had a close connection between unionism and the political parties, nor have the parties themselves been formulated along the ideological spectrum which is general in Europe. The reasons for the absence of a labour party in the United States have often been examined: the absence of past structures; the small industrial labour force when the vote was obtained; the political attitudes of individualism and pragmatism; and to no small extent the degree of particularism within unionism and its lack of any claim to represent interests outside work. But the net result is that the American labour movement has found it very difficult to exert political power except in vary favourable circumstances, such as those of the Rooseveltian New Deal coalition. Yet there is no doubt that if an organisation is to maintain its economic power it must be able to exert political power also, and this is the problem of the American movement. The most consequential battles in the 1980s are likely to be fought out in the political arena, and recent trends in political philosophy in America are not encouraging. It is not necessarily the case that labour has changed its perspectives, but it may well be that the political system itself has changed, and that labour as an old political block has been able to do relatively little about it, although there is also no doubt that its own lack of cohesiveness, its inability to organise much beyond the traditional manual working class, and its continued taint of excessive power and corruption as far as the general public is concerned, have not helped. King (1978, p.371) has suggested two major changes in political ideas within the American political system, neither of which have been advantageous to the unions:

> The first is the decline of the idea of the New Deal as the principal organizing themes of American political life. The central idea of the New Deal was a simple one; that the Federal Government could and should be able to solve the country's economic and social problems . . . The second outstanding change in the realm of ideas is the altogether new emphasis on the value of participation in politics. In the 1960s it came to be thought good for both participating individuals and the polity that ordinary men and women should have a direct say not merely in the choice of public office holders but in the making of public policy.

Both these trends have tended to reduce the political power of labour. The New Deal ideology was essentially based upon economic issues in which labour could pose as defender of the underdog generally, and as for the second labour is effective only if acting as a monolithic block. The new style politics has several other characteristics detrimental to labour. One is the decline of party structures, with the commensurate decline in the significance of manifestos and political programmes, and a second is the rise of pressure groups. On this latter point pressure groups have of course almost always existed but were previously largely self-interested as business, labour, agriculture and the professions all illustrated, but more recently many interest groups are idealistic and the rise of dozens of competing issues and groups means that there tends to be a great deal of single-interest issues and cross voting between issues. As a result coalitions of the kind which labour needs to be able to spread its political power over a range of different activities cannot easily be built. In these developments it is not altogether easy to see what would have been the appropriate course of events for the labour movement, short of the massive difficulties of starting a new political party or at least trying to take over the Democratic Party.

It should not be thought that the unions are entirely without influence in the political sphere; indeed Lewin (1978) has argued that they are more successful in this area than they are in the economic area of wages and fringes or in the area of non-economic working conditions. It is certainly true that a great deal of regulatory legislation has been passed in the United States in the last two decades or so. Indeed so many have been the regulatory programmes that Kochan (1980) has argued that the basic premise underlying the National Labor Relations Act, the promotion of the process of collective bargaining but neutrality with respect to the substantive outcome, should be viewed as mere historical rhetoric rather than as an accurate representation of present-day reality. Much of the legislation was promoted by or at least accepted by the unions, and it is perhaps paradoxical that the unions may in practice have lost rather than gained from such intervention. On the one hand, the legislation is causing a major impact upon existing voluntary institutions and thus to an extent taking over the role of the union through collective bargaining. If workers want their job-related conditions improved, and legislation brings them up to a certain standard, there would appear to be less reason why they should join unions, whose historical function has been the remedying of these job-related conditions. The capacity and autonomy of the industrial parties to create a separate system of industrial justice for the shop floor is no longer as appropriate when public laws are impinging upon this area, and this detracts to a very considerable extent from one of the major strengths of the American system of industrial relations, that the parties could create and monitor their own industrial relations system. On the other hand, the fact that such legislation needs to be passed at all is a condemnation of the inadequacy of collective bargaining, and therefore of the role of unionism. Moreover, many aspects of recent law are aimed at controlling unions in the interests of individuals as well as employers *vis-à-vis* both individuals and unions. American labour's strength depends upon the law, lacking sufficient economic or political power, but although a policy set up in 1935 can sustain the industrial relations system for so long, eventually it requires renewing through further backing from the political system. But labour seems unable to push through those aspects of legislative change which would further its own position, whilst those which it is able to achieve often seem to detract from its own appeal to non-unionists.

Conclusion

What then should American labour do? What new policies would give it some hope of achieving a revitalisation in the 1980s? Some commentators have argued that it should become involved in the betterment of the quality of working life, but while there has been some superficial move in this direction, for the most part American unions have tended to distrust the co-operation with management which would be required. A further possibility would be a move towards industrial democracy, the sharing of power in the managerial decision-making process. But this again is an area which strongly differentiates American and European unions, since there has been very little interest in this area in the United States. American unions are more than happy to leave the job of managing to management; in the words of Thomas Donahue of the AFL-CIO: 'We do not seek to be a partner in management — to be most likely the junior partner in success and the senior partner in failure. We do not want to blur in any way the distinctions between the respective roles of management and labor in the plant.' The result is that American labour is stagnant in policy terms, having neither an alternative policy philosophy, nor any real programme of extending beyond the narrow bounds of collective bargaining at plant levels. There is indeed a paradox here. It can be argued that it is precisely because unions in America have been unswerving in their affirmation of private property, the capitalist system and the prevailing system of government that they can be taken for granted by politicians and outflanked by managements, since they offer no alternatives and pose no threat. Their social role is being pre-empted by other institutions and they appear to have become increasingly instrumental agencies to their members. It is far from easy to see a way out of this policy box for American labour short of some type of economic situation which in the 1930s created a willingness to accept radical change.

Bibliography

Ashenfelter, O. and Pencavel, J.H., 'American Trade Union Growth,

1900-1960', *Quarterly Journal of Economics*, *83* (August 1969)

Bok, D. and Dunlop, J.T., *Labor and the American Community* (Simon and Schuster, New York, 1970)

Commons, J.R., 'American Shoemakers, 1648-1895', *Quarterly Journal of Economics, XXIV* (November 1909)

Freeman, R.B. and Medoff, I.L., 'New Estimates of the Distribution of Private Sector Unionism in the US', *Industrial and Labor Relations Review, 32* (2) (January 1979)

Hoxie, R.F., *Trade Unionism in the United States* (D. Appleton and Co., New York, 1920)

King, A., 'The American Polity in the Late 1970s: Building Coalitions in the Sand' in King, A. (ed.), *The New American Political System* (American Enterprise Institute, Washington, 1978)

Kochan, T.A., 'How American Workers View Labor Unions', *Monthly Labor Review, 102* (April 1979)

—— *Collective Bargaining and Industrial Relations* (Richard D. Irwin, Homewood, Ill., 1980)

Lewin, D., 'The Impact of Unionism on American Business: Evidence for an Assessment', *Columbia Journal of World Business* (Winter 1978)

Roomkin, M. and Juris, H.A., 'Unions in the Traditional Sectors: The Mid-Life Passage of the Labor Movement', International Industrial Relations Association *Proceedings* (1978), pp.212-22

Ross, A.M., *Trade Union Wage Policy* (University of California Press, Berkeley, 1948)

Slichter, S.H., Healy, J.J. and Livernash, E.R., *The Impact of Collective Bargaining on Management* (Brookings Institution, Washington, DC, 1960)

7 WEST GERMANY

Eric Owen Smith

Introduction

Against an oscillating economic background of spurts in expansion and spasms of chaos, the long-term growth of German trade unions has displayed four basic features. First, the degree of disunity within the movement. Secondly, the negative attitude of employers. Thirdly, the active role played by the state and the law. Fourthly, developments in industrial democracy or 'co-determination'.

Following the repeal of the Anti-Socialist Act in 1890, which had driven the movement underground, trade union membership doubled within a decade. By 1913 total membership had doubled again to reach 3 million, or 10 per cent of the labour force. In 1922 unionisation stood at 9 millions, or 30 per cent. It then hovered around the 4/5 million mark until the Nazis seized power and banned the movement. Following the Second World War trade unionisation reached over 40 per cent of the labour force. (Kendall; Roll; Taft.)

Trade Union Growth

c. 1871-1945

In spite of determined opposition from both the state and employers during the Imperial era, the German trade unions, although weakened by internal division, found themselves ultimately catapulted into significant positions of social and political influence after the 1918 revolution (Grebing).

However, the unions became part of the state apparatus during the Weimar Republic. The divisions within the movement grew worse. These divisions were based on both political and religious differences. Rank and file revolutionary fervour was transformed into disillusionment as time elapsed. The decline of revolutionary fervour can be gauged from the trend in strikes. These fell from about 5,000 in number in 1922 to under 500 in 1931 — a figure which resulted in Germany being top and bottom respectively of the trend in the number of strikes when compared to France, Sweden, the UK and the USA. In 1924 over 36 million working days were lost — the highest in German history (Hopkins, pp.219-20; Taft, pp.293-4). There was opposition from the

national union organisations to the extension of the works council
principle. They feared that the councils would either become the tools
of management or, alternatively, revolutionary weapons along the lines
of 1918. The experiences with works councils and, for that matter,
the compulsory arbitration and conciliation machinery were to remain
in the memory of trade union leaders.

Post-1945

Because of their resistance to National Socialism, the trade unions were
involved in the restructuring of German industry. Nevertheless, trade
union bargaining power was rather narrowly circumscribed until the
Allies imposed currency reform in 1948. Initially, trade unions were
allowed to organise only at plant and local levels. Trade union demands
for economic democracy and socialisation after the Second World War
echoed those of the post-First World War period. There was an even
larger majority of German political opinion which was anti-capitalist
and there was widespread support for public ownership. British support
for such measures had to be qualified as a result of American opposition.
German proposals along these lines were continually turned down
(Anthes, pp.80-84). In 1949, however, the Christian Democrats
(CDU/CSU) appointed a neo-liberal Economics Minister (Professor
Erhard) and they dropped their nationalisation proposals in favour
of the social market economy. Ten years later the Social Democrats
(SPD) and, to a certain extent, the trade unions were to do the same.

The Trade Unions. The wage freeze inherited by the Allies rendered
collective bargaining over money wages of secondary importance in
trade union policy until the relaxation of the freeze in November 1948.
The re-emergence of this bargaining function, along with the mounting
conviction that their political influence was waning, were behind trade
union attempts to avoid the divisions of the pre-Hitler period. An
emphasis was placed on the non-religious and party political neutral
nature of the new organisations which left them to pursue their own
independent social and economic objectives.

By far the most important step in this respect was the founding in
the British zone of the DGB — the equivalent of the TUC or North
American AFL-CIO. Hans Böckler, who was to lead this organisation,
favoured a powerful centre with regional and occupational branches.
The occupations would be grouped according to whether they were
manual workers, white-collar employees or *Beamte* (a classification
of some employees in the public sector). Böckler's proposals were

vetoed by the British occupation authorities who saw the proposed organisation as being potentially too powerful. Moreover, a British trade union delegation had advocated a small number of unions, each one of which would have complete autonomy over the industrial affairs of their members. In 1947 the revised constitution for the DGB was approved and 15 industrial affiliates were established in the British zone. Each affiliate accepted the philosophy of 'one union for each plant'. Following, first, the linking with unions in the American and French zones, as well as, secondly, the failure to agree terms for an amalgamation with the Communist-dominated unions in the Russian zone and, thirdly, the elections to the Bonn Parliament in August 1949, the DGB became the new Federal Republic's trade union federation with Böckler as its chairman. Its headquarters are in Düsseldorf where its Ruhr power base after the Second World War was also situated. A sixteenth union was formed when Textiles and Clothing split from Leather.

Proposals for a white-collar union (DAG) were drawn up in Hamburg (still the location of its headquarters) as early as 1945 and were approved by the British military authorities in 1946. The DAG was as anxious as the DGB to avoid disunity, although it could *not* accept the industrial union principle. Several conferences between the DGB and DAG culminated in 1948 with an offer from the DGB to accord *exclusive* organising rights in white-collar intensive sectors such as banking and commerce to the DAG. For its part the DAG insisted that it must have the right to organise all white-collar workers, *irrespective* of their industrial location. Agreement could not be reached, with the result that the DGB unions and the DAG established inter-zonal organisations and subsequently became competitors for membership. However, *both* organisations stress their non-religious and party-political neutral philosophies. They *both* also emphasise that the exist to promote the social, economic and cultural interests of their members.

A less serious threat to unity was the formation of a breakaway Christian trade union movement in 1955 (renamed the Federation of Christian Trade Unions (CGB) in 1959). Its establishment was opposed by prominent Christian trade unionists who wanted to avoid a divided movement. The breakaway from the DGB was partly caused by what some Christian trade unionists regarded as an anti-CDU campaign by the DGB during the 1953 federal elections, although this party's vote increased. Other reasons advanced were the debate over the nature of defence contributions at the 1954 DGB Congress and a

controversial speech at the same congress on the political role of the
unions. Support for the CGB dwindled even further during the 1960s
(Limmer, pp.105-6) but other small unions emerged.

These developments were reflected by a fall in trade union density.
Prior to the re-emergence of the large industrial undertakings, the
proportion of the labour force organised in the Federal Republic
reached 50 per cent in 1951 – a much higher proportion than Weimar
in approximately half the land area. But by 1960 it had fallen to
40 per cent. The decline continued until 1970 but during the 1970s
there was a revival and the figure now stands at over 40 per cent
again. (Grosser, pp.308-9; Kendall, pp.109 and 112; Kerr, 1954, p.546;
Limmer, p.130; Schuster, p.61; Taft, p.301.)

The Employers' Association. During the de-nazification programme
employers had not been allowed to organise. In 1950 the Confederation
of German Employers' Associations (BDA) was formed. It differed from
its Weimar predecessor (which had been abolished by the Nazis) in that
it included in membership not just employers' associations from
industry, but also from banking, transport, insurance, commerce,
handicrafts and agriculture (Bunn, p.653). The most notable exceptions
are the iron and steel employers and Volkswagen, the latter having
traditionally negotiated its own agreements direct. Employers'
associations which bargain for public sector employers are also
unaffiliated. There are 47 vertically organised national associations
affiliated to the BDA (for example, Engineering Employers and
Agriculture and Forestry Employers); in addition there are 12
horizontally organised state (Länder) associations in membership.
Through these direct members' associations, a further 750 employers'
associations (usually regional vertical or local horizontal) are
indirectly members of the BDA. As a result, the employers are a
strongly united and disciplined body whose bargaining is centrally
co-ordinated through the BDA. *One is bound to conclude that the
employers are far better organised than the employees.*

A BDA memorandum in 1954 recommended that each bargaining
unit should establish strike protection funds; at the same time the
BDA established its own permanent co-ordinating committee. In 1956
the Ruhr coal owners were invited by their employers' association
to create a DM 6 million 'solidarity fund'. In 1961 'Solidarity between
Employers' was extended to include not engaging workers on strike at
other firms; not enticing customers of strike-bound firms; or,
conversely, not transferring orders to strike-free firms. Guidelines

were issued in 1965; in 1970 they were supplemented so as to include
unofficial strike action. (Aaron and Wedderburn, pp.44, 193 and 280;
Adams and Rummel, p.5; Grosser, pp.304-5; Hopkins, p.210,
historical.)

The BDA is opposed to any restriction of private property ownership
and it found an ally in the CDU after the latter had been converted
to the social market economy. Under the strong leadership of Adenauer,
the CDU government of the 1950s built up a strong working relationship
with the BDA and, more particularly, its sister organisation (the
Federation of German Industry: BDI). The relative political stature
of the BDA increased in the 1960s and 1970s, particularly under
Dr Schleyer who for a short time before his assassination in 1977 was
president of both the BDA and the BDI (*Die Zeit* (Hamburg), 24/77 and
36/77).

The State and the Law. The 1949 Constitution of the Federal Republic
differs from the Weimar Constitution in an important respect: there
was no attempt to enshrine the concepts of industrial democracy and
specific collective bargaining rights, much less public ownership, in this
new order. It would be left to the collective bargaining parties
autonomously to determine money wages (*Tarifautonomie*) in a spirit
of co-operation (*Mitwirkung*) and co-determination (*Mitbestimmung*)
(Bendix, pp.26-7). As a result there was no codified collective bargaining
law and a general code has been formulated from rulings made by the
courts (usually by the Federal Labour Court or the Federal
Constitutional Court). In fact the judiciary have demonstrated that
they are not bound by the text of the Constitution and that they have
the power to create law if they wish (Aaron and Wedderburn, p.195).
The founding of the Federal Republic also gave the Federal Labour
Court the opportunity to begin anew without the burdens of precedent
(ibid., p.268).

In other words, freedom of speech, assembly and association are
granted in general terms by articles 5, 8 and 9, respectively, of the
Constitution, *but the courts have asserted the right to rule on these
concepts when applied to collective bargaining.* Hence a strike is not
legal unless supported by a trade union which *ipso facto* renders
unofficial strikes, and probably sympathetic strikes, illegal (Kendall,
p.125). A political strike is similarly unlawful – the only exceptions
being, first, a short 'demonstration' stoppage and, secondly, a possible
right under article 20(4) of the Federal Constitution to resist anybody
who attempts to overthrow the constitutionally established order

(Aaron and Wedderburn, pp.328-30; Bendix, pp.40-1). This article probably takes into account the attempted Kapp *Putsch* and the Nazi seizure of power. Peaceful picketing may be justified under the constitutional right of freedom of speech, but all employees who want to work must have free and secure access to the premises of an employer. Case law prohibits both force and mass picketing. However, whether *groups* of workers may pass a picket line, and whether insults hurled by a picket threaten secure access, are uncertain areas (Aaron and Wedderburn, p.274).

If the negotiation of *new* agreements results in a dispute of interests, the parties are considered to be at liberty to pursue sanctions, provided such sanctions are 'socially adequate'. The labour courts work from the premise that since all industrial disputes cause economic disruption, strikes are undesirable (ibid., pp.195 and 267; Bendix, p.37; Kendall, p.116; Rajewsky, p.67). All other means of resolving a conflict must have been explored before a strike is called. This in turn requires both parties to avoid industrial sanctions during the *currency* of an agreement — the so-called relative 'peace obligation', a concept which originated in Germany (Aaron and Wedderburn, pp.169-70; *Die Zeit*, 46/80, p.28).

Labour courts therefore play a crucial role in the Federal Republic. They operate at local, state and federal level and are composed of professional judges and lay wing members. In addition, the so-called Big Senate, also at federal level, makes rulings on subjects of fundamental importance — such as cases on the holding of strike ballots and lockouts. The labour courts will hear cases brought as a result of either individual or collective disputes of rights. In the former case an employer/employee relationship is usually involved, although rival work groups may also take their disputes to the court. When the court arbitrates on collective disputes it does so either on the basis of a collective agreement or on the basis of the employer/works council relationship (Ramm).

Developments in Industrial Democracy. When the British created the German Steel Trusteeship Administration, in order to decartelise this industry, they invited trade unionists to participate in the process. In 1947 eight large concerns were broken down into 24 smaller companies, each with the two traditional boards. (The supervisory board (*Aufsichtsrat*) meets about four times annually and concerns itself with long-term strategy. A collegiate management board of about three persons (*Vorstand*) elects a 'spokesman' and takes day-to-day responsibility for management (Lawrence, pp.40-1).) The supervisory board of each new steel company was composed of five employee representatives, five shareholders' representatives and an eleventh member from the Trustee Board. The management board was expanded to include a union-nominated labour director who was to co-operate closely with the works council. Members of the works council were elected representatives of both manual and white-collar workers. This council provided two members of the supervisory board; a further member was provided by the industry's union and the DGB supplied one member directly and nominated the fifth.

In 1950 it became clear to the unions that legislation which did not envisage employee representation on supervisory boards was a distinct probability. Strike ballots were therefore conducted in the iron and steel and in the coal industries, the so-called *Montan* industries. There were majorities of over 90 per cent in both industries in favour of strike action if the CDU government did not recognise the system of industrial democracy already practised in iron and steel and also extend these rights to coal — an industry in which the unscrambling process had been even more difficult. Adenauer, the Federal Chancellor at that time, expressed the view that such a strike threat was political in character. Ultimately, however, he was forced to make an eleventh-hour concession and in 1951 the Co-determination Act confirmed the parity, labour director and works council provisions described in the last paragraph. An 'impartial' eleventh man on the supervisory board, however, was now elected by at least a majority of three on each side; otherwise a complex mediation procedure is required. Moreover, two representatives on the supervisory board are proposed by the works council, two by the union and a further 'outsider' by the DGB. These provisions were extended to the coal industry by the same Act with the result that the strike threat was lifted in both industries. (Hirsch-Weber, 1959, pp.92-3 and p.151ff; McPherson, 1951, pp.24-5; Schuster, pp.37-8; Sturmthal, p.61; Taft, p.310.)

This still left the rest of German industry without legislation on co-determination. Hostility between the employers and unions increased as a national two-day newspaper strike, protest strikes and demonstrations were mounted to secure the same co-determination rights as those secured in the *Montan* industries. Co-operation was also withdrawn from government committees. A vitriolic criticism of the post-war co-operation between the unions and the British occupational forces was launched in the BDA's journal (Hirsch-Weber, 1959, p.113). The trade unions were to emerge from the conflict discredited, in spite of their insistence that their claim did not represent an abuse of power in view of their contribution to Germany's economic recovery (Anthes, p.92). Moreover, the Works Constitution Act of 1952 was a diluted form of its 1951 predecessor. Employee representation was one-third of the supervisory board of joint stock companies outside of the *Montan* industries; there was no labour director; works councils were given slightly more authority than under the 1920 Act, since they were given social, economic and personnel functions; employee candidates for the supervisory board were suggested by the works councils; the effect of the 1952 Act was therefore to render the unions largely ineffective at plant level.

Although during the controversy preceding the 1952 Act a threatened general strike did not materialise, the BDA nevertheless suggested that action be taken against the printing union because of the two-day stoppage it had called. Following a number of adverse lower court decisions and various expert professors' opinions – including one written by the future president of the Federal Labour Court – the printing union voluntarily paid damages in an out-of-court settlement (Aaron and Wedderburn, pp.327-8; Bunn, pp.664-5; Rajewsky, pp.36-8). Moreover, the former chairman of the printing union, who, following Böckler's death a few weeks after the agreement on the 1951 Act, had been elected chairman of the DGB, was ousted from his post in favour of the IG Metall chairman who had taken part in the more successful 1951 campaign (Hirsch-Weber, 1959, pp.110-11; Schuster, p.42). Hence co-determination, which had started life after two world wars as a compromise between conflicting political and social pressures, neither secured the envisaged transformation of society, nor the increase in union influence at plant and national level which was originally intended by its advocates (Kerr, 1954, pp.554-5).

A separate statute (Employee Representation in the Public Sector, 1955) was enacted to cover the public services. Full co-determination rights were not granted, although similar bodies to works councils were to be established. The only exception was the railways where one-quarter of the supervisory board are employee representatives and a labour director is one of the four management board representatives. The Co-determination (Supplementation) Act, 1956, specified that parity of representation in the supervisory board must be observed if more than 50 per cent of the operations of a company were in the *Montan* industries. Such a requirement had become necessary because of the spate of mergers in these industries.

Trade Union Structure

Following the affiliation of the police union in March 1978, the DGB (*Deutscher Gewerkschaftsbund*) had 17 affiliates with a record total ot 7.75 million members. The affiliated unions are listed in their 1978 rank order (with 1950 data for comparison) in Table 7.1.

Table 7.1:DGB Affiliated Unions

| Union | Membership | | | | | |
| | 31 December 1978 | | | 31 December 1950 | | |
	Number	Per cent of total	Rank	Rank	Number	Per cent of total
Metal Workers (IGM)	2,680,798	34.6	1	1	1,352,010	24.8
Public Services, Transport and Omnibus Crews (ÖTV)	1,099,396	14.2	2	2	726,004	13.3
Chemicals, Paper and Ceramics (IGC)	650,675	8.4	3	5	409,998	7.5
Construction, Quarrying and Building Materials (BSE)	517,842	6.7	4	7	405,536	7.4
Post Office Workers (DPG)	428,878	5.5	5	9	190,500	3.5
Railway Workers (GdED)	414,195	5.3	6	4	426,059	7.8
Coal Mining and Power (IGBE)	362,148	4.7	7	3	580,661	10.6
Commerce, Banks and Insurance (HBV)	314,244	4.1	8	14	63,600	1.2
Textiles and Clothing (GTB)	290,143	3.7	9	6	409,924	7.5
Food, Drink and Catering Industries (NGG)	252,440	3.3	10	8	256,186	4.7
Education and Science (GEW)	158,734	2.0	11	15	61,037	1.2
Police (GdP)	152,486	2.0	12		—	
Printing and Paper Manufacture (IGD)	145,980	1.9	13	11	133,074	2.4
Timber and Plastics (GHK)	145,076	1.9	14	10	189,661	3.5
Leather (GL)	55,068	0.7	15	13	100,412	1.9
Arts (GK)	42,109	0.5	16	16	41,924	0.8
Market Gardening, Agriculture and Forestry (GGLF)	41,311	0.5	17	12	103,404	1.9
Totals	7,751,523	100.0	17	16	5,449,990	100.0

Sources: DGB, *Geschäftsbericht 1950-51*, p.797; DGB, *Nachrichten-Dienst*, 49/79; Institut der Deutschen Wirtschaft, *Zahlen 1979*, Tables 83-4. (Writer's translation in all three cases.)

The difficulties involved in defining an 'industry' for the purposes of trade union organisation, and the consequent need for a DGB inter-union demarcation disputes procedure, will be clear from the titles of the unions (DGB *Geschäftsbericht 1975-77*, p.436; Taft, p.304). Moreover, when the police union was formed in the early 1950s it was prevented from becoming a DGB affiliate because the ÖTV claimed that it was the strongest and most suitable union for all public sector employees.

The 16 unions which affiliated to the DGB on its federal-wide foundation have had a diverse subsequent experience in terms of membership. Perhaps surprisingly in view of the high level of cultural activity in every German city, plus the growth in television and film acting, the Arts union had almost the same membership at the end of 1978 as it had had at the end of the DGB's first year in 1950. In fact its membership generally declined until 1970. Perhaps one reason was competition from the DAG. Less surprising on grounds of changes in the economic structure is the fact that membership in mining, agriculture, textiles, leather and timber has secularly declined. Membership in metal, the public services, commerce, education and the Post Office sectors has, on the other hand, increased. Net gainers over the period 1950-78, in spite of the 1974 recession having caused losses from which they had not fully recovered by 1978, were chemicals, construction and printing. Relative increases in white-collar and female unionisation also reflected changes in the structure of the labour force. They can be clearly seen in Table 7.2.

The recession of the late 1960s exacerbated a decline in total affiliated membership which began in 1966. In fact the 1965 level was not exceeded again until 1970. Seen in these terms the effects of the 1974 recession did not have such a serious impact on total membership — by 1976 there had been an almost complete recovery. The only other year when there has been an absolute fall in membership was 1959 (Jühe, p.62).

Secular expansion and contraction of membership is not the only relevant factor when estimating a trade union's potential bargaining power. Perhaps even more important is the level of organisation compared to the level of employment in an industry ('density'). Three industries are very highly organised in this sense. They are mining, the railways and Post Office employees, all of which probably have over 75 per cent of eligible employees in membership. Industries with roughly 40 to 50 per cent density are metal, the public services, chemicals, printing and leather. Something like a third of the employees

Table 7.2: Proportionate Membership of the DGB Affiliates (%)

Type of employee	1950			1978		
	Male (1)	Female (2)	(1) + (2) as % of total membership	Male (3)	Female (4)	(3) + (4) as % of total membership
Manual employees	70.2	13.0	83.2	59.0	10.3	69.3
White-collar employees	7.7	2.8	10.5	12.7	7.3	20.0
*Beamte**	5.8	0.5	6.3	9.2	1.5	10.7
Total male/female	83.7	16.3	(100.0)	80.9	19.1	(100.0)

*This group of public sector employees will be defined below. It can be noted at this stage that *Beamte* are virtually confined to five unions. They constitute two-thirds of the postal membership; most of the education and police membership; half the railway membership; and about 100,000 of ÖTV.

Sources: Calculated by the writer from the DGB publications cited at the foot of Table 7.1.

in textiles, timber, education and the arts are organised, whereas low densities are to be found in construction, catering, commerce and agriculture (ibid., pp.62-78, with added estimates for DAG and DBB – see below). The federal state containing the Ruhr district (North Rhine-Westphalia) has well over 2 million members, while the other large engineering (including motor vehicles) states of Bavaria and Baden-Württemberg have over 1 million trade unionists each (ibid., p.79).

The ascendancy of the metal workers (IGM) has been a feature of DGB affairs. Together with the public service employees (ÖTV), IGM holds almost an absolute majority of affiliated membership. With one further ally, therefore, DGB proceedings could be dominated. The same thing could be said about the establishment of a pay norm at the beginning of each round of annual wage bargaining. IGM's current private sector ally in wage bargaining is probably the chemical workers union, although ÖTV remains an important pacesetter (Clark, p.249; *Die Zeit*, 39/79, p.25; Hirsch-Weber, 1959, p.51; Kerr, 1954, p.540; Reichel, p.480).

When the chairman designate of the DGB (an official of the Post Office Union and an SPD deputy) let it be known in 1969 that he planned to strengthen the power of the DGB over its affiliates, the IGM prevented his ultimate election. However, the IGM did not succeed in swaying the DGB on the question of nationalisation (Grebing, pp.177-8; Limmer, pp.115-24; Schuster, pp.57-61). This conflict resulted in the construction union – with only 18 per cent of its industry organised – persuading the 1963 Congress to adopt the policy of contributing to the process of regulating the existing society (Limmer, p.132). Nowadays virtually all the top union officials tend to see their role in this context. The DGB and its affiliates are themselves huge property owners. They own Europe's largest property developer (*Neue Heimat*); they also own the *Bank für Gemeinwirtschaft* which since its establishment in 1950 has become the Federal Republic's fourth largest commercial bank; their life and property insurance company, which also acts as building society, is a DM 50 million undertaking. In addition there are tourist, printing, advertising and co-operative retailing companies (Hesselbach; *The Economist* (London), 30 September 1978, pp.86-7). Parity employee representation was introduced into the property and insurance companies as well as the bank between 1968 and 1970. (The DAG is also active in the property, travel and insurance markets.) Trade union leaders sit on the supervisory boards of these and other companies.

The success of the DAG (*Deutsche Angestellten-Gewerkschaft*) has been somewhat limited. First, the proportion of white-collar employees in the labour force organised by the DAG has secularly fallen from 10 per cent in 1951 to 5 per cent in 1978 (IdDW, Table 84). Secondly, the DGB unions have doubled their white-collar organisation during this period (from 10 per cent to 20 per cent of their membership – see Table 7.2). Even the DGB rate of growth, however, was not sufficient to achieve anything more than a constant proportion of white-collar employees organised in DGB unions. This was because the number of these employees increased by 172 per cent between 1950 and 1978 (3.2m to 8.7m), whereas the number of manual workers increased by only 8 per cent (9.9m to 10.7m) (BfA, Table 2.6). As a result white-collar union density has fallen from nearly 30 per cent to 23 per cent – indeed, white-collar density now stands at almost half the level of 1931, when females in this type of union represented 22 per cent of those organised (Hirsch-Weber, 1959, p.150). There has been a gradual fall in the participation rate of males in the labour force, whereas the participation rate of females has tended to remain fairly constant at about 30 per cent (BfA, Table 2.3). The unions have complained, however, about the difficulties involved in recruiting women.

If Table 7.3 is compared with Table 7.1, it will be seen that the chief areas of competition for members are commerce, banking and insurance (i.e. HBV in the DGB). The only other area of any significance is the public service, although ÖTV (in 1978) had 455,827 white-collar employees in membership. Relations between the DAG on the one hand, and HBV and ÖTV on the other hand, have deteriorated in recent years.

There are three associations affiliated to the CGB (*Christlicher Gewerkschaftsbund Deutschlands*) – one for manual workers, one for white-collar employees and one for public service employees. These three associations have, in turn, 18 trade unions in membership: 9 manual; 6 white-collar and 3 public service unions. Total membership of these unions is 250,000. They are accorded negotiating rights in a number of industries. Coverage in the manual workers' association is of an industrial nature, reflecting to a large extent the predominantly manual worker organisations in the DGB (construction, metal, chemicals, mining and so on). The German Association of Commercial and Industrial White-Collar Employees was founded in Hamburg in 1950 in order to restore the former association of German clerks and its emphatic opposition to socialisation, Marxism and all forms of collectivism. It acknowledged the 'national characteristics of Christendom', the nation being a fundamental fact (Hartfiel, pp.154-5;

Table 7.3: Occupational Membership of the DAG

Occupational group	31 December 1978				30 September 1951	
	Male	Female	Total number	Per cent	Total number	Per cent
Commercial staff	99,939	93,194	193,133	40.1	148,400	43.2
Banks (private and municipal)	29,076	14,405	43,481	9.0	22,200	6.5
Insurance	18,583	10,123	28,706	6.0	24,800	7.2
Public service	74,128	53,076	127,204	26.4	74,800	21.8
Technical staff and *Beamte**	53,191	4,672	57,863	12.0	37,200	10.8
Master-craftsmen**	16,844	142	16,986	3.5	28,100	8.2
Shipping	7,542	203	7,745	1.6	8,000	2.3
Mining	6,226	284	6,510	1.4	—	—
Totals	305,529	176,099	481,628	100.0	343,500	100.0

* To be defined below.

** The structure of apprentice/journeyman/master is still observed — see Dittmar, pp.52ff, and Lawrence, pp.158-9.

Sources: Dittmar, p.154, and DAG *Pressedienst* 3/79 (writer's translation and calculations).

Kerr, 1954, p.542; Schuster, p.118). Secondly, the Association of Female White-Collar Employees is the only German trade union exclusively for women. It was founded in 1951 according to an old tradition 'guided by the thought of national solidarity, carried by the spirit of Christian ethics' (Hartfiel, p.156).

Beamte (or public servants) are a unique German institution. They represent a social stratum in their own right. They receive a contract on appointment which specifies lifetime tenure, statutory pension rights and guaranteed salary levels. In return, they are required to accept certain limitations on their private lives. Occupations classified as *Beamte* are not confined to civil servants, the armed forces, judges, the police and customs officials. Teachers, university professors, federal bank, Post Office and railway officials are also *Beamte*. The unions representing *Beamte* are sometimes thought of as being purely lobby-organisations. They are probably more successful in maintaining parliamentary representation than the trade unions which negotiate collective agreements (Jühe, p.154; Keller, p.164; McPherson, 1971, pp.122-7).

Beamte are also highly organised: three out of every four of the 2 million *Beamte* (10 per cent of the labour force) are members of trade unions, compared to roughly one in two manual workers and about one in four white-collar workers. Table 7.4 shows that the DGB has been as successful as the DBB (*Deutscher Beamtenbund*) in organising *Beamte*. There are two types of *Beamte* organisation. The first is the professional association — that is to say an organisation which prefers the term 'association' to that of 'trade union'. Some of these associations are independent, others are affiliated to a central organisation. By far the largest central organisation is the DBB (800,000 members) which was established in 1950. A small minority of its affiliated membership (see Table 7.4) are not *Beamte* and the associations responsible for such membership take part in the appropriate negotiations between the relevant employers' associations and other trade unions.

The most important independent association is that of the armed forces (DBV — 235,000 members). This association is the first of its kind in German history. Both active and former personnel — irrespective of rank — are eligible for membership and there are specialised departments for each service. Other independent associations are those of judges and attorneys (12,000) and university professors (8,000).

The other type of *Beamte* organisation carries the title 'union'

Table 7.4: Proportion of Manual Workers, White-Collar Employees and *Beamte* organised in trade unions in 1978

	Beamte		White-collar employees		Manual workers		Totals	
Employed labour force [a]	absolute	2,269,000		9,396,000		10,016,000		21,681,000
	in per cent	10.47		43.34		46.20		100.00
Trade union members	absolute	per cent	absolute	per cent	absolute	per cent	absolute	per cent
DGB[b]	832,088	50.52	1,548,947	71.65	5,370,438	98.16	7,751,523	85.53
DBB[c]	731,671	44.43	54,000	2.50	15,000	0.27	800,671	8.63
DAG[c]	–	–	478,735	22.15	–	–	478,735	5.16
CGB[b]	83,200	5.05	80,100	3.75	85,900	1.57	249,200	2.69
Total	1,646,949	100.00	2,161,782	100.00	5,471,388	100.00	9,280,129	100.00
Density (i.e. proportion of the labour force organised) Total		72.59		23.01		54.63		42.80
DGB		36.67		16.49		53.62		35.75
DBB		32.25		0.58		0.15		3.69
DAG		–		5.10		–		2.21
CGB		3.67		0.85		0.86		1.15

Notes: a April 1978.
b 31 December 1978.
c 30 September 1978.

Source: Institut der Deutschen Wirtschaft, *Zahlen 1979*, Table 84 (writer's translation).

and is affiliated to the DGB. As noted at the foot of Table 7.2, these unions are: education, police, Post Office, railways and ÖTV. All of them, to varying degrees, also organise white-collar employees and, with the exception of the educational union, manual workers. This again results in multi-purpose organisations which are represented on a number of negotiating bodies. ÖTV may also often find itself technically negotiating in both the private and public sectors, since a number of municipal enterprises are registered in the legal form of private corporations. These DGB unions (with the probable exception of the newly affiliated police union) have challenged the long-held legal opinion that *Beamte* do not have the right to strike. Work-to-rules have been staged in the Post Office, on the railways, in tax offices and, during peak holiday periods, by air traffic controllers. This, of course, constitutes a form of industrial action but confrontation has been generally avoided by federal and state authorities. A strike ballot for a one-day warning strike was prepared by the education union in 1972.

Works Councils

During Weimar, the main union organisation was 'squeezed into a narrow corridor between the works councils caring for the daily plant interests of the workers and the SPD catering for visions of social reform' (Kerr, 1954, p.545). Although the works councils were theoretically the 'long arm of the union' reaching into the plant, they were an arm without a hand (ibid., p.538).

After the Second World War, works councils again sprang up spontaneously in many plants. (The councils had been abolished by the Nazis in 1933, but their members had continued to act as unofficial advisers to their fellow workers.) Legal recognition of the reconstituted councils was granted by the Allies in 1946 (Sturmthal, p.54; Taft, p.308). The 1952 Act kept the unions out of plant bargaining and they had to wait a further 20 years before legislation somewhat more in accordance with their aspirations was to be passed — a development which will be further explored in the next section. In effect, therefore, bargaining has been carried out at *two* levels. The *first* level is the regional agreement negotiated by the relevant trade union and employers' association, while the *second* level involved grievance handling and supplementary bargaining between the works council and the individual employer. This has caused wage drift (*European Trends*, No. 46, February 1976, p.34; Kendall, p.127; Kerr, 1954, p.537; Miller, p.339). Hence the unions

have been kept, to pursue the earlier metaphor, at arm's length.
Contact with the rank and file member tends to be minimal and the
unions have become centralised and bureaucratic (Kerr, 1954,
pp.540-1; McPherson, 1951, p.23; Miller, p.343).

Unions have nevertheless attempted to develop a distinct system
of work place representatives. Such attempts gathered real momentum
after the 1967 recession (Miller). Until this recession the trade unions
had never really given up hope of exercising a higher degree of control
over the councils. In any case a very high proportion of works
councillors are also active trade unionists. Moreover, many councillors
also hold positions on the trade unions' works committees. But these
councillors tend to identify with their company. This is particularly
true of the chairmen: the considerable developments that have been
made in extending the recognition of lay union representatives at
plant level have tended to be vitiated by works council chairmen
who take the view that their full-time role within their company or
plant is of more value in enchancing the welfare and financial gains
of their constituents. (*Die Zeit* series 'Between Two Stools' 42/78 to
49/78 inclusive; Hartmann, 1979, pp.78-81; Miller, p.340 and
pp.346-7.)

Council chairmen become entrenched. Many company council
chairmen tend to be also involved at the level of their own plant as
works council chairmen. In addition, it is not unusual to find that they
are also members of their company's supervisory board. This type
of contact with management is to most chairmen the only positive
method of ensuring their company's continued prosperity. Because
chairmen are generally the repositories of such vast amounts of
information, they become career specialists in this function. There
is overwhelming evidence that tenure and these qualifications
go together in large-size firms (Hartmann, 1979, pp.74-8).

Trade Union Policy

The Main Bargaining Issues

By the middle of 1979 DGB unions had secured pay increases
averaging 4.6 per cent — approximately the same as the rate of
inflation. This compared with 5.2 per cent in 1978 and 6.7 per cent
in 1977 which, while representing some real gains, were still not the
primary cause for concern by the authorities (*Report* 6/79, West
German Embassy, London). An even bigger policy problem is that
pay for hours worked is constituting a smaller and smaller proportion

of total labour costs. For example, in engineering (if one assumes pay
for hours worked = 100), the index for indirect labour costs (or
'fringe benefits') in 1970 = 47.6. By 1978 it had reached 68.2. This
latter index yields the following when subdivided: holiday and sick
pay 27.3; holiday and other bonuses 13.5; and social security
contributions 27.4. Pay for hours worked has increased by 86 per
cent since 1970; other labour costs have risen by 166 per cent
(Himmelmann, 1979, p.259; Incomes Data Service (London)
International Report, No.78, p.5). The clear trend is one of
introducing both extra holiday pay and annual bonuses. Moreover,
in the next few years both white-collar and manual employees (who
usually have the same holiday entitlement) will become entitled to
six weeks' annual holiday. The trade unions are also seeking a further
reduction in the length of the working week. Finally, German
unions are both a party in the field of collective bargaining within a
given society and a movement for social reform. (Hirsch-Weber, 1963,
pp.279-80 and p.281; Kerr, 1954, p.536 and p.555; Limmer, pp.143-8;
Roll, p.92.)

The Main Bargaining Tactics

The Collective Agreements Act 1949 (as amended in 1952, 1969 and
1974) lays down the possible contents of a collective agreement. It
also regulates the applicability of the agreement, defining the
parties (trade unions and employers' associations) who may conclude
such agreements and finally provides that all agreements must be
registered at the Federal Ministry of Labour. These agreements are
detailed, diverse and numerous. Something like 30,000 are registered
in the specially created section of the Ministry. Some may be in
respect of only a particular region's wage agreement, applying to a
particular industry during the current annual wage round
(*Raumlohnabkomnen*). More rarely there will be similar agreements
with federal-wide application (*Tarifverträge*). Finally there will be
a whole series of more comprehensive and general agreements (for
three to five years) which cover holiday pay, lengths of holiday and
so on (*Manteltarifverträge*). Once registered, agreements are legally
binding on both parties and both the federal and *Länder* governments
have powers to enforce the conditions therein as statutory minima.
(Aaron and Wedderburn, p.132; Hofmeier, p.5; Kendall, p.124;
Kerr, 1954, p.539; Reichel, p.469.) The employer, but not the union,
may register plant agreements (Reichel, p.473).

 In addition, the Federal Labour Court laid down a rigorous case law

on the conduct of industrial disputes and the DGB and BDA both built
up their own strict codes of practice. The emergence of case law
coincided with a hardening of attitudes on the part of employers
(Cullingford, pp.26-7). The trend in unofficial action significantly
showed a marked upward trend from 1964 onwards, even though
unofficial strikes are strictly speaking illegal (Clark, p.243; Hofmeier,
p.6; Kendall, p.130n). In 1974 the DGB revised its voluntary code
of conduct in three important respects. First, strikes could be used
to achieve legislative aims and strike action could be used if
negotiations seemed to be serving no useful purpose – as opposed to
strikes being a measure of last resort; secondly, the DGB maintained
that there was no law to support the Federal Labour Court's 1958 ruling
that strike ballots can be defined as industrial action – affiliates
should therefore feel free to prepare for industrial action in this or
any other way; thirdly, in the event of employers retaliating with a
lockout, affiliates should lay down rules on whether and how selective
emergency work should be carried out by their members (Incomes
Data Services (London) *Report*, No.192, p.23).

It has been seen in the previous sub-section, however, that the
collective bargaining system has been delivering the goods either
because of, or in spite of, the unofficial trend in strike action.
Possibly as a result of this factor, the Federal Republic loses
comparatively few days per worker through strike action. Finally, all
unions have strict rules about the procedure to be followed before a
strike is called, including in most cases a 75 per cent majority of those
voting in a strike ballot and, in the case of the DAG, only a 25 per cent
majority in favour of ending the strike (Dittmar, pp.152-4).

Moreover, the silence of the constitution on the question of the
lockout has not prevented the Federal Labour Court from ruling in
1955 (and 1971) that employers have the right to *defend* themselves.
In effect, this has inhibited unions from staging selected strike action
at strategically important plants, which would have enabled them to
reduce the costs of strike action. In such circumstances the employers'
association may legally encourage a lockout of any or all union
members in as many plants as it choses. The Labour Court's ruling
has consistently been challenged on three counts. First, that a lockout
is *not* analogous to strike action. Second, the employer's *bargaining
power* lies in his ability to withdraw or reduce employment
opportunities and his pricing decisions affect real wages. Third, the
balance of power is already *unequal*, with the employer having the
advantage (*Die Zeit*, 13/78, p.17). Further, all the costs of strike action

fall on the union, because there can be no call on public funds (supplementary benefits, etc.) or tax refunds in the event of strike action. However, another factor which more conceivably reduced trade union bargaining power was a decision of the Federal Labour Court in 1967 that closed shops are contrary to the constitution (Cullingford, pp.14-15). Where union density is high, however, the law may on occasions be disregarded (Miller, p.340).

In the first significant post-war dispute over pay and conditions of service, the issue was one of equality with white-collar workers, particularly in the terms of sick pay. The strike — although it had national implications — took place in the northernmost state of Schleswig-Holstein. It began on 24 October 1956 and ended on 14 February 1957. It involved 34,000 engineering workers and affected 38 plants. The strikers, who were members of IG Metall, received the equivalent of half pay from the union during the strike. The employers formed a 'solidarity fund'. The strike committee, besides publishing a four-page daily newspaper, ran a huge entertainment programme for strikers and their families. A majority of 88 per cent had voted in favour of strike action; the first proposals by the mediator were rejected by 97.4 per cent. On 30 January 1957 IG Metall signed a compromise agreement only to have it rejected by a 76.2 per cent majority. The union's advice was again rejected in early February, but the majority fell to 57.7 per cent and this meant a return to work (the necessary majority for continuing the strike was 75 per cent). There were two important consequences. First, a major step towards the equality with white-collar workers (which was subsequently realised when an Act governing sick pay was introduced by the federal government in 1957). Secondly, in 1958 the Federal Labour Court declared that the first strike ballot had been held five days before the peace obligation had expired, although the union had denied this. The court found for the employers and awarded them DM 18 million damages against the union. However, the employers did not press for payment but settled for a conciliation agreement. (Aaron and Wedderburn, pp.41n, 133 and 153; Cullingford, p.25; Grosser, p.312; Kendall, p.125; Rajewsky, pp.69-74; Schuster, p.54.)

The next serious confrontation occurred in 1963, this time in the Nordwürttemberg-Nordbaden region where both IG Metall and the employers (led at this juncture by Herr Schleyer — see page 181) take equally militant lines. Indeed, it is often said that when this annual phase of collective bargaining is completed an acceptable pattern for the rest of the economy will normally have been drawn up. The employers planned a wide offensive for 1963 and instead of a few key firms being strike bound (as the union had intended when it received an 85 per cent backing for the strike) 900 firms employing 450,000 in two regions staged a lockout for the first time since 1928. IG Metall then held a strike ballot in the Ruhr, and other DGB unions pledged support, but the Economics Minister acted as conciliator and persuaded both sides to accept a compromise 5 per cent increase.

In 1957-8 and 1963 the decisions of the labour courts and the tactics of employers reduced the *official* strike propensity. However, in 1968 the dramatic recovery of the economy from the 1967 recession brought about increases in profits which outstripped the increase in wages. Hence by September 1969 there was a rank and file revolt. The number of working days lost in 1969 was a negligible factor (249,000); it was the unofficial nature of this short period of strike action which was the significant feature. IG Metall and the coal miners' union were both obliged to renegotiate agreements (Cullingford, pp.30-32). Greater rank and file pressure was exerted on trade union leaders after 1969. In 1971, 4.5 million working days were lost through lockouts (1.9 million) and strike action (2.6 million) – the highest total in the post-war history of the Federal Republic (BfA, Table 3.4).

Confrontations during the 1970s involved at least four important bargaining considerations. First, in the case of the somewhat abortive chemical workers strike in 1971 there was inflexible opposition from the employers to a pay claim. The opposition was on the grounds that financial losses were being incurred. Large dividends were nevertheless declared (Cullingford, pp.46 and 52; Dzielak, p.63ff; Ebsworth, pp.66-7). A similar situation obtained during the north German dock strike of 1978. Secondly, the ÖTV strikes in 1974 were in effect caused by a government pay policy designed to keep down this public sector wage settlement (Clark, p.254). Thirdly, a threat of technological unemployment in the printing industry has been the primary cause of the fairly frequent confrontations in this industry (Himmelmann, 1977). A similar fear provoked the IG Metall strikes in north Baden in 1978 (*Die Zeit*, 15/78). Lockouts were again used during the printing and engineering strikes in 1978. It induced both unions to file 35,000 law suits to have lockouts declared illegal. (In June 1980 the Federal Labour Court confirmed its 1955 and 1971 rulings that retaliatory lockouts are legal.) Fourthly, the steel industry strike in late 1978 was called to press a claim for a

35-hour week in order to offset the effect of mounting redundancies. The claim failed and the employers again responded by locking out twice as many employees as those on strike. This time rank and file anger also turned on IG Metall after a settlement was reached. This gave a fillip to union attempts to renegotiate its procedure agreement so that warning strikes can be held during negotiations. At the end of 1979 an agreement was reached which limited the duration of the peace obligation to six weeks — two weeks before the expiry of an agreement and four weeks afterwards.

Third-party involvement, via conciliation and arbitration, has been an important strike substitute, particularly in important controversies (Kerr, 1952, p.333; Hofmeier, p.8; Reichel, p.483). In 1968 — according to one of the few pieces of empirical research in the area — there were 293 arbitration agreements between trade unions and employers' associations. They covered about 10.3 million employees (Königsbauer, p.15). Perhaps 5 per cent of all wage settlements are reached by means of arbitration. There had been well over 1,000 arbitrations by 1972 (Külp, p.15). The Federal Labour Court 'demands that a strike is preceded by an arbitration procedure' (Bendix, p.44). It is only after this stage that both parties are released from their peace obligation. The DGB and BDA concluded a basic arbitration agreement in 1954 and this model was adopted in agreements among their affiliates. This gave rise to a voluntary system which contrasted to the compulsory Weimar system, although the Federal Ministry of Labour had threatened an Arbitration Act when a voluntary system did not initially materialise after a 1950 agreement between the DGB and BDA (Aaron and Wedderburn, p.297).

Politicians will generally offer their services as mediators after a strike has commenced and the normal arbitration procedure has been exhausted. At the time of the first post-war threatened lockouts in 1962, the prime minister of Baden-Württemberg (Dr Kiesinger — a future chancellor) persuaded the parties to return to the negotiating table. During the more bitter, and escalating, 1963 strikes and lockouts, the federal Minister of Economics (Professor Erhard) intervened and chaired meetings between the two parties. The Minister of Labour in North Rhine-Westphalia involved himself in the 1976 printing and the 1978-9 steel strikes and lockouts. The mayor of Hamburg intervened during the 1978 docks strike.

Until 1974 there was no machinery for arbitration of interest-disputes in the public sector (McPherson, 1971, pp.190-1). Major disputes had not previously occurred in this sector. The 1974 strikes and a number of work-to-rules in recent years, however, followed the general pattern of a relative increase in militancy. As a result of the 1974 strikes, an arbitration agreement was reached by the parties in the public services sector. It was used for the first time in 1976 (Keller, p.167).

Concerted Action

In 1967 there was, by German post-war standards, quite a serious recession. The Economics Minister of the time therefore introduced the Promotion of Economic Stability and Growth Act. This Keynesian-based Act sought among other things to establish the voluntary co-operation of the trade unions in a type of incomes policy (Lembruch and Lang, p.202; Hudson). Employers and government would also be represented. Hence a formal attempt at wage restraint was channelled through an institution known as 'Concerted Action'.

Informal efforts in this direction had been attempted as early as 1960 and 1963, but they were without any real measure of success (Cullingford, p.34). However, the first two years of Concerted Action were successful in terms of wage restraint: there was an almost staggering correlation between government guidelines and actual basic wage and salary movements (Clark, p.248). Not surprisingly, when economic growth began to exceed the growth in real wages, there was some rank and file disenchantment. As profits increased with the rapid economic recovery in 1968 and 1969, rank and file discontent could ultimately be no longer suppressed. The result was the September 1969 strikes.

The wage restraint effects of Concerted Action as such were less successful after 1969. There was a change in the DGB approach: every effort was made to include variables other than money wages. Long-term policy issues, as well as prices and profits, received attention from the union side. In effect Concerted Action became a forum for an exchange of general information.

In 1977, the trade unions boycotted the 40th session of Concerted Action. This was as a protest against an employers' challenge in the courts of the statute which extended co-determination rights. Following the failure of the challenge, preliminary contact between the employers and trade unions to discuss economic problems began again, although a full, formal resumption of Concerted Action was ruled out.

Further Developments in Industrial Democracy

The setting up of the Biedenkopf Commission in 1968, together with
an SPD/FDP coalition after the 1969 federal election, eventually led
to the 1972 Works Constitution Act and the 1976 Co-determination
Act. There had been elements of a Pyrrhic victory in the 1952 Act. The
main trade union criticisms of the practice of co-determination were that
the minority of employees on supervisory boards felt that they lacked
real influence; interests could be better represented on the works
councils; shareholders retained their option to veto new investment;
even in the *Montan* industries, the labour director was concerned only
with *consequences* of commercial and technical decisions -- the latter
being taken by his fellow directors; works' councillors and trade unions
lacked information because of the restrictions in terms of secrecy placed
on their representatives on supervisory boards (Däubler). For these
reasons, the DGB was quite adamant that parity representation should
be extended to all supervisory boards.

The position of the labour director would still present particularly
difficult problems. The trade unions tended to regard him as their
representative on the management board. However, while nominated by
labour he is responsible to, and can be removed by, the entire board.
His well paid and influential position undoubtedly tends to make him
a member of the managerial class (Kerr, 1954, p.558). Moreover,
when the *Montan* Act of 1951 was placed on the statute book there
were 71 mining and 34 steel companies. Many mergers between 1952
and 1968 reduced the number of companies subject to this Act to 31 in
mining and 28 in steel (Adams and Rummel, p.6). Labour directors
often became directors of personnel affairs in individual plants. By the
middle of 1969, the critical state of the German coal industry resulted
in many mines being fused into once consolidated company which
now includes 94 per cent of the productive capacity in mining
(Hartmann, 1970, pp.139-40). Again this resulted in the functional
demotion of 28 labour directors. Finally, a major controversy was
caused in 1980 when Mannesmann argued that the *Montan* model no
longer applied in its case. This was because steel had come to represent
a fairly small proportion of total turnover.

The Biedenkopf Report (1970) gave a clear endorsement to the
success of co-determination in coal and steel. In industries outside of
the *Montan* sector, however, a 7:5 ratio on the supervisory board (in
favour of shareholders) was advocated. Two of the members would
jointly be chosen by the employer and union (Cullingford, p.68,
Kendall, pp.135-6). Perhaps the Commission was more impressed by

the pacifying effects which co-determination had on organised labour than by the sense of participation which it imparted to individual employees. On the other hand, the Commission indicated how collusion between the board of management and the works council tended to pre-empt even the somewhat limited powers of the supervisory board. Finally the joint management-labour 'Economic Committee' was considered to be superfluous because information was exchanged at other levels (Hartmann, 1975, pp.56-7).

Attempts were made in the 1972 Act to extend the roles and rights of trade unions at plant level. A trade union can now initiate proceedings in the labour courts, a majority of a sizeable work group (as opposed to one quarter of the whole works council under the 1952 Act) can vote for attendance of the union at council meetings; timely invitations to *each* individual council meeting must, however, be sent and 'the employer retains considerable control over the entry of the union official to the plant' (Roberts, pp.349-50). The Economic Committee became an obligatory, employee-only body under the Act. Where a works council is larger than nine members strong, a Works Committee deals with the day-to-day business of the council. A company with several plants is obliged to recognise and facilitate the election of a company-wide council. Councils are also legally entitled to be informed of management's *intended* actions. Finally, there was recognition for the rights of minority workers (foreign workers, young persons and the disabled).

When the 1976 Act reached the statute book, it provided for a 6:6 supervisory board ratio for firms employing between 2,000 and 10,000 employees. Over 10,000 to 20,000 employees meant that the ratio would be 8:8 and 10:10 for firms with over 20,000 employees. This Act thus created a third system: the *Montan* system remained intact, while firms employing between 500 and 2,000 employees retained the 1952 Act's one-third representation. If there are 10 workers' representatives under the 1976 Act, 3 are from the unions and 7 are chosen from the employees — one of whom must be a senior executive. The shareholders' representatives are elected at the company's AGM. A chairman and his deputy are then elected by a two-thirds majority of the supervisory board. In the event of deadlock the shareholders provide the chairman, the employees his deputy. A two-thirds majority on the supervisory board is also required for the appointment of the management board. If necessary, the chairman has a casting vote. Finally, the labour director is appointed on the same terms as other members of the management board.

The biggest stumbling block is the representation of senior executives. In effect, this organised group has become yet *another* social and industrial entity (Bendix, p.136; Hartmann, 1975, p.63; Roberts, p.359). Election procedures and the role of the labour director are further contentious issues. In the eyes of the DGB the new Act has resulted in only a diluted form of parity representation on the supervisory board. For some employers, the Act represented a fundamental attack on property rights and they took the matter to the Supreme Constitutional Court (Bundesminster für Arbeit, 1979, pp.263-7). The Court ruled in 1979 that the Act was a 'vehicle for peaceful social order'.

Conclusion

Inter-union competition has played a role in the lack of success in organising the growing proportion of white-collar workers. The unique German institution of *Beamte* also causes organisational problems. Although not a serious problem as yet, the Christian wing of the movement is still an alternative for DGB members. An alleged growing radical influence in the HBV has already caused some relatively minor disaffection to the DAG. The 1980s will in any case produce a new generation of union leaders who were not active during the post-war reconstruction. From the point of view of trade union bargaining power, the existence of works councils has further undermined the movement.

There is evidence of some increase in rank and file militancy of late, but the Federal Republic's strike record remains low by international standards. A number of constraints operate which would in any case tend to reduce strikes: case law developments, lockouts, arbitration, strike ballots and rising real wages. There was an extension of co-determination rights during the 1970s.

Bibliography

Aaron, B. and Wedderburn, K.W., *Industrial Conflict: A Comparative Legal Survey* (Longman, London, 1972)

Adams, R.J. and Rummel, C.H., 'Workers' Participation in Management in West Germany . . .', *Industrial Relations Journal, 8* (1) (Spring 1979), pp.4-22

Anthes, J. *et al.*, *Mitbestimmung: Ausweg oder Illusion?* (Ro Ro Ro Tele) (Rowohlt Taschenbuch Verlag, Reinbek bei Hamburg, 1972)

Bendix, D.W.F., *Limits to Co-determination?* (Institute of Labour Relations, University of South Africa, Pretoria, 1978)

Bundesminister für Arbeit und Sozialordnung, *Mitbestimmung* (Bonn, 1979)

—— (BfA), *Statistisches Taschenbuch* (1980)

Bunn, R.F., 'The Federation of German Employers' Associations: A Political Interest Group', *Western Political Quarterly, 13* (3) (September 1960), pp.652-69

Clark, J., 'Concerted Action in the Federal Republic of Germany', *British Journal of Industrial Relations, XVII* (2) (1979), pp.242-58

Cullingford, E.C.M., *Trade Unions in West Germany* (Wilton House Publications, London, 1976)

Däubler, W., 'Co-determination: the German Experience', *Industrial Law Journal, 4* (4) (1975), pp.218-28

Dittmar, R., *Die Deutsche Angestellten-Gewerkschaft* (Droste Verlag, Düsseldorf, 1978)

Dzielak, W., *Belegschaften und Gewerkschaft im Streik* (Campus Verlag, Frankfurt/Main, 1978)

Ebsworth, D., 'Lay Officers in the German Chemical Workers' Union', *Industrial Relations Journal, 11* (4) (Sept./Oct. 1980), pp.63-70

Grebing, H., *The History of the German Labour Movement* (Oswald Wolff, London, 1969)

Grosser, A., *Germany in Our Time* (Penguin Books, Harmondsworth, 1974)

Hartfiel, G., 'Germany', in A. Sturmthal (ed.), *White-Collar Unionism* (Illinois UP, 1966), pp.127-63

Hartmann, H., 'Co-determination in West Germany', *Industrial Relations, 9* (2) (1970), pp.137-47

—— 'Co-determination Today and Tomorrow', *British Journal of Industrial Relations, XIII* (1) (1975), pp.54-64

—— 'Works Councils and the Iron Law of Oligarchy', *British Journal of Industrial Relations, XVII* (1) (1979), pp.70-82

Hesselbach, W., *Public, Trade Union and Co-operative Enterprise in Germany* (Frank Cass, London, 1976)

Himmelmann, G., *Der Bürger im Staat, 27* (3) (1977)

—— - - Ibid., *29* (4) (1979)

Hirsch-Weber, W., *Gewerkschaften in der Politik* (Westdeutscher Verlag, Köln und Opladen, 1959)

—— 'Die Gewerkschaften: Interessengruppen oder sociale Bewegung?',

Gewerkschaft Wirtschaft Gesellschaft (Bund-Verlag, Köln, 1963), pp.275-82

Hofmeier, K., 'Partners or Adversaries', *Sozial-Report*, 4-76(e) (Inter Nationes, Bonn-Bad Godesberg, 1976)

Hopkins, S.V., 'Industrial Stoppages and Their Economic Significance', *Oxford Economic Papers, 5* (3) (June 1953), pp.209-20

Hudson, M., '"Concerted Action": Wages Policy in West Germany, 1967-77', *Industrial Relations Journal, 11* (4) (Sept./Oct. 1980), pp.5-16

IdDW (Institut der Deutschen Wirtschaft), *Zahlen* (Deutscher Institutes-Verlag, Köln, 1979)

Jühe, R. et. al., *Gewerkschaften in der Bundesrepublik Deutschland: Daten Fakten Strukturen* (Deutscher Institutes-Verlag, Köhn, 1977)

Keller, B., *Der Bürger im Staat, 27* (3) (1977)

Kendall, W., *The Labour Movement in Europe* (Penguin Books, Harmondsworth, 1975), pp.89-139

Kerr, C., 'Collective Bargaining in Postwar Germany', *Industrial and Labor Relations Review, 5* (3) (April, 1952), pp.323-42

—— 'The Trade Union Movement and the Redistribution of Power in Postwar Germany', *Quarterly Journal of Economics, 68* (4) (1954), pp.535-64

Königbauer, G., *Freiwillige Schlichtung und tarifliche Schiedsgerichtsbarkeit* (Gustav Fischer Verlag, Stuttgart, 1971)

Külp, B., *Der Einfluss von Schlichtungsformen auf Verlauf und Ergebnis von Tarif- und Schlichtungsverhandlungen* (Dunker und Hamblot, Berlin, 1972)

Lawrence, P., *Managers and Management in West Germany* (Croom Helm, London, 1980)

Lembruch, G. and Lang, W., *Der Bürger im Staat, 27* (3) (1977)

Limmer, H., *Die Deutsche Gewerkschaftsbewegung* (Günter Olzog Verlag, München-Wien, 1966)

McPherson, W.H., 'Co-determination: Germany's Move Towards a New Economy', *Industrial and Labor Relations Review, 5* (1) (October 1951), pp.20-32

—— *Public Employee Relations in West Germany* (Institute of Labor Relations, University of Michigan, 1971)

Miller, D., 'Trade Union Workplace Representation in the Federal Republic of Germany', *British Journal of Industrial Relations, XVI* (3) (1978), pp.335-54

Rajewsky, X., *Arbeitskampfrecht in der Bundesrepublik* (Suhrkamp Verlag, Frankfurt, 1970)

Ramm, T. in B. Aaron (ed.), *Labor Courts and Grievance Settlement in Western Europe* (California UP, 1971)

Reichel, H., 'Recent Trends in Collective Bargaining in the Federal Republic of Germany', *International Labour Review, 104* (6) (December 1971), pp.469-87

Roberts, I.L., 'The Works Constitution Acts and Industrial Relations in West Germany: Implications for the United Kingdom', *British Journal of Industrial Relations, XI* (3) (1973), pp.338-67

Roll. E. in H. Marquand, *Organised Labour in Four Continents* (Longmans Green, London, 1939), pp.63-116

Schuster, D., *Die Deutschen Gewerkschaften seit 1945* (Verlag W. Kohlammer, Stuttgart, 1973)

Sturmthal, A., *Workers' Councils* (Harvard UP, 1964)

Taft, P. in W. Galenson (ed.), *Comparative Labor Movements* (Prentice Hall, 1952), ch. 4, pp.243-312

NOTES ON CONTRIBUTORS

E. Owen Smith (BA(Econ.), PhD) Senior Lecturer in Economics, Loughborough University. Served apprenticeship before receiving higher education. Research experience at Mannheim and Freiburg Universities. Previous publications include works on both British and German collective bargaining. Experienced arbitrator and mediator.

Les Cupper (BEc, MEc, DipEd) Senior Lecturer in Industrial Relations and Co-ordinator Labour Studies Programme, University of Melbourne, Parkville, Victoria, Australia. See Bibliography of Chapter 1 for sample of publications.

June M. Hearn (MA, PhD) Senior Lecturer in Industrial Relations, Graduate School of Business Administration and Industrial Relations Course Director for Advanced Management Education, University of Melbourne, Parkville, Victoria, Australia. Some of her publications are listed in Chapter 1.

J.R. Hough (BA, MSc, PhD) Senior Lecturer in Education and Economics, Loughborough University. Worked in insurance before attending university. Has studied at the Sorbonne. Publications on French economy. Consultant to UNESCO.

G.C. Allen (FBA) Emeritus Professor of Political Economy, London University. Internationally acknowledged expert on Japan. Has published numerous works on the Japanese and British economies. Recipient of the Order of the Rising Sun and Japan Foundation Award.

T.L. Johnston (MA, PhD) Professor of Economics, Heriot-Watt University, 1966-76. Chairman, Manpower Services Committee for Scotland 1977-80. Appointed Vice-Chancellor of Heriot-Watt University, 1981. Author of the standard work in English on collective bargaining in Sweden. In addition has edited and translated into English many of the seminal documents covering new initiatives in Swedish labour relations. Has wide experience as an arbitrator and mediator, and as chairman of Wages Councils.

Andrew W.J. Thomson (MA, PhD) Professor of Business Policy,

University of Glasgow. Educated at Oxford and Cornell Universities taking a PhD in Industrial Relations at the latter in 1968. Has spent two periods in 1973 and 1977 teaching industrial relations at the University of Chicago. Main publications include books on the Industrial Relations Act, grievance procedures and collective bargaining in the public sector. Is a member of the ACAS panel of arbitrators.

NAME INDEX

SUBJECT INDEX

References to general themes
recurring throughout the book (for
example, trade union growth) are
listed under the appropriate heading.
References specific to a particular
country (for example, Omi Silk
Company, Japan) are listed under
that country's heading.

arbitration *see* third party involvement
Australia: bibliography 40-2;
  compared to: France 2, UK 14;
  conclusion 40; introduction 1-2,
  13-14; Labour Party 14, 16, 17;
  Liberal-National Party 21, 24

ballots: Australia 25; UK 130, 140-1,
  146, 149; USA 165-6;
  W. Germany 183, 184, 185, 186,
  187, 189, 190, 204
banking and commerce: Australia
  18, 27; UK 138; W. Germany
  180, 181, 186, 187, 189, 190,
  204
bargaining power *see* employers'
  bargaining power; trade union
  bargaining power
building industry: Australia 17, 19,
  30; Japan 83; Sweden 102; UK
  138, 139, 140; USA 158, 168;
  W. Germany 186, 187, 189
business unionism (USA) 171-2

capital substitution 6, 10, 142
central union organisations:
  Australian Council of Trade
  Unions (ACTU) 16, 26-32, 35,
  37, 38, merger with ACSPA 26-8;
  other central organisations 27-8;
  France 43, 55, CFDT 44, 46-7,
  52-61, 69, CFTC 44, 46-7, 55-61,
  CGC 47, 55-6, CGT 44, 46-7,
  52-61, 69, CGT-FO 45, 47,
  52-61, FEN 45, 46; Japan: All-
  Japan Congress of Industrial
  Labour Organisations 78, All-
  Japan General Federation of

Labour 78, Japan Labour Federation 74, present-day organisations 82; Sweden 101, 110-11,
  LO 98-104, SACO/SR 104,
  107-8, TCO 104-7; UK Trades
  Union Congress (TUC) 2, 43, 104,
  127, 132, 134, 135, 136-40, 145,
  146, 147, 179; USA: AFL 45,
  156-7, 158, 159, 160, 161,
  AFL-CIO 160, 161, 166, 167,
  170-1, 176, 179, CIO 159-60,
  161; W. Germany: CGB 180,
  190, 192, 193, DBB 192, 193,
  DBV 192, DGB 179, 180, 184,
  185, 186-9, 193-4, 197, 199,
  200, 201, 204
clerical workers and unionism:
  Australia 17; Sweden 101, 105;
  USA 168; W. Germany 190, 192
closed shop: Australia 10, 18;
  Sweden (absence of) 3, 110; UK
  10, 146-50; USA 10 (bargaining
  units) 159, 160; W. Germany
  (illegal in) 10, 198
co-determination *see* industrial
  democracy
collective bargaining: Australia (shift
  to) 33-4; degree of centralisation
  in 9, 13, 102, 103, 106, 114-15,
  119-20, 129, 169, 173, 196;
  economic implications 6, 140;
  France 43, 50, 62; Japan 76, 83;
  Sweden 100, 102, 103, 106, 107,
  112, 114-15, 116, 119; theory of
  9, 10-11; UK 129, 140, 149;
  USA 156, 161, 162, 168, 171,
  172-3, 175; W. Germany 179,
  182, 196, 199-200
communism and trade unions:
  Australia 17; France 2, 45, 62,
  66-7, 69; Japan 78, 79; UK (ETU
  affair) 123; USA 161
conciliation *see* third party involvement

demarcation disputes *see* inter-union
  disputes
dual labour markets 2-3, 89-90, 92,

For Product Safety Concerns and Information please contact our EU
representative GPSR@taylorandfrancis.com
Taylor & Francis Verlag GmbH, Kaufingerstraße 24, 80331 München, Germany

www.ingramcontent.com/pod-product-compliance
Lightning Source LLC
Chambersburg PA
CBHW050432280326
41932CB00013BA/2079

9 781032 394442